The
Everyday
Advocate

The
Everyday
Advocate

Standing Up for
Your Child with Autism

Areva Martin, Esq.

NEW AMERICAN LIBRARY

NEW AMERICAN LIBRARY
Published by New American Library, a division of
Penguin Group (USA) Inc., 375 Hudson Street,
New York, New York 10014, USA
Penguin Group (Canada), 90 Eglinton Avenue East, Suite 700, Toronto,
Ontario M4P 2Y3, Canada (a division of Pearson Penguin Canada Inc.)
Penguin Books Ltd., 80 Strand, London WC2R 0RL, England
Penguin Ireland, 25 St. Stephen's Green, Dublin 2,
Ireland (a division of Penguin Books Ltd.)
Penguin Group (Australia), 250 Camberwell Road, Camberwell, Victoria 3124,
Australia (a division of Pearson Australia Group Pty. Ltd.)
Penguin Books India Pvt. Ltd., 11 Community Centre, Panchsheel Park,
New Delhi - 110 017, India
Penguin Group (NZ), 67 Apollo Drive, Rosedale, North Shore 0632,
New Zealand (a division of Pearson New Zealand Ltd.)
Penguin Books (South Africa) (Pty.) Ltd., 24 Sturdee Avenue,
Rosebank, Johannesburg 2196, South Africa

Penguin Books Ltd., Registered Offices:
80 Strand, London WC2R 0RL, England

First published by New American Library,
a division of Penguin Group (USA) Inc.

First Printing, April 2010
10 9 8 7 6 5 4 3 2 1

 REGISTERED TRADEMARK—MARCA REGISTRADA

LIBRARY OF CONGRESS CATALOGING-IN-PUBLICATION DATA:

Martin, Areva.
    The everyday advocate: standing up for your child with autism/Areva Martin.
        p.   cm.
    ISBN 978-0-451-23021-8
    1. Autistic children—Care.   2. Parents of children.   3. Patient advocacy.   I. Title.
    RJ506.A9M37557   2010
    618.92'85882—dc22   2009047873

Set in Celeste
Designed by Sabrina Bowers

Printed in the United States of America

PUBLISHER'S NOTE
This publication is designed to provide accurate and authoritative information in regard to the subject matter covered. It is sold with the understanding that the publisher is not engaged in rendering legal, accounting, or other professional services. If you require legal advice or other expert assistance, you should seek the services of a competent professional.

While the author has made every effort to provide accurate telephone numbers and Internet addresses at the time of publication, neither the publisher nor the author assumes any responsibility for errors, or for changes that occur after publication. Further, publisher does not have any control over and does not assume any responsibility for author or third-party Web sites or their content.

The scanning, uploading, and distribution of this book via the Internet or via any other means without the permission of the publisher is illegal and punishable by law. Please purchase only authorized electronic editions, and do not participate in or encourage electronic piracy of copyrighted materials. Your support of the author's rights is appreciated.

To Ernest, Michael, Morgan, and Marty—
my everyday advocates

Contents

Foreword

In my own life, I have had the opportunity to witness the powerful impact a few dedicated advocates can make in the lives of those with autism. I've seen horrifying living conditions eliminated, abusive institutions shut down and unfair social systems exposed all because of their passion and determination.

Change is not always easy; change is not always fast; but any change in the fundamental quality of life for those with disabilities rests almost entirely on the work of everyday advocates. The astonishing effectiveness of their efforts has inspired me from the very beginning.

Thirty-two years ago, I visited Camarillo State Hospital with a childhood friend who worked in the autism wards. The hospital was a desolate, isolated compound surrounded by cactus, with several wards full of small and beautiful children with autism. Some of the children exhibited self-injury, beating their heads against concrete walls or pulling out large clumps of hair. Untrained orderlies provided ineffective treatments, such as dragging them away from the walls or pulling their hands away from their heads. Other children engaged in aggression, biting anyone who tried to interact with them. These children had all the teeth in their mouth removed, but they continued to bite! One young boy sat in a semicircle in the "classroom" masturbating, only stopping each time the aide approached him, then rapidly returning to the activity as soon as the aide walked away. It was bad. It was worse than bad. It was horrible. But, for kids with autism, that was the best there was back then.

After touring the units, my friend introduced me to a man who had a laboratory at the hospital. He was a psychology professor whose lab was conducting research that proved that the procedures used in the mental hospitals were not only inhumane, but also ineffective. I didn't know it at that time, but seven years later he would become my husband. As a naive but ambitious twenty-two-year-old student, I confessed that I wanted to volunteer at the state hospital and work with those adorable little children who never had the chance to leave a gated area and were confined to rooms with no toys, no carpets, and just a few pieces of mismatched furniture. To my shock he replied, "You don't want to work here. The only reason we have our lab here is to get rid of this place." Not long after that, the hospital was closed, primarily due to his lab's advocacy. Advocacy is a wonderful thing. I will always admire my husband for his tireless effort to make the world a better place for individuals with autism by closing down the mental hospitals. Children with autism are rarely institutionalized now.

Areva Martin is another person I admire greatly, and it is a great privilege to write the foreword for *The Everyday Advocate*. Hardly a week goes by that I don't hear her name mentioned in connection with some altruistic cause—the cover of the *Los Angeles Times* for exposing the unfair system that children of color with autism face, a fund-raiser she's holding for disadvantaged individuals with disabilities, a committee she's chairing, a town hall meeting she's holding, a family she's helping, a conference she's organizing. . . . Areva is passionate, dedicated, and committed to helping individuals with autism and other disabilities. In addition to her accomplishments as a renowned lawyer and advocate for the disabled, she has also walked the walk, which is equally important. The firsthand stresses, challenges, and joys that families face are expressed throughout the chapters of her book. This isn't just a book about being an advocate, which is important in its own right. It's also a support guide—the author *knows* how it feels to not be told all the options, to have to change a system that isn't working, to motivate people to provide the best possible services for individuals on the spectrum, and to approach an often lacking system in a responsible, intelligent manner. Personal examples from her work as an attorney, as well as her work as a parent, make her book both unique and user-friendly.

Of course advocacy can also be a bad thing, if it is not done thoughtfully, carefully, and systematically. Over the years I have seen many families and professionals lose credibility—and lawsuits—because they didn't understand the importance of documentation, because they fought with the very people that were their biggest supporters, because they sought procedures that weren't scientifically documented, because they wanted everything—to the point that they spent their time "advocating," instead of understanding what was best for a child. This is why *The Everyday Advocate* is so important.

It provides step-by-step procedures and recommendations for advocating on a daily basis, and making change in a way that is logical, scholarly, and effective. *The Everyday Advocate* presents this crucial information in an entertaining and friendly way, with personal stories sprinkled throughout its pages, which makes the book hard to put down.

There are lots of books that are designed to help parents navigate the legal system and advocate for the best program possible for their child. Most are complicated and simply restate the law. *The Everyday Advocate* is different. It provides a comprehensive approach that helps a family develop a strong foundation. It doesn't just state what the laws are; it provides families with a road map to navigate the system as well as deal with the emotions that go along with advocacy, in an entertaining and supportive way. In short, Areva's advice, wisdom, knowledge, and expertise clearly make *The Everyday Advocate* a must for anyone who has, or works with, a child with disabilities. The vital information in this book will most certainly help families pave the way for positive change.

So ask yourself: Does my child have a school program that is enriching and appropriate? Is my child included with typical children at the level that I would like? Do we have a comprehensive social program that targets both my child and my child's peers? Does my child have a positive behavior support plan to decrease problem behaviors? Is my child receiving enough opportunities for communication throughout the day? Is my child's progress being monitored on a regular basis? Are the goals that are being worked on meaningful and practical? Are the staff that work with my child well trained? Are my child's goals coordinated across the day?

If you answered "no" to *any* of these questions, *The Everyday Advocate* is a must. And even if you can answer "yes" to all those questions, face the fact that many children don't have the excellent program your child has, and most adults on the spectrum do not live the lives that they deserve. Most live in group homes, few get married or have meaningful romantic relationships (even though most report a desire), and few gain meaningful employment. This means continued advocacy for all of us.

The Everyday Advocate is a comprehensive guide for helping your child *and* paving the way for future generations of children with autism.

—Lynn Kern Koegel, PhD, Koegel Autism Center,
University of California, Santa Barbara

The
Everyday
Advocate

Advocacy Makes a Difference

*What's remarkable is not how many failed in the face of
discrimination, but rather how many men and women
overcame the odds; how many were able to make a way
out of no way. . . .*

—*Barack Obama*[1]

As a parent or caregiver of an autistic child, you are in a rare and
wonderful position to make a meaningful contribution to the
world. The long years of love, sweat, tears and joy that lie before
you as you advocate for your child are sure to have ramifications for others, who will gratefully benefit from your efforts.

History has already shown us that advocacy on behalf of those who
are less fortunate has profound and far-reaching effects. Unlike those
who have fought for human rights at times in the past, you don't have
to wonder if your efforts will be in vain. You can be certain that, in
the end, you will make a difference—because all of the progress that has
been made in advancing human rights has been because of advocates
just like you.

As remarkable as it seems, equality in America—for special-needs children and adults—was guaranteed only twenty years ago. On July 26, 1990,
the landmark Americans with Disabilities Act (ADA) was signed, taking a
sledgehammer to a wall that had "for too many generations, separated
Americans with disabilities from freedom they could glimpse, but not
grasp."[2]

The law promoted the integration of those with disabilities* into every aspect of daily life—communities, workplaces, schools and services. Although no single piece of legislation can change long-standing biases and misperceptions,[3] it was hoped that increased contact with disabled children and adults would gradually create greater acceptance.

As he signed the legislation, President George H. W. Bush said, "We rejoice as this barrier falls . . . claiming together, we will not accept, we will not excuse, and we will not tolerate discrimination in America."[4]

This was the kind of rhetoric that resounded through the sixties. In that great era for civil rights, Attorney General Robert Kennedy spoke passionately on behalf of "the excluded" in our society. Thurgood Marshall fought powerfully for the integration of schools. Joan Baez led a crowd of 300,000 people, singing "We Shall Overcome" at the Lincoln Memorial during the March on Washington, where Martin Luther King, Jr., began a speech with the words, "I have a dream. . . ."

Thanks to a fervent groundswell of advocacy that was felt around the world, the Civil Rights Act of 1964 was passed, prohibiting discrimination on the basis of race, religion, national origin or gender. But people with disabilities were left out.

My grandmother was one of them.

At twenty-eight years old, she had been shot and paralyzed from the waist down. Afterward she was confined to a hospital for seven years—not because she needed the medical care, but because of sheer logistics. She simply couldn't get around! No government regulations had been passed to require access ramps or elevators in public buildings. Today, paraplegics can participate in the Special Olympics in lightweight magnesium wheelchairs with titanium bearings for exceptional speed and agility. Vans fitted with hydraulic lifts are commonplace and, in many states, subsidized by the government. But in my grandmother's day, the wheelchairs themselves were obstacles. Heavy and unwieldy, they were often too wide for standard doors. When she was finally allowed to go

---

* The Equal Employment Opportunity Commission determined that a wide range of conditions *automatically* fall under the scope of the ADA, including "such contagious and noncontagious diseases and conditions as orthopedic, visual, speech and hearing impairments, cerebral palsy, epilepsy, muscular dystrophy, multiple sclerosis, cancer, heart disease, diabetes, mental retardation, emotional illness, specific learning disabilities, HIV disease (whether symptomatic or asymptomatic), tuberculosis, drug addiction, and alcoholism." 28 CFR 35.104(1)(ii); EEOC Compliance Manual (No. 915.002), March 14, 1995, pp. 902–21; *see also* Memorandum: "Legislative and Regulatory History—Foundation for the Proposed ADA Restoration Act," p. 4.

home, my grandmother could barely turn the chair around in the house, much less move freely from room to room. I remember that when I was a little girl we had only one family friend strong enough to lift the massive steel wheelchair into the trunk, then pick her up and carry her from the apartment to the car. Going out was so labor-intensive that this vital, healthy woman, who raised me, didn't leave the house more than once a month.

Public buildings were completely inhospitable to people with disabilities then. Even if they could have gotten through the front doors, almost every aisle, doorway, elevator, telephone, bathroom and service counter would have been inaccessible. As a result, many talented, eligible people with disabilities were unable to make use of public services and locked out of meaningful jobs. Public schools were not open to children with disabilities. A fully integrated life in the community was out of the question.

It took persistent advocacy for things to begin to change.

In 1953, when her athletic, fourteen-year-old son, Ed, contracted polio and became a quadriplegic confined to an iron lung, Zona Roberts stepped up. First, she hired a tutor. And then—although the Internet would not be available for thirty years—an electronic home-to-school connection was set up, so Ed could finish high school. When he enrolled in the College of San Mateo, Zona accompanied him, pushing the heavy manual wheelchair through narrow school halls.

When a professor saw that Ed had a passion for political science and was one of the smartest students he'd ever taught, he encouraged Ed to transfer to the University of California at Berkeley. Although the university gladly admitted him, the administrators balked when they realized he was quadriplegic. It took a legal battle for the university to make good on the promise of admission. Lack of awareness about disabilities was so common at the time that newspapers ran the story with the headline, *Helpless Cripple Goes to School.*[5]

In 1970, Ed Roberts became the first severely disabled person to attend a university. It was a tremendous victory that would open doors for others to pursue their education. But the need for advocacy never let up. When Ed arrived at UC–Berkeley, he was surprised to find himself isolated—given accommodations in the hospital instead of the dorms. As soon as more students with disabilities enrolled, Ed organized a group called the Rolling Quads to advocate for their right to live alongside other students.

Along with Judy Heumann, he started the independent living movement (ILM) that created a fundamental shift in attitudes toward disability. Calling for "civil rights, not charity," it rejected the idea of sequestering the disabled away in nursing homes and rehab facilities. Instead, the ILM emphasized advocacy through political lobbying and public education to increase awareness. The dignity of independence, Roberts said, was *at least* as important as—if not more important than—physical reparation.[6]

In the years that followed, huge milestones were laid on behalf of the disabled, each of them achieved with advocacy. When people speak up, astonishing progress can be made. New perspectives are adopted, new laws are written; then more advocacy is needed to see that the laws are put into effect. Successful advocates learn to pace themselves, knowing that each challenge will be followed by another. But every milestone paves the way for the next.

Before children with autism could attend public schools and those in wheelchairs could access public buildings, civil rights had to be won for millions of Americans. Before Rosa Parks could ignite a Montgomery Bus Boycott, the Supreme Court had to strike down the Alabama law that made segregated bus service mandatory. Before Martin Luther King, Jr., could march on Selma to register voters, the Supreme Court had to find the Southern Democratic Party's exclusion of African-Americans unconstitutional. Before the Civil Rights Act of 1964, the Supreme Court had to strike down the laws allowing for the segregation of schools.

In the struggle for disabilities rights, the most historic shift occurred with the passage of Section 504 of the 1973 Rehabilitation Act. It was the world's first civil rights provision for people with disabilities. Never before had those with disabilities been viewed as a legitimate minority group, deserving of basic civil rights protections. This new "class status" made it possible to prove discrimination against a recognized group.

Under Section 504, any organization that received federal funds— such as hospitals, universities, libraries, national museums, government institutions and public transportation services—was required to provide access for people with disabilities. It was a huge breakthrough and meant that people like my grandmother would be able to live more active, normal lives.

But complying with the law was expensive. In many cases, it meant that ramps had to be built; wider doorways had to be installed; and additional training had to be given to staff in order to accommodate special needs. Aware of these difficulties, the government didn't enforce the law.

The hard-won rights in Section 504 might never have been put into effect had it not been for the advocacy of Frank Bowe, a professor at Hofstra University, who rallied people with deafness, mental retardation, muscular dystrophy and other disabilities to hold sit-ins at federal buildings. By April of 1977, Americans were used to sit-ins and marches, but they weren't used to this. The sight of hundreds of disabled people showing up in New York, Washington, D.C., and San Francisco to defend their rights in wheelchairs, on portable respirators and on crutches[7] had a powerful effect.

At the U.S. Department of Health, Education and Welfare in San Francisco, more than one hundred disabled demonstrators refused to leave until new regulations were signed that guaranteed Section 504 would be put into action. To this day, it is the longest sit-in at a federal building in history.[8] And it worked.

Like the civil rights activists before them, these bold advocates prepared the ground for the next milestone. By the time the ADA was passed in 1990, it had been preceded by decades of campaigning and demonstrations that changed people's attitudes and broadened their understanding.

When the bill itself was introduced, advocates with disabilities came from around the country to talk to members of Congress, explaining why each provision was important to address a very real barrier in their lives. Many of them slept on floors by night and visited congressional offices by day. People who couldn't come to Washington told their stories in letters, attended town meetings and made endless phone calls. To establish the need for the protection of the ADA, a national campaign was initiated to write "discrimination diaries" telling about instances of poor access and daily discrimination.

One young woman with cerebral palsy described at the congressional hearings how a local movie house would not let her sit in the theater. When her mother called the theater to complain that that kind of attitude "sounded like discrimination," the theater owner replied, "I don't care what it sounds like." When the president and members of Congress heard the story, they used it to symbolize that America "does care what it sounds like" and would no longer tolerate this type of discrimination."[9]

For months, Justin Dart, chair of the Congressional Task Force on the Rights and Empowerment of People with Disabilities, continued to hold public hearings across the country. Thousands of people with disabilities attended with their friends and families to advocate the need for the civil rights protection that was later embodied by the ADA.

These early advocates for disability rights were pioneers. Different times call for different kinds of advocacy. Parents today are not called upon to march in the streets or stage sit-ins to secure rights for their disabled children. Laws are now in place that guarantee those rights. But the laws alone are not sufficient.

History shows clearly that action always requires an advocate. It is solely because of the courage and commitment of brave advocates that a promising quadriplegic can study political science at a preeminent state university, a young girl with cerebral palsy can go to a movie in her own hometown, and an autistic child can attend a public school with his peers.

Parents with the courage and commitment to take up the mantle of advocacy and speak out for their autistic child stand shoulder-to-shoulder with those who have made great strides in human rights throughout history. Advocacy makes a difference—whether on the grand stage of sweeping social change or in the everyday life of a single child. As parents, caregivers and friends of any individual with a disability, in some way, we are all called upon to be everyday advocates.

PART I

The Call to Advocacy

CHAPTER 1

Facing Facts:
Getting a Diagnosis

When our son was born, yards of pink fabric, headbands and girlie accessories made room for trucks, cars and trains. We knew right away that Ernest Martin III (affectionately known as "Marty") would be the darling of the family. We could always find his two proud sisters peering over the edge of his crib, stroking his head. They completely adored him. As soon as he was old enough to sit up, we would often find the three of them huddled together in front of the television watching a Disney movie or splashing around in the pool. Seeing them playing so happily together brought a special joy to our hearts.

It was like that for almost two years. Then things began to change. At first, it was just a suspicion that I couldn't quite articulate, but as the mother of two healthy girls, I knew in my gut that something was wrong. When you're around a child every day, everything about him is imprinted on your mind—how he speaks, what makes him laugh, who he'll run to if he scrapes his knees. You think you see him so clearly, but a gradual change can be hard to notice, because you make the adjustment over so many days and weeks. It's easy to accept and make excuses for a child you love, no matter how quirky his behavior. It's much more difficult to stand back and see that something is strange.

It didn't seem that odd when Marty collected colored pencils and bottle tops. But then I had to acknowledge that it didn't stop there: on the floor of his room were piles of objects—pencils, forks, socks— meticulously stacked to form enormous towers. Over the next few weeks, he started spending more time in his room and stopped playing with his sisters altogether. Instead of chattering and laughing all day, Marty barely spoke at all. And even when we called his name, he wouldn't meet our eyes.

After a normal pregnancy, delivery and his first eighteen months of life, Marty was changing into a boy we'd never seen before. Although well-meaning friends assured me that everything was fine, I looked, with a heavy heart, for other possibilities.

WHAT'S HAPPENING TO MY CHILD?

Identifying what's abnormal as opposed to what's simply atypical is no easy feat, even for parents who have watched other children develop. Diagnosing autism is not as easy as reading a checklist and ticking off boxes. For some families, it literally takes years to receive an accurate diagnosis. Most children exhibit signs before the age of two months, but many others show no symptoms until between the ages of four and six, when school begins. Autism is a complex neurological disorder. It's also a spectrum disorder, which means it can present itself in different ways in different children, with symptoms ranging from mild to severe. Still, being honest with myself, I had to admit that many of the changes I'd noticed in Marty could be explained by what I'd heard about autism.

If I was still clinging to the dream that Marty's early days as a typical boy were a guarantee of a healthy future, my research quickly snapped me out of it. I soon learned that it was not uncommon for parents to report that their child hit all the early milestones—they sat up at six months, crawled at nine months, walked at twelve months, babbled words at sixteen months, and spoke in full sentences at eighteen months—and then retreated into a shell.

One of the things that provokes so many theories about the causes of autism is that so many children with autism seem to be developing normally until a particular event takes place—like receiving a childhood vaccination between six and twenty-five months. Then, almost overnight, their disruptive behavior, piercing screams, inconsolable tantrums, or unintelligible babbling begins.

Experts struggle to explain why there has been such an explosion in the number of children being diagnosed with autism in recent years. Some attribute it to our improved ability to accurately diagnose the condition. Others say that environmental factors—such as pollutants and chemically processed foods—are the culprits. In the disability community, many believe that autism is caused by mercury or other contaminants found in vaccinations.

WHOM CAN YOU TRUST?

If you haven't already, you'll soon discover that there are many claims about cures for autism. Hyberbolic oxygen chambers, chelation therapy, and special diets all have their supporters. The media regularly tells stories of children who were diagnosed with autism but miraculously "recovered."

Don't buy into the hype. You would not be tempted to believe in miracle cures for diabetes, cancer or any serious medical condition; don't fall for it with autism. To be the best advocate for your child, you must have good, reliable information and a team of credible professionals you can trust. Anything less is a formula for frustration and disappointment.

Of course, it is important for qualified scientists to search for answers and for parents to report any information that might help, but I believe that too much speculation about causes and cures is a distraction. I would rather spend my time attending to the day-to-day reality of living with autism. The parents I know who focus on addressing the practical issues—such as accessing services and integrating their child into their family and community—express the greatest level of acceptance and the least amount of anxiety and stress.

When I looked for explanations, I found very few. The Centers for Disease Control and Prevention (CDC) have declared autism a national health crisis. Yet there is still no central clearinghouse of information.

Every time I found a reliable source, it seemed to lead to another source with information that was conflicting or difficult to understand.

This neurological condition has confounded doctors, scientists and health-care workers alike. Despite more than sixty years of research, scientists still do not know what causes the disorder. And there is no cure.

Although it was first identified in 1943, by 2006 it had reached epidemic proportions. In 2007, the official CDC estimate placed the prevalence of autism at one in 150 children. By October of 2009, a new study by the American Academy of Pediatrics found that the parent-reported rate of autism was one in every ninety-one children (one in every fifty-eight boys). The same month, the CDC announced that new figures would be released from their Autism and Developmental Disabilities Monitoring (ADDM) Network at the end of 2009, but preliminary results showed that approximately one percent of children have autism spectrum disorder. This is significantly higher than the rate shown by their studies only two years ago.[1] Experts in Cambridge, England, studying this disease now believe that as many as one of every thirty-eight boys born today in the United Kingdom will be affected.[2] In states like California, there has been an increase in autism of well over 1,000 percent in the past twenty years—a twelve-fold increase that means two children a day will be diagnosed with autism.[3]

Because autism is a complex disorder that takes place across a spectrum, it is especially difficult to diagnose. Children present a myriad of characteristics—from restricted movements to repetitive behaviors to severe insomnia. No two children diagnosed with autism are alike, nor do they have exactly the same symptoms. One child may be nonverbal and have a variety of self-stimulating behaviors, such as hand flapping or spinning; another child might be able to carry on a conversation about complex scientific and mathematical models, but be unable to button his jacket or ride a bicycle.

Children with autism often have what are known as comorbid conditions, such as attention deficit disorder (ADD) or obsessive compulsive disorder (OCD). ("Comorbid" simply means they may have another, unrelated disorder along with autism.)

Autism is often characterized as being mild, moderate or severe. Those children with the mildest form of autism (known as "high-functioning") and better language skills have been said to have Asperger's syndrome, although there is a current debate about the usefulness of this term.[4] Pervasive developmental delay (PDD) is a broad medical term used to describe a number of developmental disorders including autism, Asperger's syndrome, Rett's disorder, childhood disintegrative disorder and pervasive developmental disorder not otherwise specified (PDD-NOS).

Although it is happening less frequently, children with autism have often been diagnosed with mental retardation. It's so common that the assumption that autism goes hand in hand with mental retardation has become one of the biggest myths about the disorder.

There is an important difference between autism and mental retardation. A child with mental retardation has an extremely low IQ but demonstrates relatively steady skill development and learning capacity. Children with autism typically show uneven skill development with deficits in certain areas, most frequently in their ability to communicate with or relate to others. They may have distinctive—even extraordinary—skills in other areas. An extremely small number of children are "autistic savants" with genius-level skills in a single subject.

The inaccurate diagnosis of mental retardation often occurs when experts use intelligence tests that require good verbal skills. Since most children with autism have verbal deficits, they score poorly on such tests. However, when experts use tests that rely on abstract reasoning and nonverbal skills, the same autistic children may demonstrate average or above-average intelligence.

In her study of autistic children, Meredyth Goldberg Edelson found that only 19 percent had below-average intelligence, leaving 81 percent with average intelligence or higher. She observed that many of the studies conducted thirty-five to forty years ago were "based on faulty data or no data at all . . . No one had ever systematically analyzed the evidence in support of those claims." Many times, when the researchers found a child who, due to poor verbal skills, couldn't be tested, they simply assumed the child was retarded and gave him a low IQ score. Even if children have been correctly diagnosed with mental retardation, we know today that they still have a vast potential to develop, despite their cognitive deficits.[5]

Regardless of the outcome, it is vital that the diagnosis be measured against the parents' observations and knowledge of the child. An incorrect diagnosis can lead to years of ineffective and inappropriate treatments.

MORE FACTS ABOUT AUTISM

One in every ninety-one children born today will have autism.

For boys, the ratio is even higher: One out of every fifty-eight boys is autistic.

Autism is the fastest-growing developmental disability in the United States (10 to 17 percent per year).

More kids are diagnosed with autism than diabetes, AIDS and cancer *combined*.

More than one and a half million people in the United States have autism.

These facts about autism are staggering, but it's the crisis going on in your own home that can feel overwhelming. Like most parents, I found myself struggling with the painful realization that my little boy might never talk, attend school with his sisters, or ever have a friend, while at the same time coping with a completely foreign world of acronyms and agencies to try to figure out what to do about it.

There was so much to learn, so many decisions to make and, unfortunately, so little time. What I didn't know seemed almost endless. But what I did know was that I had a short window of opportunity to take action.

EARLY DIAGNOSIS

One thing was increasingly clear to me: With autism, early diagnosis is crucial. Birth to age three is a critical time in any child's development. A delayed diagnosis may compromise his chances for success.

It's natural to be afraid of getting a diagnosis. How could a parent not be afraid of learning that her child has an incurable condition filled with challenges? At some point, however, the fear of finding out is exceeded by the agony of not knowing. Watching, day after day, as a child retreats further into a shell; waiting, with a heavy heart, for the familiar smile that never comes anymore; hoping that none of it means anything when you know in your heart that it does—these moments breed fear. And every minute we indulge them costs our child time that could have been spent in treatment.

As painful as it is, parents have to face the facts. If a child has autism, it is not going away. There is nothing we can do to change that reality.

Some parents are told that it's better to avoid "labeling" children— particularly boys—and, even more particularly, African-American boys (who are twice as likely as their white peers to be labeled as "disabled" and placed in special education). Others fear that once a child is diagnosed, their educational and employment records will be tainted for life. One of my son's teachers actually told me this. It's absurd. The fact is, thirty years from now no one will care whether Marty was diagnosed in kindergarten with autism, learning disabilities or any other disorder.

On the contrary, embracing the diagnosis and starting intervention services can help a child grow and blossom. Intensive, well-designed, timely intervention can improve the prospects—and the quality of life— for many children. Without it, they are significantly at risk for cognitive, social, or emotional impairment. Well-implemented programs can brighten a child's future and lead to greater independence, enabling her to be included in her community, and live a more productive, fulfilling life.

NEED FOR ADVOCACY

Unfortunately, getting a diagnosis is not as simple as calling a doctor and getting an appointment for an evaluation. Surprisingly enough, many parents report that they are met with resistance at every turn.

Most private insurance companies, for example, don't pay for these exams. Trying to get coverage can cause frustrating delays. Ultimately, parents may have to find a way to pay these costs themselves. (The issue of insurance coverage for evaluations and treatment of autism is covered in detail in Chapter 8.) In order to determine whether or not your private health insurance company or HMO covers evaluations, you have to be prepared to make some calls and do some homework to find out what's possible for your child.

Another obstacle is the misinformation, ignorance and intolerance that abound, even among the teachers, doctors, caregivers and other experts we've learned to trust. It is not uncommon for parents to share their concerns with one of these experts, only to be told prematurely that there's nothing wrong. When a parent is already living in a quiet state of anxiety, these reassurances can delay their efforts just enough to miss out on an early diagnosis. In our family, listening to the soothing words of well-meaning friends—instead of taking action—cost us time that could never be recaptured.

The more information I amassed about this disorder, the more I began to realize that it was going to be up to me to make things happen—not only to find the best doctors, but to find a way to get on their busy calendars; not only to find the best school, but to get my son enrolled; not only to understand what the best intervention and treatment options were, but to make them a reality for Marty.

Getting all of this accomplished was not going to be a matter of luck, good intentions or connections. If I wanted to succeed, I couldn't just hope for the best. I was going to have to take charge and become an advocate for Marty. Every single day.

I issue the same challenge to you. If your child is autistic, it is not the end of the world. Autism is not a death sentence; it's a way of life. But it can't be approached casually. If you want to succeed in getting the care and services your child needs, you have to take charge, even if that style feels completely foreign.

This is going to take more than you expect—more inner strength, more time, more money, and more patience. It's going to require you to change and grow to accommodate it, to find a place in the world for your child and guard it with your life. And I know you can do it!

Some families fall apart from the strain, but the durable ones find a way to plunge their roots more deeply with every blow. With the skills of an advocate, you can be one of the parents who grow stronger and more adept at coping with unexpected obstacles as the years go by.

By the time I met Dr. Dwayne and Naomi Cox, their nine-year-old son, Dwayne, Jr., had been in public school for one year. Although he was in a special education class, no one had put together the many signs that he was on the autism spectrum.

DJ was incredibly bright, but his mother did notice subtle things: the inappropriate use of toys; lack of imaginative play; rigidity with his daily routines; difficulty paying attention; obsession with facts; and tantrums during transitions. Naomi also knew Dwayne, Jr.'s lack of language was a red flag, but her answer was to have every physical examination possible, including taking him to an ear, nose and throat specialist. She even had his eyes checked!

Ironically, his ability to function well was an obstacle to his diagnosis. Dwayne, Jr., was enrolled in a very expensive preschool, and for two years, not even the sophisticated staff noticed his symptoms. Finally a teacher expressed concern that during circle time Dwayne, Jr., walked around the edges of the room and that he avoided any type of eye contact at all costs; she suggested that he be evaluated. The evaluator said he had a form of "developmental delay," and Naomi and Dwayne decided to move their son to a different school. They weren't ready to challenge the diagnosis and to dig deeper.

By that time, Dwayne was in kindergarten. He continued to excel academically. His first- and second-grade teachers marveled at his academic prowess and raved about how well mannered and polite he was. These glowing reports were bittersweet, since his parents quietly nursed their concerns that something was wrong. Dwayne, Jr., had begun to flap his arms, to focus excessively on objects and to disengage from his family, his peers and even his younger brother. He continued to excel in school, yet he had no friends and spent most of his school day alone in a corner.

As Naomi later admitted, she and her husband were in denial, trying to soothe themselves with the things that were going well. After all, Dwayne could read and write; he not only managed his classroom assignments, he had mastered the majority of them. At two different private schools, five teachers had given him high marks and praise. Sure, he was different, but he'd always been different. Even as an infant, he was constantly moving and distracted. His speech was delayed, but family members said there was no cause for alarm, since several male relatives had had delayed speech.

Despite Dwayne, Jr.'s strengths, by the time he entered the third grade, his parents could no longer ignore his symptoms, but after years of conflicting feedback about their son, they felt exhausted and frustrated. Although they were used to taking charge in their own professional spheres, they quite naturally approached their son's condition like laymen, like the worried parents they were. What they really wanted was to be able to turn to an expert and say, "Please tell us what's wrong!" But in Dwayne, Jr.'s case, the experts couldn't seem to agree.

When Naomi and Dwayne came to me for consultation, they didn't want to overlook any genuine problems, but they were discouraged by years of inconsistent information and contradictory advice. They explained to me that his preschool teacher had noticed problems, but his first- and second-grade teachers had been certain nothing was wrong. Now his third-grade teacher was urging them to seek yet another evaluation. The whole thing had, quite naturally, left them worried and confused.

I advised Naomi and Dwayne not to go to a diagnostic exam without first doing some critical homework:

- Gather all of the information from the various tests.
- Compare that information with their own notes about Dwayne, Jr.'s behavior.
- Write down a series of pointed questions to find out from the next evaluator whether the test results, the information from the experts, and her notes about Dwayne, Jr.'s behavior were consistent with their own observations.

After following this advice, Naomi and Dwayne obtained an evaluation that focused on their son's behavior, his splinter skills and, most important, his learning style. This evaluation was the key—not only to a better understanding of the disorder, but to making decisions about what interventions would best help him address his difficulties with speech and language, social interaction and attention.

Getting a thorough and accurate diagnosis and treatment plan was the first step in Naomi and Dwayne's journey to helping their son. As a result of implementing the plan, they saw marked improvement in his language skills and behavior. He was able to transition from activities without throwing tantrums and he was far more attentive in class.

Dwayne's diagnosis came nearly six years after he entered preschool. This was, in part, due to the understandable optimism and wishful thinking of his parents, but in large part the delay was a result of the many misconceptions about autism and the complexity of making a diagnosis, even when there are warning signs.

Well-intentioned teachers and relatives can often thwart a timely diagnosis. Preoccupation with the mastery of routine skills, such as counting and word memorization, can also keep both teachers and parents from recognizing the signs of autism.

Still, Dwayne's story has a happy ending. Although he was not diagnosed at the critical early intervention age of eighteen to twenty-four months, his parents were aggressive in securing services for him once they got a diagnosis. He's now in seventh grade in a private school setting. Although he continues to need support, he has made tremendous progress. For the first time, he is not an isolated kid with great academic skill; he also has friends.

A diagnosis of autistic spectrum disorder is complex. Any physician or therapist will automatically be inclined to see things according to his or her own bias, unless extenuating facts are presented.

This is why parent advocacy is vital.

Rather than assuming that an expert, in a single evaluation, will make a connection between all the relevant behaviors and any other data from tests or reports, parents must do their homework. And they must be prepared to challenge a diagnosis if it is not consistent with their own knowledge about their child. Naomi wasn't prepared to do that when Dwayne, Jr., was younger, but by the time he was entering third grade, she was ready to step up as a parent advocate. As a result, she approached the evaluators differently. Instead of waiting to hear their opinions about her son's behavior, she went to each evaluation with the connections already mapped out.

Parents are in the best position to do this because they have been puzzling out these connections for months or years. The depth of your knowledge about your own child can never be matched by the evaluator, no matter how skilled he or she is. As an advocate, you can lead and direct the evaluations with specific questions. You can point out connections that the evaluator may have missed. Keeping your mind open to other possibilities, you should go to each exam with a set of questions, key points and issues to be reviewed. There are simply too many possibilities and too many opportunities for error and confusion to sit passively by, hoping for an answer.

As Naomi discovered, strong advocacy can help focus the evaluation and improve the odds of achieving an early and accurate diagnosis.

RECOGNIZE THE WARNING SIGNS

The CDC and many other national and local agencies issue developmental checklists that provide specific, month-by-month descriptions of the milestones a child should be achieving each month.

MILESTONES CHECKLIST

Center for Disease Control www.cdc.gov/ncbddd/actearly/milestones/index.html

Parents can select the age of their child and fill out a milestones checklist. The result can be printed and saved. It's a simple way to document the important milestones a child is meeting.

We naturally think of a child's growth as height and weight, but from birth to five years, a child should be reaching milestones in how he plays, learns, speaks and acts. A delay in any of these areas could be a sign of a developmental problem, even autism. The earlier these developmental delays are recognized, the greater the options for the child's future.

The Mayo Clinic provides a list of characteristics that may indicate autistic spectrum disorder. If a child's behavior matches these characteristics, that is not a diagnosis. Instead, it is a sign that parents should get a comprehensive diagnosis for the child.

Warning Signs: Social Skills
- Fails to respond to his name
- Has poor eye contact
- Appears not to hear others at times
- Resists cuddling and holding
- Appears unaware of others' feelings
- Seems to prefer playing alone, retreats into his own world

Warning Signs: Language
- Starts talking later than other children
- Loses previously acquired ability to say words or sentences
- Does not make eye contact when making requests
- Speaks with an abnormal tone or rhythm, may use a singsong voice or robotlike speech
- Can't start a conversation or keep one going
- May repeat words or phrases verbatim, but doesn't understand how to use them

Warning Signs: Behavior

- Performs repetitive movements, such as rocking, spinning or hand flapping
- Develops specific routines or rituals
- Becomes disturbed at the slightest change in routines or rituals
- Moves constantly
- May be fascinated by parts of an object (e.g., the spinning wheels of a car)
- May be unusually sensitive to light, sound and touch, yet oblivious to pain[6]

Most children with autism are slow to acquire new knowledge or skills. Another symptom, as doctors at Mayo have observed, is difficulty sharing experiences with others. When a parent reads to them, children with autism are unlikely to point at the pictures or interact with the parent.

In *Raising a Sensory Smart Child*, Lindsey Biel and Nancy Peske tell a story that is, unfortunately, very common. When their child, Cole, was still only a few months old, Nancy and George noticed that he was missing developmental milestones. Later, when most toddlers were adding words and sounds to their vocabularies, Cole seemed to "lose every vocabulary word as soon as he learned it." But like hundreds of other parents whose sons exhibit developmental delays, Nancy and George were told that boys develop later, so they should "wait and see." At Cole's two-year checkup, the pediatrician finally suggested the couple get an evaluation from a speech pathologist. Unfortunately, Nancy and George couldn't find one with an opening less than four months away. Nancy posted a desperate query on an online message board for parents asking what she should do. A helpful mother wrote back, saying that, "every state provides a free evaluation and free or low-cost services for children under age three who may have developmental delays." Nancy and George scheduled a two-hour evaluation in a matter of weeks and discovered that Cole needed early intervention—both speech therapy and occupational therapy.[7]

FIND A PHYSICIAN TO DIAGNOSE YOUR CHILD

Before taking Marty to get a diagnosis, I learned about the importance of early intervention. That knowledge helped me overcome any of my own urges to deny that anything was wrong. Once I became aware of the time factor, I was eager to get an evaluation, but finding someone with the expertise to provide an accurate assessment was not as simple as looking under "Autism Evaluations" in the phone book or calling a regular pediatrician. Many pediatricians, nurse practitioners and internists don't have any experience in diagnosing autism. But they can make a referral to someone skilled in this complicated specialty. When I went through this process myself, we were fortunate that our pediatrician knew a highly qualified specialist who could evaluate our son. In the years since then, I've spoken with hundreds of parents who had to do a lot of legwork to find the right person to evaluate their children.

Whenever I speak to the clients in my special-education law practice[8] or the parents who come to my Special Needs Network[9] for help and support, I recommend that they give their pediatrician very specific information about what they're looking for: a pediatrician with a specialty in either developmental pediatrics or neurodevelopmental disorders (and preferably a board certification in one of these areas); or a psychiatrist or psychologist with expertise in evaluating developmental disorders. Knowing exactly what you're looking for can eliminate frustrating obstacles and dead ends.

Other professionals, such as speech pathologists, occupational therapists and physical therapists, may be on an assessment team, but rarely have the qualifications to make a definitive diagnosis of autism. If a pediatrician or primary care physician cannot make a recommendation, call the local public school and ask for a referral from the school's psychologist. It's best to avoid picking an unknown evaluator from the Internet or the phone book, but when that is the only option, these reputable Web sites offer resources for parents to find doctors for special-needs children:

Autism Speaks:[10] http://www.autismspeaks.org
American Academy of Pediatrics:[11] http://aap.org
American Board of Pediatrics: https://www.abp.org/ABPWebStatic
American Board of Psychiatry and Neurology:[12] www.abpn.com

IMPORTANT QUALIFICATIONS

In addition to finding someone with experience and expertise in evaluating developmental disorders, here are some other important considerations in choosing an evaluator:

1. How long has the doctor been in practice?

2. How long has he worked with autistic spectrum disorder (ASD) patients?

3. How long has he had a certification in his specialty?

4. What percentage of his patients have developmental disabilities?

5. What age children does he typically evaluate?

6. Has he been practicing in the community long enough to be well connected to local services and treatment programs?

7. What tests does he use? Why?

8. If the tests are positive, does he provide treatment?

When you consult an expert, notice whether the waiting room is friendly to an autistic child. It should not be too busy or noisy. There should be toys in the room that might interest an autistic child. The expert's personal qualities should also be taken into account. Is she patient, empathetic and hopeful? Does she address your child directly and interact easily? Ask the doctor if there is an observation room where you can watch the interaction that takes place between the doctor and your child. You may even ask if you can videotape the evaluation. It is important that you feel comfortable asking questions and feel that your concerns are being heard. If the doctor makes it hard to ask questions and does not listen to your concerns, keep looking.

WHAT TO SAY. . .

When Physicians Postpone Examinations

Trust me. This will happen. Parents must learn to keep moving, without breaking stride. Go in strong. Successful advocates turn hesitation into action. Knowing what to say can—and does—help.

PHYSICIAN: "There is a waiting list for an appointment."
PARENT: "Please put us on your waiting list. But in the meantime, can you give me two referrals? It's important that we see someone right away."
PHYSICIAN: "A child must be diagnosed before intervention can begin."
PARENT: "I know that getting a diagnosis is important, but that process can take time. Right now, my child is not speaking. We'd like to begin speech therapy immediately."
PHYSICIAN: "Wait and see if the symptoms subside in a few months."
PARENT: "Developmental disorders don't subside. My child has already missed several developmental milestones. The sooner we intervene, the better."

PREPARE FOR THE DIAGNOSIS

First, you should know that four diagnostic tools are generally used to make a diagnosis: parent observations; general developmental tools; ASD screening tools such as the Checklist for Autism in Toddlers (CHAT), the Modified Checklist for Autism in Toddlers (M-CHAT) and the Childhood Autism Rating Scale (CARS); and direct observation of your child by an expert in the field of autism evaluation. The exams often take two to four hours and may even take place over several visits. Costs vary, but should range from $1,600 to $2,400.

Unlike a physical medical exam, where a doctor uses a stethoscope and other tools to determine whether a child has an ear infection or swollen tonsils, the evaluation to determine whether your child has autism depends on you.

You will be asked to answer a long series of questions about your child. Prepare yourself to provide detailed information about your child's speech and daily behavior. The best way to ensure that the information you give is specific and accurate is to keep a journal from the moment you suspect that your child may not be developing typically.

Record in this journal every conceivable detail about your child. Makes notes about his daily schedule, sleep patterns, diet and eating habits, words he uses or stops using, responses to simple commands, crying spells or tantrums. If you notice any other unusual behavior, such as flapping his arms or stacking objects into towers, jot it down. Be sure to note the date and time this behavior started and how often it occurred. Without a journal, these kinds of details will be missed.

Your personal journal also becomes documented evidence of what has been happening with your child. Keeping clear records like this can debunk any notion that you are exaggerating or mistaken in your observations.

When you go to the evaluation, take any other relevant documents as well, including reports from school, day care or any other setting in which your child may have received instruction; medical reports outlining the immunization schedule; and a list of your child's medical conditions and medications taken at any time.

With this documentation, you will be prepared to get the diagnosis your child needs to start making real progress. As a parent advocate, you will learn to focus on one task at a time to keep from feeling overwhelmed. The first one is getting a diagnosis.

As time goes on, you will learn to surround yourself with a reliable team of doctors, caregivers, friends, supporters and other advocates who can offer insight and advice. You will come to trust yourself more, as you surmount one obstacle after another. By applying the principles of advocacy, you will begin to have more success in commanding the attention of administrators who are accustomed to dismissing parents. You will become an expert in the issues regarding your child. You will learn to think clearly and speak with authority. All of these things will give you more confidence. As a stronger parent and accomplished advocate, you will even come to educate others around you—from the misinformed stranger who thinks your disruptive child only needs discipline to the misguided physician who assumes he knows what's best for your child. Your transformation into a staunch parent advocate will not happen overnight. You will grow into the role with time and experience.

The implications of autism for your child's life and your own will take years to grasp. There is an enormous amount of information to learn, but you don't have to get up to speed right away. Throughout the course of this book, you will be introduced to the information that has been most vital to my family, as well as to the clients at my law firm and the Special Needs Network. And you will learn the skills of advocacy that will make you a powerful force in protecting your child's rights and getting things done on her behalf.

10 THINGS YOU SHOULD KNOW FROM DAY ONE

1. Statistics only predict norms: Every child is unique.

2. Stop comparing to other kids: Improvement is the best measure.

3. Don't give in to needless panic: Check with a professional before getting alarmed over information found on the Internet.

4. Keep records: In addition to your notebook, there is a wide array of technology available, such as regular and digital video cameras. Record disconcerting behavior/incidents and let the doctors see exactly what is happening.

5. Be fearless: Don't be afraid of the system or of being disliked.

6. Verify everything: Well-meaning professionals aren't always right.

7. Know your child loves you: Autistic children show love differently. It's up to you to find and cherish those cues.

8. Believe you can do this: It will get better.

9. Accept help: Learn to let go a little.

10. Enjoy your child every day: Remember the gift of having this child you love.

PUTTING IT INTO ACTION

1. Make a list of at least three experts in your area who specialize in autism. Visit their Web sites or contact their offices to get information on their rates, availability and expertise. You may not need these professionals now, but it is a way to start building your database of resources for future use.

2. If you have a child who may be on the autism spectrum, visit one of the Web sites mentioned in this chapter and review the developmental milestones. Has your child met the appropriate milestones for her age? If you are uncertain, discuss the milestones with a qualified professional.

3. Start videotaping your child when he is exhibiting behavior that concerns you. This information can be invaluable to you, as well as the doctors, therapists and others who assess his progress.

4. Share the information in this chapter with a friend or relative who needs support or information about obtaining a diagnosis for autism.

CHAPTER 2

A New Perspective:
Stepping Up

G etting an accurate diagnosis is a turning point. In practical terms, it means that you can stop wondering what's wrong and start learning everything you need to know about your child's condition. Instead of searching for a way to make sense of unexpected quirks and inexplicable behavior, you finally have an explanation.

It should be a relief. But it can come as a shock.

I'm no stranger to hardship. You don't go from being raised by a disabled grandmother and a night-shift janitor, to a Harvard Law School honors graduate who runs a successful law firm in LA, without sweat and tears. After coming so far, I thought I could handle anything. Then I had an autistic child.

When I first learned my son's diagnosis, I couldn't even say the word "autism" without breaking down in tears. For months, I had put off going to a specialist for a diagnosis, hoping that whatever was happening with Marty would simply go away.

If I hadn't already had two daughters, I might have managed to stay in denial a little longer. But Marty was my third child. His two older sisters had given me models of what normal development for a two-year-old looked like. At this age, both Morgan and Michael had been speaking in complete sentences. Morgan had even potty trained herself by then. One day, she had simply declared she was ready to move on to "big girl" pants and refused to wear diapers anymore. Her older sister, Michael, was asking so many questions at this age that we were sure she was destined to be an attorney like her mom and dad.

Kindhearted friends reassured me. Boys always talk later than girls. If Marty preferred to play by himself and hoard a collection of plastic spoons and straws, maybe he was just independent and inventive. How I wanted to believe them! But in my heart, I knew that none of their assurances could explain what was happening with my son.

When my husband, Ernest, and I finally met with Dr. Diane Henderson, a developmental pediatrician, she told us gently that she suspected Marty had autism. This was her compassionate way of easing the blow. She recommended that we get a second opinion, but we didn't need to. I knew her diagnosis was right. But hearing it was a shock. As she described the condition, I sat in stunned silence, with the word "autism" playing over and over in my head. Minutes later, when I touched my face, I found it was covered with tears. When we left her office, I drove to a nearby parking lot, stopped the car and wept.

I was so afraid for my son—not only for what he might go through, but for how other people might treat him. It took months of love and support from many family members before I could share the diagnosis with anyone else. Right-brained pragmatist that he is, Ernest kept saying, "You might as well tell people he has autism. If they can't accept Marty, they can say good-bye to the Martins. We're a package deal." He kept encouraging me to be more open about it, but I wasn't ready.

"There's no need to call it *autism* . . ." I told myself. After all, I could truthfully say he was still getting tested and the doctors weren't quite sure about the true nature of his condition. Somehow the vagueness seemed to leave more room for hope.

Most of all, I didn't want to risk the horrible possibility that someone would hear the word "autism" and assume that Marty was doomed.

Like many parents, I also felt a profound sense of loss. We had not lost Marty, the boy we all loved and adored, but so many wonderful things we had hoped would be a part of his experience—going to school with his sisters, playing sports, taking a girl to the prom, attending college, starting a career—had been swept away with a single word.

It was far better—even crucial—to have a diagnosis. But as the implications began to sink in, my fear and resistance were gradually replaced with grief.

A HEALTHY SENSE OF GRIEF

Grief is the appropriate response to loss. It's the emotional suffering you feel when something or someone you love is taken away.

It is natural for parents to mourn the news of their child's incurable disorder and the loss of the child they expected. You may associate grief with the deaths of loved ones (and such a loss does often cause intense grief). But grief can accompany the loss of:

relationships	friendships
health	cherished dreams
employment	attachments
financial stability	security

Decades ago, Elisabeth Kübler-Ross, MD, identified the stages of grief in her famous book *On Death and Dying*. Others have built on her work to give us insight into the ways we respond to tragedies in our lives. In coping with the diagnosis of autism, parents may experience many of these stages, in any order. In fact, it's common to have good days and bad—moving back and forth between them—as we struggle toward acceptance.

Stage One: Shock, Denial, Isolation

"My child doesn't have autism. He's just different."

In this stage, we protect ourselves by using denial and isolation as a buffer, to keep us from being overwhelmed by the full extent of this new reality. It is a survival instinct—the equivalent of putting our arms up to cover our face when something rushes toward us too quickly. It allows us to modulate our exposure, so we can take it in at our own pace.

Stage Two: Awareness and Emotional Release

"Is this my fault? Did I do something to cause my child to have autism?"

When we feel safe enough to acknowledge the reality, our emotions take over. We can feel anger and guilt. We may try to deflect those feelings by blaming someone else or even bargaining with God in exchange for a different outcome.

Stage Three: Depression

"Nothing will ever be the same. The future is grim."

Ultimately, we are left to face the reality. Our denial and isolation have bought us a little time to get used to the idea. We've had a chance to vent, but then a feeling of pain and hopelessness can sweep over us.

Stage Four: Acceptance

"Autism is a challenge, but we can cope with it together."

In this stage, we come to terms with reality. Our acceptance gives us enough relief that we can start to engage in social activities again. We're able to talk about the situation without as much pain and find a way to feel hopeful for the future.

Acceptance is the goal, but each of these stages is perfectly normal and healthy.[1]

The most damaging response is to suppress these feelings or hold on to the grief too long. When a parent pushes away any fear, frustration, anger or resentment he may be feeling, those emotions can break out in other ways. Anxiety attacks, insomnia, weight fluctuations and chronic depression can indicate that a parent has been overwhelmed and is not making a fluid progression through the stages of grief. Consultation with a therapist or medical professional can help get things back on track.

It's important to honor your genuine feelings, whatever they are, and not try to make them into something you think you ought to feel. Everyone comes to terms with this diagnosis in their own way. My husband cried with me in the parking lot after we heard Marty's diagnosis, but after that he never looked back. He was ready to move with all deliberate speed to learn about the therapies and treatments, find appropriate programs and wade right into the autism information maze. I needed more time than that. You may too. But the truth is, the longer you spend in guilt and self-pity, the longer you delay the ability to vigorously help your child.

USE ADVOCACY TO ALLEVIATE DENIAL

Advocacy can help you move past denial more quickly. Directing your energy toward an issue, rather than away from it, can be so empowering that it motivates you to do even more.

1. Talk to someone you trust about what you are observing in your child. Find someone who will not try to persuade you to take a particular action, but will simply listen.

2. Journal your observations. Review what you write three or four times a week.

3. Make yourself familiar with the medical literature on autism and its many causes and symptoms.

4. Attend a workshop or seminar on the topic. Getting more information will help you have a better understanding.

5. Visit a preschool or classroom with typical children. Seeing other children who are comparable in age will help you have a frame of reference for your child's behavior.

Get in the habit of asking what you can do, instead of ruminating or dwelling on your sense of frustration, anxiety or uncertainty. One of the finest skills an advocate can develop is the ability to act effectively despite those feelings. Cultivate this skill and you will become a powerful advocate for your child. As you practice you will also move toward acceptance.

FOOLING OURSELVES

For many parents, Stage One is the most difficult. Because we have all heard that denial is a common response to grief, most of us are alert to the tendency to fool ourselves in the obvious ways. Even if we try to deny it for a while, sooner or later, we at least manage to admit that something is wrong.

But denial is insidious. It can take many forms. Refusing to call the condition by name and clinging to false hope are two of the most common forms of denial.

Denial Posing as Discretion

Denying that a serious medical condition or developmental disability exists is no cure. It actually perpetuates a myth that is harmful to both the child and the family.

Sometimes a spouse or family members are so frightened by the idea that something could be wrong that they try to keep you from getting a diagnosis. It's as if they're clinging to the hope that if they don't name it, it isn't real.

I understand this fear. I was worried too that if we used the label "autism," Marty would be stereotyped and subjected to social isolation. It seemed safer and more discreet to avoid using the term.

Avoiding the diagnosis doesn't alter how your child is received by peers and other adults. Even those who are unfamiliar with the technical name for the disorder will know that the child is different from her peers. A child who withdraws from other people or engages in self-stimulatory behaviors—such as spinning—will continue to do so with or without the label. And the behavior speaks for itself. A rude, insensitive person will criticize, humiliate or taunt anyone with unusual behavior, whether they are disabled or not. In fact, the failure to give a name to the behavior can make matters worse. Confronting the issue head-on, getting a proper diagnosis and embracing the child's differences allow parents and family members the opportunity to raise awareness, and to educate themselves and others.

We are social creatures, who learn how to act—and even how to feel—by observing the people around us. When a family embraces a child and loves him unconditionally, regardless of his unusual behavior, it models that response and gives everyone permission to do the same. It's amazing how others respond to a child when it is clear that the family has accepted and adjusted to the child's disorder.

Getting to that point can be difficult and happens over time. This journey will undoubtedly be marked with pain and disappointment, but it will also be filled with many victories and sweet moments to be treasured over a lifetime.

Denial Posing as Optimism

Rarely do parents pretend there's nothing wrong when a child is exhibiting the symptoms of autism. But they can fool themselves in other ways. As if they're determined to "overcome" the diagnosis by sheer persistence, some parents spend hundreds of hours getting second, third and even fourth opinions, hoping to find a way out—another evaluation that minimizes the symptoms, a training method that promises to eliminate the unwanted behaviors, a medical breakthrough that offers relief.

It's a way of accepting and yet not accepting the diagnosis.

In their unrelenting search for alternatives, these parents are demonstrating the courage, tenacity and dogged determination that would make them excellent advocates in getting the services they need to help their child. Instead of using this invaluable energy to make life better for their child with autism, however, they focus on trying to eliminate the condition altogether. Only a parent can know where to draw the line between looking for new possibilities and making the best of things as they are. But it can help to realize that, sometimes, optimism is denial in disguise.

Denial Posing as a Miracle

Every week, I get several calls from clients, relatives of clients, my own relatives and friends, asking me if I have seen the latest report of a child who has apparently been cured of autism.

As I said in Chapter 1, too much emphasis on causes and cures can take us away from the everyday realities our children face—regardless of what caused their condition or whether it will eventually be cured. I would rather spend the bulk of my time working to improve the life of my own child and other children with autism today.

It's encouraging to hear of the wonderful "recovery" of someone who has had a spontaneous remission or a successful chemotherapy treatment for cancer. Most of us also know of good people who have lost their battle with diseases, despite receiving state-of-the-art treatment. And it's no surprise that there are also lots of stories with happy endings for children who have autism. How we hear these stories can tell us a lot about whether we are using the hope of a miracle cure as a kind of denial.

In her book *After the Diagnosis*, Dr. JoAnn LeMaistre talks about people whose reactions to a diagnosis fall at opposite ends of the spectrum. Some move directly to depression, resigning themselves to a gloomy sense of helplessness. Others cling to a Pollyanna approach that is fueled by joyous testimonials that "tug at the heartstrings" of everyone who reads them. Besides creating false hope by overplaying the likelihood of complete recovery, the Pollyanna approach invalidates the genuine sadness and depression that are a healthy part of the grief process.[2]

As mature adults, our experience tells us that, realistically, a particular intervention or treatment will be a great success for some children and not so great with others. Autism outcomes, like cancer outcomes, can vary widely. In the case of autism, the outcome depends on a number of factors, including the level of delay a child has, the age at which he or she is diagnosed, the type and quality of the intervention provided, and the level of familial support, among others. Recognizing this is no reason to give up hope or imagine the worst.

Unfortunately, parents are often told early on that they need to pick sides—either accept the medical evaluation of the scientists at the Centers for Disease Control and Prevention, who say there is no cure; or align themselves with the movement popularized by the actress Jenny McCarthy, who believes complete recovery is possible. I don't think parents should be forced to pick a side. The reality is that hope is an important element to helping your child succeed, and you can never be wrong in hoping for the best outcome.

If a report comes out saying that a new drug or therapy has helped increase language in children with autism, by all means investigate the study and determine—in collaboration with your team of experts—whether the treatment makes sense for your child. By doing so, you don't have to form any particular judgment about whether autism can be cured. You just have to believe in exploring treatment options that are likely to lead to success.

WHAT ARE YOU REALLY SAYING?

Stories of miracle cures can have a surprisingly negative impact on the very children parents are trying to protect.

In recent years, some adolescents and adults with autism have begun to describe how it feels for people to say they have "a disability" or "a problem," when it doesn't feel like that to them at all. For her *New York Times* article, "How About Not 'Curing' Us?" Amy Harmon spoke to an autistic boy in the Catskills named Jack. "We don't have a disease," Jack and his classmates agreed. "So we can't be 'cured.' This is just the way we are."[3]

Across the country a new movement is taking shape among those with high-functioning autism and Asperger's syndrome. Inspired by the student-activist days of the sixties, they claim the right to neurodiversity as a basic civil liberty and think of themselves as the Autistic Liberation Front.

At the 1994 International Conference on Autism in Toronto, autistic activist Jim Sinclair addressed himself to parents in a moving presentation entitled "Don't Mourn for Us."

> Look at your grief from our perspective. . . . Autism isn't something a person *has*, or a "shell" that a person is trapped inside. There's no normal child hidden behind the autism. Autism is a way of being. It is *pervasive*; it colors every experience, every sensation, perception, thought, emotion, and encounter, every aspect of existence. . . . It is not possible to separate the person from the autism. Therefore, when parents say, "I wish my child did not have autism," what they're really saying is, "I wish the autistic child I have did not exist, and I had a different (non-autistic) child instead." . . . This is what we hear when you mourn over our existence. This is what we hear when you pray for a cure.[4]

TAKING THE BLAME

Although the desire to blame someone can be a part of the emotional release in the second stage of grief, it can also exist without any connection to grief at all. When it is wrongly directed toward a vulnerable parent, it can be especially destructive.

A few years ago, I spoke at a conference for parents in a large church in Los Angeles. The audience asked me spirited questions about the causes of the autism epidemic. There was familiar speculation about whether autism was caused by immunizations, toxins or something in the environment. A few parents may have been looking for the emotional release of blaming an external source. But most of the questions were asked by eager parents with an intimate knowledge of autism, who genuinely wanted to know what was causing the increase in this condition.

After about an hour, a delicate woman in the back stood up to speak. Her voice was shaking and she was visibly crying. The hundreds of clamoring parents in the room instantly yielded the floor.

The young mother said that this was the first time she had spoken in public about her daughter, who had been diagnosed with autism as a toddler four years ago. As soon as she heard the diagnosis, this young mother sought counsel from the pastor of her church.

What her pastor told her shocked us all. He said bluntly that her daughter's autism was God's way of punishing her for her sins, and the only way her daughter could be healed was for her to repent and commit her life to God. She was weeping uncontrollably as she told us she had spent the last four years believing that she was responsible for her daughter's condition.

Her story brought tears to our eyes. We were all horrified to hear that a man in his position could behave in such a cruel and irresponsible way. The toll it had taken on this young mother was painful to see. As I walked over to console her, other mothers stood up and said that they had placed blame on themselves in a similar way. Some had spent months, and even years, believing that they were responsible for their child's condition.

It's only human to lash out at others or blame ourselves when we feel frustrated and trapped. One mother put it like this:

> If you knew what caused it, you could fix it, right? So it's your husband's fault because you told him not to tickle the baby so much, or because everybody on his side is a little weird, or it's your fault because you had that glass of wine with dinner in the second trimester, or you kept working so late into your pregnancy, or you weren't

overjoyed when you found out you were pregnant.... Blame can cause damage that's hard to repair.[5]

It's bad enough for parents to blame each other. When a pastor, a colleague, a family member or even a total stranger takes it upon themselves to blame the parents, it can be hard to bear. Some of the women in the church that night said that they had actually been accused of not nurturing their child enough as an infant, a notion advanced in the 1940s by Dr. Leo Kanner. Because it put the blame on allegedly cold mothers with "a genuine lack of maternal warmth" (many of whom had other children who were not autistic), it soon came to be called the "refrigerator mother" theory. Since that time, the blame has fallen on older-aged fathers, television watching, food allergies, household chemicals, wireless technology and children themselves, if they spend too much time indoors. As recently as November 2008, scientists at Cornell University said that increased rainfall could be the culprit.[6]

WHAT TO SAY. . .

When People Blame You

Many people still believe that autism is caused by a mother's failure to nurture her child after birth. Accusations like this can be hurtful and intensify feelings of guilt in a parent. Rather than simply turning away, consider adopting the active stance of an advocate. As an advocate, you can view these comments as an opportunity to educate and inform people about their misconceptions.

COWORKER: I am so sorry to hear that your child has autism. My cousin's son was diagnosed last year. I heard it was because my cousin went back to work too soon after his birth.

PARENT: Sixty years ago a doctor wrote a paper saying that autism was related to whether a mother was sufficiently nurturing to her child. His research was completely unfounded. Fortunately, we now know that autism is a complex neurological disorder. So you can rest assured that your cousin had nothing to do with her baby's condition.

FRIEND: Did you see that special on television about the little boy
who was cured of autism after his mother cuddled with him every
night and read him stories? Maybe that would work with your
child.

PARENT: I missed that special, but trust me, cuddling and reading are
not cures for autism. There is no scientific evidence suggesting
that mothers can cause or cure a child of autism.

RELATIVE: They say something goes wrong during pregnancy to
make a child autistic. Did you eat any food or take medication
that could be responsible for your son's autism?

PARENT: I took great care of myself during my pregnancy. But there
is absolutely no causal link between a mother's prenatal care and
autism. The experts speculate that autism is related to a combination of genetic and environmental factors. I can't control either
of those things.

IT'S OKAY TO FEEL DEPRESSED

Depression is a healthy response, a normal stage of grief. Obviously,
I'm not encouraging you to deliberately stir up a sense of depression by
running worst-case scenarios over in your mind or seeing only the negative side of the situation. Although the stages of grief are quite universal,
no two people respond in the same way and no two situations affect you
in exactly the same way.

Some people move through the feeling of depression fairly quickly.
They do feel the isolation, the sadness and the helplessness, but their
attention turns readily to acceptance and action. You may be one of
those people. Just be sure that you're not one of the ones who shut down
depression so completely that they don't even know they're feeling it.
This stage of grief can't be suppressed. It's much simpler to let yourself
feel it than to wait for that upset emotion to break out into your life
when you least expect it—causing sudden accidents, angry outbursts,
toxic bitterness and inexplicable health problems.

No one wants to feel depressed, but the fact remains that it can be an
appropriate response. When you reach this stage of grief, you may have
a desire to shield yourself by not discussing the situation for a while. It's

okay to decide that telling friends and talking with experts can come later. Allow yourself space.

Be gentle with yourself. If you are feeling sad, it's because—right now, at least—this situation upsets you. Maybe it won't later. Maybe the good outweighs the bad and you'll discover that. In the end, you'll want to look for the bright side and learn what a powerful difference you can make in your child's life. But experiencing your feelings—whatever they are—is the only real way to get there.

It's not unusual to have contradictory feelings. One part of you may feel depressed or afraid the diagnosis of autism means you'll no longer have a life. At the same time, another—equally legitimate—part of you may disagree. ("How can you be depressed? Did you only want a perfect child?")

Sometimes, even when you think you've moved past the grief, you can feel a sudden wave of sadness when you see other children your child's age, talking and playing together. In the beginning, when the diagnosis is new and you're at your most vulnerable, the happiness of other healthy children can be hard to bear. It can lead to resentment, envy, depression and even anger.

It can be hard to own up to such feelings—most of us would like to be above that kind of "pettiness"—but the truth is, we feel them anyway! In our competitive society, we all want our children to excel—to get the best grades, be the star athlete, get accepted by the top schools. Even when we know in our hearts that these things aren't what really matter, it can be painful to give up the dream.

CREATE YOUR OWN PERSPECTIVE

Unless you find another dream for your child, depression is inevitable. Until you adopt a new perspective, you will constantly be measuring your child against an unfair standard that should never be applied to him. When other parents mention the achievements of their children, you'll feel embarrassed by your own child. How can you stand up for a child who embarrasses you?

Defining your own perspective is one of the secrets to being an unshakable advocate for your child. It will also serve as a helping hand to lift you out of depression. When you recognize that you, and only you, can decide what's best for your child, what's appropriate for him in every area—from education to medical care to socialization to behavior in public to quality time with your family—you can relax and start to trust yourself. When other people insist that they know best, remind yourself that, regardless of their opinions, you have a privileged perspective based on your intimate knowledge of your own child.

Over the years, as many of your choices prove right, you will increasingly validate your confidence in the choices you make and help yourself maintain your own stable, loving perspective on your child.

First of all, when you encounter people—and you will, no matter what you do!—who make obnoxious, uninformed comments, don't take it personally. Don't let yourself fall prey to their antiquated theories or ignorant remarks. You have to protect your own well-being, so you can be physically and emotionally strong enough to care for your child. There is never any reason to relinquish control over your feelings to others.

Sometimes you may have to reach deep to find a way to hold your ground, but every time you succeed, you get a little stronger. Over time, you'll begin to notice that it's gotten harder for other people to throw you off balance, no matter what their position of authority or what remarks they make.

Second, don't just ignore other people's hurtful assumptions or comments; take charge of the situation instead. Even the most obnoxious person can be turned around very quickly when you offer a candid explanation. By demystifying autism with clear, honest information, you let them in and diminish their need to gossip or make disparaging remarks while they try to figure out what your child's behavior means.

Whether they admit it to themselves or not, people are afraid of the unknown. Explaining what autism is and debunking the myths they may have heard will go a long way toward shifting their attitudes. Sometimes a creative analogy can give them a familiar way to think about it.

Years ago, a charming essay by Laura Krueger Crawford began to circulate on the Internet. It's a beautiful model of the kind of warm acceptance, wit and humor that can win people over and soften hearts.

My son is now eight and, though we have come to accept that he will always have autism, we no longer feel like citizens of a battle-torn nation. With the help of countless dedicated therapists and teachers, biological interventions, and an enormously supportive family, my son has become a fun-loving, affectionate boy with many endearing qualities and skills.

In the process we've created . . . well . . . our own country, with its own unique traditions and customs. . . . Let's call it Schmolland.

In Schmolland, it is perfectly customary to lick walls, rub cold pieces of metal across your mouth and line up all your toys end-to-end. . . . It is quite normal to repeat lines from videos to express emotion . . .

Other families who are affected by autism are familiar and comforting to us, yet still separate entities. Together we make up a federation of countries, kind of like Scandinavia . . . we share enough similarities in language and customs to understand each other, but conversations inevitably highlight the diversity of our traditions.

"Oh, your child is a runner? Mine won't go to the bathroom without asking permission." "My child eats paper. Yesterday he ate a whole video box." "My daughter only eats 4 foods, all of them white." "My son wants to blow on everyone." "My son can't stand to hear the word no. We can't use any negatives at all in our house." "We finally had to lock up the VCR because my son was obsessed with the rewind button." . . .

I will never stop investigating new treatments and therapies that might help my son. But, more and more, my priorities are shifting from what "could be" to "what is." I look around at this country my family has created, with all its unique customs, and it feels like home.[7]

ACCEPTANCE

Eventually you may be comfortable enough to take the initiative and start telling people that your child has autism before they even ask. Once the mystery is removed, people can be remarkably kind and sympathetic.

If you have difficulty talking about your child's diagnosis, you may want to start with a safe environment and move outward. Begin by talking to a group of parents and experts whom you trust and who also understand the issues. With them, you will be able to rely on their sensitivity if the conversation is more upsetting than you might expect and touches on your pain, guilt and fears.

It's perfectly normal to be cautious about sharing your feelings about your child at first. Even when you decide you would like to turn to friends, finding the right confidants may be a matter of trial and error. Like many mothers I've spoken to, Bonnie Berry LaMon told me she felt utterly lost and alone when she learned her son Jesse's diagnosis. She worried that his autism might be related to the fact that she gave birth at age forty, or had a high-powered career that came with a lot of stress. Bonnie was a partner at one of the nation's largest law firms and managed the careers of Grammy award–winning artists. While she was pregnant with Jesse, she was navigating the complexities of intellectual property and financing multiyear record deals. In the months after he was born, she spent long hours at the office, catching up. Although she thrived on the pressure, she wondered if it had had a negative impact on her son.

When he started to display unusual behavior, Bonnie did research online and found thousands of articles and studies, but much of it left her confused. Jesse was extremely verbal. He could spell and read, but like many children with autism, he often found it difficult to answer questions, respond to his name or make the transition between simple activities. His symptoms did not fit neatly into any of the categories of literature on autism she found. Jesse's preschool teacher told her that a diagnosis of autism would be harmful over the course of his education, since he would be labeled and relegated to special classes.

With such conflicting information, Bonnie found it difficult to talk to friends about Jesse's behavior. In addition, like many parents who are accustomed to having all the answers and running the show, talking about her emotions, fears and sense of lack of control was challenging. Although she told a few close friends, their sympathy didn't offer the kind of assistance she needed.

When Bonnie came to me, I reassured her that she was not the only parent feeling this kind of conflict. Many others like her had joined my nonprofit organization, the Special Needs Network. Finding people who have had similar experiences can provide real comfort. Bonnie was eager to try it.

When she saw that other parents—many of whom, like her, were accomplished professionals—had the same questions and concerns, she realized that she didn't have to go it alone. In this environment, she could talk honestly about Jesse's condition without worrying about criticism, judgment or even naive questions ("What do you mean, your son can't use a fork? He's four years old, isn't he?"). She could admit that Jesse—even at age four—was still having problems going to the toilet by himself, brushing his teeth and dressing himself.

She drew strength from learning more about possible outcomes and opportunities for success. Bonnie also bonded with other parents whose stories of their children's strengths and challenges made it easier for her to discuss her son's condition with extended family members, coworkers and others in her immediate circle. Bonnie could answer questions about her son's condition more confidently, laugh off any insensitive comments and in general stride into her role as advocate.

Besides the Special Needs Network, another thing that helped Bonnie move more swiftly toward acceptance was her consultation at my office. Not everyone realizes that an initial consultation with an attorney is often free of charge. It does not commit you to a contract or a course of action. In some cases, you may pay for an hour's consultation, but in others, the attorney will simply limit the time they discuss your case—in person or by phone—to thirty minutes. Even that brief meeting yields important information and can give you direction when you need it.

HOW TO FIND LEGAL SUPPORT

Every time I appear on the Dr. Phil *show as the autism expert, I'm flooded with calls afterward. People who have seen me on the show express their relief. Most of them say they haven't been able to find an attorney who is knowledgeable about special needs.*

Others call to tell me, "We have one attorney in our town who focuses on children's rights at school. But she works for the school district!" Or they say they've finally found an attorney who knows about special-needs children, but he's too expensive and they can't afford his advice.

One of the reasons this deluge of callers can't find an attorney in this field is that very few of them exist. I couldn't find one either, when I first learned Marty's diagnosis!

Yes, even in the city of Los Angeles, where there are more than five hundred thousand attorneys, I could find only a handful who specialized in special rights for children. Many of them were working only part-time in the field. Ultimately, I drove to the San Fernando Valley to meet with an attorney. Because I'd heard horror stories about the difficulty of getting interventions and services children were entitled to, I wanted advice from a knowledgeable expert who could warn me about potential minefields or dead ends.

Knowing firsthand how hard it was for parents to find the vital information they needed, as I explored the field I wanted to share everything I was learning. First, I expanded my legal practice to include special-needs children. Then I began to speak everywhere I could, to educate others about what I'd learned—and continued to learn every day. Whenever I saw a new opportunity to help, I took it.

Not long after I expanded my legal practice, I realized that one of the biggest things parents were lacking was a community of others going through the same struggles on a daily basis. The Special Needs Network was set up to help parents move through their grief by bringing them together in small groups, town hall meetings and other forums with other parents and experts. You can start a similar support group in your own area—you don't need any special training to do it!

If you discover that you cannot find a special-needs attorney in your own town, check the bar associations of the nearest urban area. The bigger cities are more likely to have at least a few attorneys who are qualified to give you advice for a special-needs child. They may be willing to meet for a consultation by phone.

Even if you are looking for an attorney to represent your child in your local court or school district, it is possible to hire an attorney who is licensed out of state. It's common practice for attorneys to form temporary affiliations with local law firms so they can file documents and negotiate cases in other states. Not all attorneys do it, but you can find out with a single phone call. Don't hesitate to ask. Legal advice about the complicated morass surrounding autism—in terms of rights, medical treatments, education, caregivers and a host of other issues—can prove invaluable.

Remember, you don't have to go it alone. If you are willing to ask for help and to surround yourself with people who can provide support, you will have an easier time than if you stay isolated. Your ability to move toward acceptance can be greatly eased by cultivating social support around you—either among your own friends and family or through organizations like the Special Needs Network.

THE CALL TO ADVOCACY

Accepting that your child has autism takes courage and a strong dose of faith—the ability to believe that the four-year-old who is completely nonverbal today will one day learn to communicate.

Based on my personal and professional experience, I can tell you with certainty, you will be amazed at the progress your child makes. I have watched nonverbal children blossom into conversationalists and uncoordinated children participate in Olympic games.

You must learn to walk a fine line, to be as realistic and as flexible as possible. Keep in mind that some of the greatest success stories in history took a lot longer than expected. Don't ever give up on your child. Don't be deterred for a minute if he is not acquiring a skill as quickly as you would hope. It's to be expected.

As a parent, you will gradually make the shift from accepting the diagnosis to "living with autism." This means being able to adjust to the child who refuses to get on the school bus; unclogging your sink ten times in one week after your child has stuffed it with every imaginable object, including small plastic toys; leaving your sister's wedding early because your child can't tolerate the noise from the band; and packing extra clothes for every outing because your child can't resist jumping into any water he sees.

The good news is that a child with autism is constantly changing. Many of their early behaviors evolve or disappear entirely as they receive interventions and the environment around them changes. Children with autism have many strengths and unique characteristics. Parents must learn to identify and cultivate those traits in their children, while guarding their exceptional vulnerabilities. This challenging task is best addressed by mastering the skills of advocacy.

Becoming an advocate will never change the condition, but it can utterly change your perspective and that of everyone you come in contact with.

As you gradually release the dreams you had for your child before the diagnosis, you will move through the difficult stages of grief toward the calm of acceptance. Then you will be ready to take on the new role that this diagnosis asks of you.

"We need you," Jim Sinclair said in his plea to parents. "Your world is not very open to us, and we won't make it without your strong support. . . . Take a look at your autistic child again and . . . [t]hink to yourself:

> "'This is not my child that I expected and planned for. This is an alien child who landed in my life by accident. I don't know who this child is or what it will become. But I know it's a child, stranded in an alien world, without parents of its own kind. . . . It needs someone to care for it, to teach it, to interpret and to advocate for it. And . . . that job is mine if I want it.'"[8]

As the mother of an autistic child, I know how much this new job asks of a parent. I have felt for myself what a blow this diagnosis can be. Despite my deep, unqualified love for my son, it has literally forced me to find a new strength inside.

Learning how to advocate for my son has been the biggest challenge of my life. But now Marty is ten years old. In the years since his diagnosis, I've spoken with hundreds of parents who have children with special needs. It's been a wonderful opportunity for me to help. Along the way, I've become a recognized expert myself.

As a result of standing up for my own child and standing up for the children of my clients, I know exactly what it takes. I can clearly describe the road ahead—pointing out many of the pitfalls and showing you how to avoid them, explaining definitively what works and what doesn't.

Because I was so frustrated myself at the lack of clear information when I needed it most, you will be given concrete tools for navigating the laws, institutions and decision makers that so greatly affect your child's life. In the very next chapter, "Advocacy 101," you'll be introduced to the skills you need to become a powerful advocate for your child.

If I can move from anguish to advocacy, so can you. It isn't easy, but I'm going to show you how. Now let's roll up our sleeves and get down to business.

PUTTING IT INTO ACTION

1. Start a journal to track all of the milestones your child reaches. This will make you more aware of his progress and help you gain a better appreciation for the wonderful growth that is possible for him.

2. Write down your feelings in relation to having a child with autism. Don't be afraid to acknowledge feelings of sadness, hopelessness and even despair. But if you find that your journal entries are *primarily* focused on feelings of sorrow, consider talking with someone you trust, such as a friend, minister or a professional counselor.

3. Write a list of all of the wonderful things you love about your child, such as her smile, her pretty white teeth, her curly hair and her dimples. Review this list when you are feeling sad. Simply reflecting on your child's positive attributes will induce a state of happiness.

4. Plan a family meeting with your immediate and close extended family members. Talk about the diagnosis and your feelings. This is a safe environment, and talking about what's going on with your child will help you begin to move from anguish to advocacy.

5. Imagine your own "nation," in the tradition of Laura Krueger Crawford. Define your own language and rituals. Make a game of it that the entire family can join in. Let siblings and other relatives take turns creating new words and activities that exist in the land of your family.

CHAPTER 3

Advocacy 101:
The Principles of Advocacy

Advocacy is often associated with lawyers, lobbyists or politicians. In fact, hardly a day goes by that we don't see a parade of advocates on the news. Usually, they are men in dark suits with crisp white shirts, taking the world by force. Most of these advocates represent businesses and governments. But they're not the only ones who can speak up and get things done. As the parent of an autistic child, you must learn to be a powerful advocate in your own right.

Caring for an autistic child requires more than good parenting. It's not enough to provide food, clothing, shelter, love and affection. Adding in good medical care and special-education facilities isn't enough either. Active intervention must become a way of life.

Too often, autism is accompanied by scarce resources, inconsistent information, negative stereotyping, constant rejection and startling ignorance. Health-care workers who are normally compassionate may suddenly demonstrate prejudice toward an unruly autistic child. Because your child learns differently, schoolteachers may completely dismiss her potential.

In addition to prejudice there is the problem of misinformation or lack of information. Astonishing as it seems, I have met school administrators who were completely unfamiliar with the Individuals with Disabilities Education Act (IDEA), which governs education for children with special needs, and the ADA, which prohibits discrimination against anyone with disabilities. Every week, I see frustrated parents in my office who have been denied their rightful services due to a bureaucrat's inaccurate information, poor understanding of the law or inadequate staffing.

Parents who face obstacles like these require extraordinary resilience and tenacity. From a complicated negotiation with professionals to a personal insult based on ignorance, the struggle itself can bring up painful emotions. I know this only too well from personal experience.

When Marty was three years old, I enrolled him in our neighborhood preschool. One of his therapists suggested I arrange playdates with some of his classmates. My daughter Morgan had a friend with a younger brother who was in Marty's class, so I called the boy's mother. Although the woman and I were not good friends, our children had known each other for two years, and we had shared a few meals and conversations. I knew I was taking the easy way out by choosing a parent who was sure to go along, but I wasn't looking to make a project out of this—just to get my son a playdate.

After five minutes of talking to this mother, I knew something was wrong. She asked me if we could plan the get-together on a day when the weather was supposed to be nice, since she'd heard that children with autism like to be outside . . . and that way, the boys could play in the yard, and not have to come into the house! The conversation grew increasingly offensive from there, but I was so taken aback, I didn't know what to say. The conversation continued; every time she suggested something and I agreed to it, she upped the ante.

Finally, she told me that, "since kids with autism have a difficult time with others," she assumed I was also sending along a therapist. And by the way, could we limit the playdate to thirty minutes?

Although she veiled her conditions as consideration for what was best for Marty, it was actually a horrible rejection of him. As soon as I hung up the phone, I knew I'd just learned a valuable lesson—a lesson that would not only help me become a better parent, but an even better-prepared advocate for my son. Thanks to that boy's mother, I learned that even with people I might expect to find cooperative, empathetic or receptive, I should never, ever assume I'll get the response I hope for. In the future, I knew I needed to be more prepared to deal with obstacles involving my child.

Rejection feels personal when it's directed at a child you love. As a special-rights advocate, I have consoled Supreme Court judges and CEOs as they wept over an insult to their autistic child. No matter how invincible we are in other areas of our lives, when it comes to our kids, we are *all* vulnerable.

Even parents who have successfully guided their other children through the school and health-care systems can experience frustration and resistance at levels they've never encountered before. Ordinarily, parents can choose a good school, then assume that the teachers and administrators will be knowledgeable about the best educational techniques. When they choose to teach phonics or prefer new math or set a certain time for recess, parents can generally trust their decisions. With a special-needs child, parents have to get a lot more involved than that.

Teachers in mainstream schools are likely to have very limited knowledge and even less experience with autistic children. Even in schools devoted to special-needs children, the range of opinions about the best approach varies widely—and the stakes are much higher. It's no longer a matter of whether a child is sounding out his words with phonics or not. The choices a school makes may affect his ability to speak or connect with others. Suddenly, it's up to you to discover what the options are, know what resources are available and take action to get the results you want. Those are the traits of an advocate.

You may not be accustomed to shouldering this level of responsibility, but you *can* become a powerful advocate, just as I did. For almost a decade, I have taught literally thousands of parents to master the skills that enabled them to stand up for their autistic child. You can do this. And when you do, you will join a proud tradition.

Advocates are the ones who speak up against injustice, who follow their conscience and act on their convictions. As a parent advocate, you are part of a movement that has changed the face of this country. Parents like you are responsible for wheelchair ramps in public buildings, libraries filled with books written in Braille, and captions on television programs. Becoming an advocate can not only make the world better for *your* child; it can have far-reaching ramifications for society.

THE SEVEN PRINCIPLES

Advocacy is not a lofty idea. It is practical work in the trenches. These seven principles can be a guide to what an advocate does—and what an advocate becomes, as a result of applying these principles.

1. Take Responsibility   *Be a leader*

2. Learn   *Be an expert*

3. Think Critically   *Be discerning*

4. Speak with Authority   *Be proactive*

5. Document   *Be prepared*

6. Collaborate   *Be a team builder*

7. Educate   *Be a voice for your child*

Advocacy Principle 1
Take Responsibility: Be a Leader

Perhaps the simplest way to step into your new role as an advocate is to think of yourself as a leader. It's said that leaders take action when no one else can or wants to. When they see that something needs to be done, they do it.

By taking it upon yourself to make things happen, you accept a role of leadership. This mental shift will have a direct impact on how you position yourself in all of your encounters—with doctors, teachers, caregivers, therapists and everyone else who offers services to your child.

Taking responsibility is one of the key attributes of an advocate. All the other principles of advocacy follow from this. As the parent of a child with autism, you cannot afford to passively sit by and hope for the best. You have to take action and initiate change. An advocate doesn't waste time and energy blaming others. You recognize that it serves no purpose and only bogs things down further. When things are not working well, you take responsibility for changing it. Like any good leader, an advocate doesn't *wait* for things to improve, but *acts* to improve things.[1]

The alternative is untenable. Failing to accept responsibility will not only leave parents at the mercy of a system that is not conducive to getting the best care for their child, but it can also have negative consequences for the parent. James J. Messina, PhD, director of psychological services at St. Joseph's Children's Hospital, warns parents that, by not taking responsibility, they run the risk of becoming:

- Overly dependent on others for recognition, approval and acceptance.
- Chronically angry or depressed over how unfairly they have been treated.
- Fearful about taking risks or making decisions.
- Guilt-ridden in their need to rescue others
- Unable to trust other people or to feel secure.[2]

Blaming others and avoiding responsibility will only make things worse. When you can make things significantly better by stepping up and accepting your role as a leader, why not embrace it wholeheartedly?

According to research by the Leadership Institute at the University of Southern California, character is the most important element that determines a leader's effectiveness. Leaders rarely fail because of lack of knowledge or technical incompetence; they fail from lack of character.[3] Long before you become an expert on autism and learn to deal with the maze that surrounds it, you can bring your own strength of character to the task. Your commitment to your child will help you rise to the occasion. I have seen so many parents find resources in themselves that they never knew they had.

Know that you are on a steep learning curve and will not be able to master everything overnight. All you can do is your best. If you take responsibility where you can and resolve to improve, you will make a positive difference. As the playwright Tom Stoppard once said, "Responsibilities gravitate to the person who can shoulder them."[4] An advocate is such a person. Let that be you.

Advocacy Principle 2
Learn: Be an Expert

Once you establish yourself as an expert, the interactions you have with teachers, school administrators, doctors and other specialists will immediately change for the better. Don't worry! You don't have to be a scholar or have a doctorate degree in psychology or education to become an expert. People do it all the time. And remember, you are starting with an advantage: You are already an expert on your own child.

No one can know more about your child—his or her wants and needs, strengths and weaknesses—than you. No one can advocate more effectively than you. For a child with a disability, parents and caregivers are their lifelines—their way to gain access to a world from which they might otherwise be cut off forever.

To be taken seriously as an advocate, however, you must also know the facts. Initially, this means educating yourself about the diagnosis itself. Later it will mean learning about different treatment options and educational choices, as well as federal and state laws that provide protection to individuals with disabilities.

With targeted reading and research, you will steadily build on your knowledge. It is not important—or even possible—to know as much as every school administrator or medical specialist you encounter. It is possible, however, to do enough research to stay well-informed and prepared for every meeting you schedule.

Make a Reading List

Start by identifying the critical books, articles and other written materials on autism, special education, and individuals with disabilities. Many of the most relevant titles are listed in the appendix at the end of this book to give you a head start.

Keep in mind, however, that this is a dynamic area. The information you read even a year ago may no longer be applicable today. The Web sites of recognized organizations and institutions can give you the latest research. My own site (www.arevamartin.com), along with the Autism Speaks (www.autismspeaks.org) and the Centers for Disease Control and Prevention (www.cdc.gov) sites, can provide you with a good way to stay current.

As you have no doubt discovered, your Internet browser will gladly offer you millions of Web sites on autism every time you search. Googling "autism" recently brought up 15,900,000 results! If you are tempted to wade into this endless sea of commentary, opinion and advice, you need to do it with discernment; nothing will undermine your authority as an expert more quickly than bad information or shoddy research. In the next section we'll talk about critical thinking skills to help you choose and evaluate the information you find, but here are five steps to use each time you approach a new area:

- Read a comprehensive summary of the topic.
- Know the leading options.
- Understand the pros and cons of each option.
- Find out what others have experienced with these options.
- Locate the supporting data.

Identify Experts

From your research, identify ten individuals who are already considered experts in this field and read their Web sites, books and/or articles. If you have specific questions that match their expertise, consider contacting them by e-mail or setting an appointment to meet with them.

If there are doctors at a hospital or university who are involved in autism research you find relevant, contact them to find out how you can follow their studies. Most scientists publish their results in medical journals that can be accessed through the Internet or the institution that sponsors the project.

GETTING ACCESS TO SPECIALISTS

John Brown, PhD, assistant clinical professor, Department of Psychiatry and Behavioral Sciences, School of Medicine, UC–Davis M.I.N.D. Institute, says that researchers are always looking for ways to connect with parents of children with autism, particularly families who have multiple children on the spectrum, minority families and others who have been historically absent from research studies.

Parents who are willing to participate in such studies will have instant access to researchers, scientists and other professionals who work in the field of neurodevelopment disorders. Taking classes and enrolling in workshops given by prominent specialists are also reliable ways to make invaluable connections and learn from the best in the field.

Find out about conferences, autism magazines, publications and Listservs that provide information about autism. Many of these conferences are free for parents and offer a wealth of information. My own nonprofit organization, Special Needs Network, sponsors a free annual conference that includes the country's leading experts in the field of disabilities and education. At each workshop, parents, caregivers and other professionals are given an opportunity to pose questions and in some instances have short, on-the-spot consultations about their children.

Know the Language

My clients often worry that they will not be taken seriously at meetings with school officials, doctors and other experts because they are unfamiliar with the jargon used by specialists.

It's true; you will have to familiarize yourself with strange-sounding terms and abbreviations, such as "rec therapy," "aut," "LAS," "OT," "psych eval," "AT eval," and many more. The appendix and glossary in the back of this book give you the common terms and acronyms used by experts.

Don't be shy about carrying a cheat sheet to meetings for quick reference. Whenever you have to meet with an expert or educator, you can also take a couple of minutes and write out a statement using some of the key terms. Reading over the statement will help you feel more relaxed saying the terms, whether you repeat the statement *verbatim* at the meeting or not.

Acquiring a grasp of the basic language will allow you to feel more confident and empower you as an advocate. There are no shortcuts to the hard work it requires to become comfortable in this area.

When I was giving a ninety-minute advocacy workshop last spring, I watched a dad in the front row taking copious notes on his laptop. I was intrigued by how carefully he jotted down each and every word. Afterward, I walked over and asked if I could look at his screen. He showed me his directory. It included hundreds of files from conferences, school meetings, lectures, books and articles on autism. He told me that he took his laptop with him everywhere.

Because he came across so many new terms, he had created a document he called a word bank. Every time he was introduced to a new medical or legal term or concept related to autism, he put it in his bank, along with the definition. Later he studied the words and definitions to use whenever he talked to experts. He had learned to call various experts he met at the lectures and conferences whenever he had questions. He recognized what an invaluable resource they could be and how willing they often were to help. The word bank had dramatically improved his ability to make those connections. He said he felt that his relationships with experts had noticeably improved when he began to speak their language.

Even as you become more of an expert yourself, you will still inevitably rely on the experience and training of doctors, therapists, educators, advocates, attorneys and other professionals. But your own growing expertise will empower you. It can give you an overview of the issues, make you aware of the latest advances, improve your interactions with professionals, and increase your credibility. Building a basic foundation of knowledge can even help you ask the right questions—to find out what else you need to know!

Advocacy Principle 3
Think Critically: Be Discerning

As soon as you begin to gather information about autism, you need a reliable way to evaluate it. Otherwise, how will you know which information is likely to be valid and which is more likely to be suspect?

When we say that someone is "critical," we mean they find fault with everything. "Critical thinking" has a different connotation. It means that you evaluate and reflect before making a decision. Let's say someone tells you about a new treatment for your child. An emotional thinker may decide it's a good idea because he likes the therapist who recommended it or "had a good feeling" about it. A critical thinker takes those gut feelings into consideration as well, but takes the time to find out more, to examine the pros and cons and to check out the source before making a decision. If after gathering the available information you still don't know what to think, do not hesitate to say, "I don't have enough evidence to make a judgment about that yet." It is a sign of a careful thinker.

Expect your knowledge to deepen and grow over the years, informed by new breakthroughs in research and your own child's individual needs. In the course of your research, you will go online; read books, magazines or newspapers; and talk to other parents in person or in chat rooms and blogs. Exposed to so many sources of information, you will constantly be placed in the position of having to figure out what to believe or what to do. It's impossible to make good decisions based solely on your feelings. You must persistently make an effort to examine the evidence before forming an opinion. Bring these elements to any evaluation you make:

- Think for yourself
- Examine the pros and cons
- Notice emotional biases—in yourself and others
- Suspend judgment until all the evidence is in
- Remember how much you don't know

Whether you are faced with conflicting opinions about how to best educate your child or you are trying to decide if a new diet holds any promise, cultivate patience. Despite the urge to do things quickly, allow yourself to wait for evidence and evaluate it carefully.

Be sure to listen closely to *what* is being said, not *how* it's being said. Don't be influenced by how confidently someone makes an assertion, only by how plausible that assertion is. If you allow yourself to be caught up in other people's enthusiasm, you may miss the fact that they are leaving out important implications or making claims to know things that may not even be knowable! By taking the time to look for more evidence and think critically, you improve your odds of noticing when a position is—intentionally or unintentionally—based on bias, self-deception, propaganda, distortion or misinformation. When it concerns the well-being of your child, there is too much at stake to settle for less.

CRITICAL THINKING SKILLS

- Listen carefully
- Question deeply
- Never settle for generalizations
- Work to understand the specifics
- Consider the source

Advocacy Principle 4
Speak with Authority: Be Proactive

With practice, any parent can learn to speak powerfully and persuasively on behalf of her child in any situation—including school meetings, public places, therapy and medical appointments. When you are prepared to take responsibility and armed with the best information available, you can confidently speak with authority about your child.

Remember, you are absolutely the best person to frame your child's situation in the most compassionate way. Even if you don't normally think of yourself as courageous, you can become an outspoken advocate on your child's behalf. The parents in my classes on advocacy surprise themselves all the time.

Recently, Sonya Guzman, one of the shyest moms in the class, confessed that she could never envision herself talking in front of a crowd about any subject. And yet, when I asked her questions about her son—what he liked, his favorite toys, the names of his best friends—she lit up and took on an entirely new persona. It was such a vivid demonstration of how possible it is, even if you're painfully shy, to speak out about something (or someone) you love. Once Sonya realized how comfortable she was talking about her son, she had the confidence to try speaking about him in public and soon became a wonderful, inspiring spokesperson on his behalf.

Whatever you may think is holding you back, I promise you that when you begin to talk about a touching moment with your child, your fears will fade away. One more thing: However shy or inexperienced you may feel, your love for your child will shine through. Authenticity is unmistakable, and it holds incredible power.

WHAT TO SAY. . .

When Confronted with Opposition

Unfortunately, it is all too common for parents to encounter hostility, negative feedback and/or blatant resistance from school personnel, other parents, agencies and even family members. Here are some suggestions about how to handle it:

OPPOSITION: You again? The other parents aren't nearly as pushy as you are.

PARENT: If that's what it takes to get the services my child needs, I'm glad to be pushy.

OPPOSITION: Your child can't make use of this program. She's barely responsive!

PARENT: My child is entitled to participate. For now, I am here to

> communicate for her. With programs like yours, she may gradu-
> ally learn to do it for herself.
> **OPPOSITION:** Oh, you're bringing him with you?
> **PARENT:** Absolutely. We love having him along. He's part of our
> family.

Be Proactive

This concept is widely accepted in business management and the workplace, but rarely associated with parent advocacy.

Many parents feel so overwhelmed with emotions about their child's condition that it's difficult for them to plan and to take the initiative. Instead, they find themselves simply reacting to the never-ending onslaught from outside forces: the letter from school setting the next individual education plan (IEP) meetings held in the early spring to plan for the coming school year; the notice from the insurance company that no further therapy sessions will be covered; the call from the exasperated teacher who is overworked and undertrained for the job. On top of these stresses, one sad look on the face of a child because he has no friends can break a parent's heart.

Reactive parents tend to live in a state of perpetual upset with the school system, the doctors, the therapists and anyone else they encounter. No one can get it right for these parents. Their children never have the services they need. Ultimately, everybody is working against them. They seem to be completely at the mercy of their lives. In fact, living reactively—instead of proactively—is a choice. A terrible choice.

By contrast, parents who are proactive make things happen. These parents are also influenced by external forces, but their response to the stimuli is different. Being proactive does not mean being pushy, obnoxious or aggressive. It simply means having the courage to take the first step.

Richard and Bee Campbell did just that. When their son, Jacob, wasn't talking at sixteen months, they launched into action. Family members gave them the same misguided advice that most parents get— "wait and see," "boys talk later than girls." Rather than being passive, the couple asked their pediatrician for information on speech disorders and related conditions. Although they weren't ready to jump to the conclusion that it was autism, they wanted to know the possibilities and, more important, be prepared in the event their son's speech did not improve.

By taking the initiative and educating themselves, the Campbells were in the position to plan rather than to react. Being proactive keeps them ahead at every turn.

Advocacy Principle 5
Document: Be Prepared

In order to be proactive and speak with authority, you will need documentation as backup. Not many people work in careers that have trained them to keep the extensive records you need as the parent of a child with autism. If you find the task a bit daunting, you are not alone. But once you've had the experience of going to a file and immediately locating a vital record, your motivation will soar! Good records can allow you to confirm what was said in a meeting, track medical treatments given by a range of doctors, inform specialists of details that you would not otherwise remember, create reminders of upcoming appointments and so much more. Establishing a system is the biggest chore. When the organization is in place, it is much easier to maintain the documents you need.

Master Organization

In his book *Become a Recognized Authority*, Robert W. Bly quotes an old saying: "Experts don't know more than other people; their information is just better organized."

Organization provides the solid infrastructure of parent advocacy. Without it, vital information is lost or not accurately remembered, leads are wasted, contacts are forgotten and chaos is inevitable. Dropping notes and records into a drawer or an in-box after a meeting is not sufficient. Within an astonishingly short period of time, important documents are buried and hard to find.

It's important to have a system in place for keeping information organized. From the initial diagnosis to the multiple evaluations a child may undergo every year, it is not unusual for a child's records to contain literally thousands of pages. A surprising number of those pages will be needed for reference later. Getting organized early not only simplifies the search for important documents in months to come; it creates an ongoing sense of empowerment. With so many elements out of your hands, the act of organization can also give you a welcome sense of control. And because so many people are disorganized, you can set yourself apart as an advocate by arriving with orderly documentation.

Before buying files, labels, scanners, boxes, or cabinets, begin by thinking about the system you prefer. Everyone has his own approach. Medical records, for example, can be filed in small filing boxes labeled with the date and relevant details (such as the name of the doctor or hospital, the name of a particular examination, etc.) or placed in conventional filing folders with handwritten or printed tabs. If you prefer the versatility and space-saving quality of digitizing your child's records (and you set aside time to do it), you can use a scanner to record and save the records on your computer.

With any of these systems, labeling is key. A well-filed document without a label may be lost forever. In order to work, your strategy must be consistent. Before you begin, spend time thinking about where you will instinctively look for the documents you need. If your child has been given a screening by a speech pathologist, are you more likely to look for it under the name of the pathologist, the name of the test, the date, the broad medical files or the other files you plan to take to the school evaluation meeting? If you choose a labeling strategy and stick with it consistently, you will train yourself to find things more quickly within the system. Then you will need to maintain and reorganize the system on a regular basis, to keep it working well.

ACHIEVING BETTER ORGANIZATION

1. **Never Open a General File.** Keeping several in-boxes can be useful, if you go through them every week. A "general" file (labeled "therapy" or "medical") is better than nothing, but just barely.

2. **Create an Index.** A directory of your file folders, whether handwritten or logged on your computer, is easy to update and invaluable for helping you find files. Make sure it's easily accessible anytime you look for a file.

3. **Use Divisions.** Assume that many of your files will be filled. Plan ahead for that. Decide whether you would prefer to

break large files into smaller categories or assign them different volume numbers.

4. **Leave Extra Space.** An overfilled box or cabinet is unwieldy. Always leave space to move files in and out easily. Allow room for growth. If necessary, cull files by throwing them out or putting them in a separate archive.

5. **Archive Old Information.** Depending on the space available, you may consider keeping the files from one school year in a readily accessible place. Box and label the files from previous school years. You may still need to refer to them, but you do not necessarily have to keep them at hand.

6. **Identify Temporary Papers.** Flyers for meetings, special notices, address change cards, and other papers can be thrown out after they have been attended to. Add a Post-it or colored dot to these papers, indicating their expiration date, so you can throw them out without hesitation.

7. **Keep Files Safe.** Be sure to keep your file system secure. Consider using filing cabinets with locks or elevating them off the ground to avoid water damage.

8. **Make Filing a Habit.** Decide on a systematic way to keep your filing system intact; then promise yourself you'll do it—whether it is filing daily or weekly or as soon as documents arrive. Not many people enjoy it. But everyone appreciates being able to find important documents when they need them. It's an invaluable habit.

When you do research before meeting with experts, put notes and copies of your research into the relevant files. If necessary, create corresponding files both on paper and on the computer. Depending on the nature of the documents, they can be taken to meetings in a folder, briefcase or laptop. Make a habit of returning these documents to your filing system when you return. One of the easiest ways to lose track of important papers is to set up a system, but leave your files in different places—outside the system!

Create a Journal for Your Child

The most effective way for you to assess your child's progress is to develop a method of documenting it. The form this takes could be anything from a handwritten journal in a beautiful notebook to digital computer files stored on a memory stick. More and more parents are setting up blogs, where they track their child's daily progress, inviting family and friends to make entries. Others have made their own expanded scrapbooks, filled with notes, drawings, school papers, photographs and other mementos. Siblings and other relatives can join in too. Whatever method you choose, embrace it as a wonderful opportunity to tell your child's story.

In my classes, we call these scrapbooks "This Is Your Life" and make a point to share them with the autistic child who is the star of the story. It can be a very poignant experience for a child to see his life so wonderfully portrayed by the people who love him.

This type of journaling is also cathartic. On those days when you feel exhausted and question whether you are doing enough, glancing at a journal or scrapbook can remind you of the incredible work that you— and so many others—are doing to support your child. It can motivate you and be a great source of inspiration.

The journal allows you to present your child's strengths and challenges from your own perspective. Take this collection of your child's drawings, photographs from vacations, and certificates from summer camp to school meetings and medical appointments. Show it to new teachers, babysitters and even relatives. A quick perusal will give them a glimpse into your child's life and personality.

If any biases about autism are still lingering in their minds, this journal can offer a gentle correction to those mistaken views. It can allow them to make a subtle, but important, shift in the way they treat your child.

Keep a Record of Behavior

Along with the basic facts about the disorder, parent advocates must have the facts of their own child's specific condition at their fingertips. A central record of your child's behavior, his strengths and challenges, will be invaluable to assessors and to those on your professional team who will assist you in making important decisions about treatment.

Today your child may like to build funny towers with just about any object he can get his hands on. But tomorrow he may be lining up cars, dolls or crayons. By the time he is a teenager, he may be memorizing state capitals or repeating every word of the Discovery Channel's newest episode on dinosaurs.

Each of these phases represents a very significant change in his development that may, in turn, require a change in services or a new approach to therapy. You are the only one who knows your child well enough to explain these changes to the appropriate experts, but without documentation, even you may miss critical details.

The reality is, physicians, school administrators and other experts are busy people and will rarely listen for long. Being able to provide the basic facts in a well-organized and documented manner is an invaluable asset. It can dramatically improve the odds of finding the best solutions for a child.

Put Everything in Writing

Lawyers like to say, "If it's not in writing, it didn't happen." Make this your mantra. Learn early on to put all communications with your child's school, doctors and other agencies in writing. Even if it's two sentences, it can make a difference.

Any interaction you have regarding the care and treatment of your child by professionals should be memorialized in writing. Medical records and school reports can simply be filed, but it's up to you to create a written record of phone calls, meetings and appointments.

Requests for insurance reimbursement or school services are prime examples. When clients come to me with documentation in these matters, it makes their position immeasurably stronger. For example, write down the dates that you requested authorization for services, the type of services and the precise response you received. These are essential elements. You will have little hope of remembering these details without records and less hope of finding them if you have scribbled them on Post-it notes and thrown them in a drawer somewhere. Creating a file and putting everything in writing solves the problem easily.

Right now my office is representing a family in a dispute with a private insurer that refuses to cover a hospitalization program for their six-year-old boy with autism. In our initial meeting, each side requested copies of all written documentation regarding this issue. As attorneys know, without these records, disputes are reduced to "finger pointing and blame shifting." Our clients readily produced their notes regarding their attempts to obtain coverage, significantly bolstering our argument. It is always much more difficult to dispute something in writing.

Take Notes During Meetings

During every meeting or phone call with experts, parents should take notes. There will be too many meetings filled with technical terms and specifics for anyone to remember all the details. Keeping well-organized notes can seem cumbersome at first, but the advantages soon outweigh the inconvenience.

It has the added benefit of raising the experts' sense of accountability when they see parents taking accurate notes about the meeting. You can also use the notes to double-check that your goals for the meeting were met and your questions answered.

As a practical matter, stacks of notes from a meeting can easily be misfiled and separated, so it is important that you put the expert's name as well as the date and time at the top of the first page, then abbreviate that and put a page number on each subsequent page. For example, the top corner of the second page of notes from a meeting with a pediatrician may show a circled "2" with "Dr. Hanover, 3/15/10" beside it. If there isn't time during the meeting, add these headers before you file the notes.

Taking carefully marked notes, filing them and marking the calendar for follow-ups immediately after a meeting is by far the most effective way to reduce stress and anxiety. Missing appointments and misplacing vital information are far worse than taking a few extra moments to get it right. It is easy to verify statements and agreements if there is a record in the file at home. Without that record, it's almost impossible.

Advocacy Principle 6
Collaborate: Be a Team Builder

Throughout the course of your child's life, you are likely to interact with literally hundreds of people—from the most highly specialized diagnostic physicians to the special-education teacher's aides who accompany your child at school. Some of these people will be fleeting connections, while others will become a vital part of your team. But if you approach these interactions like an advocate, all of these relationships will benefit you and your child.

An advocate understands the value of *synergy* and works to achieve it. Synergy (from the Greek *synergia*) means working together in such a way that the outcome is greater than the sum of the parts. Grudging cooperation will not suffice. Harsh words, impatient remarks, poor communication, missed meetings, and passive-aggressive tactics have no place in the interactions of a committed advocate. These are but a few examples of how to sabotage the smooth, collaborative flow that allows the individuals to harmonize with one another—with a far greater result than any one of them could have achieved alone.

According to Stephen Covey, "Synergy is the highest activity of life; it creates new untapped alternatives; it values and exploits the mental, emotional, and psychological differences between people."[5] In his book *Seven Habits of Highly Effective People*, he directs his advice about collaboration toward people who are willing to assume responsibility. Collaboration, for Covey, is never about passive compliance. It's about leadership. As soon as you begin to collaborate, you have an opportunity to influence other people.

Parent advocates are highly motivated to claim that influence for the sake of their child. One of the most sustainable ways to get the kind of harmonious cooperation that produces synergy is to take Covey's advice and "think win/win."

The parent of any special-needs child is often under pressure, suffering from lack of sleep, and juggling unexpected demands. It would be easy to feel irritable and even entitled to consideration, after what you have to go through in any given week. Coping with that stress is both a burden and a challenge. But it should never interfere with the quality of these collaborations.

As an advocate, you have to keep the bigger picture in mind. Maintaining productive, amicable relationships will offer you huge advantages. You can't afford to sacrifice that for the sake of venting your frustrations, no matter how tired or fed up you may feel.

Fortunately, the ability to collaborate like an advocate is not dependent on your emotions; it's a skill. Once you've mastered it, you can put it into practice regardless of how you feel.

Establish Amicable Communications

Start by taking the time to meet with the teacher, physician, therapist, aide or other relevant connection. Assume that they have your child's best interest at heart and will do their best to act accordingly.

Keep in mind that your child is going to spend most of his time at school and in therapy. It is not uncommon for children between five and twelve years old to have a ten- to twelve-hour day in school and therapy! Of all the people in your child's life outside the home, his teacher and therapist will be among the most critical members of his team. Build strong relationships with them both, for the benefit of your child.

Remember that, while you have the final authority as a parent, this teacher or therapist deserves your full respect. Ask about their approach and listen attentively. Work to develop shared goals and methods of communication. By listening and taking their input seriously, you create the kind of win/win situation that will put them at ease.

A bond of trust can begin in these early meetings that will make them feel comfortable calling you or keeping you well-informed. Every patient or generous gesture on your part will encourage them to be patient and generous to you in return. Knowing that your child may well need exceptional tolerance and generosity down the line, it's wise to cultivate this ground early on.

Make a Contribution

Work to make a contribution where you can. While that is not always possible in a therapeutic setting, it is quite common for parents to volunteer to help in the classroom, to drive for field trips or to assist with students at recess. If you are a working parent whose schedule precludes you from being at the school during the day, offer to provide food for a function or make a cash donation. Look for ways to contribute resources that can help the teacher better instruct your child in the classroom.

When Karen Scott was unhappy with the level of resources at her son Henry's school, she approached the problem like an advocate. Rather than complaining about the situation, she took it upon herself to look for solutions.

She requested a meeting with the school principal about setting up a small resource center on the school campus. Before the meeting, Karen obtained donations of books, computer software and other materials to stock the room. She also obtained permission from a district administrator to hold on-site training of all staff on the many materials that would be in the center.

The meeting with the principal was a breeze. She saw that Karen had done all of the preliminary work and that the center would not disrupt routine or cost the school money. With a win/win situation, there's very little reason to disagree. Not only did Karen create a strong collaborative partner, but, in her willingness to be an advocate and take the lead, she created a model the school district now uses to set up resource centers at other schools.

Anticipate Conflict

Even a specialist in team leadership like Susan Gerke of IBM admits that "conflict is inevitable in a team . . . in fact, to achieve synergistic solutions, a variety of ideas and approaches are needed. These are the ingredients for conflict."[6]

This often comes up in the context of challenging a school district or social service agency that provides services to your child. Whether there is a dispute over the nature of services or their duration, you have to ask yourself if you can find an informal resolution or if you should initiate a lawsuit or administrative claim.

One of the first considerations, of course, is the reality that such actions are almost always expensive and time-consuming. Although the action may be appropriate on its own merits, it may be completely inappropriate in the context of more important concerns.

PICK YOUR BATTLES

Being an advocate is not a popularity contest. At some point, you will inevitably have to make decisions that will be unpopular with family members, friends, school officials or others—even if you have previously worked well in collaboration.

A conflict can quickly escalate into a formal complaint or even a lawsuit. As you decide whether or not to pursue such an action, do not base your decisions on your emotions. While your feelings give you important personal feedback about what matters to you the most, they are not a good basis for making objective decisions. For that, ask yourself the following questions:

- Have I thoroughly considered all other possible options?
- How else can my child receive substantially the same benefit?

- Is there anything I can do to improve the situation?
- Can I afford the time and financial expense of filing an action?
- What impact will the action have on my child, my family and me?

Recently, I heard the author of a popular book on autism suggest that parents who needed more money to tend to their child's needs should mortgage their homes and borrow from friends. Unless you have a method of repayment and very wealthy friends, this is simply bad advice. Likewise, getting embroiled in costly litigation, if it will cause you financial ruin, is ill-advised.

In the school context, the question becomes: Will such an action undermine the collaboration between you and your child's teachers? Will it cause the school staff to retaliate against you or your child? Will it prevent a harmonious working relationship in the future?

Legally, schools are prohibited from discriminating against parents and children when they exercise their rights under federal or state law. As a practical matter, humans often hold grudges, and filing an action can be perceived as a personal attack.

You may be surprised to hear this warning from a special-rights attorney, who often negotiates conflicts and files lawsuits on behalf of my clients. It's not my intention to discourage you from taking further action when it is warranted; I am only encouraging you to consider the implications before you act.

Raising a child with autism is a lifelong endeavor. With every decision you make, you must keep the long-term consequences in mind. If you find that the advantages of amicable collaboration outweigh the gains you could make by filing a formal claim, put collaboration first. Years from now, the compromise may have cost you far less than you expect and the benefits of synergy may have been worth far more. Alternatively, if after careful consideration you decide that filing a claim or lawsuit is the best course, be aggressive and do so without guilt or regret, knowing that your actions are designed to assist your child even if it means a loss of collaboration or hurt feelings on the part of teachers or administrators.

Advocacy Principle 7
Educate: Be a Voice for Your Child

Opportunities to educate others abound. You can speak at your local PTA meeting, school board meeting, city hall or at a social club. The more you share your experiences and expertise, the more you sensitize others to the needs of disabled children and adults. By speaking with authority, you will empower everyone who hears your story. You can also educate others by participating in walks, writing articles or blogs and speaking at conferences. All of these activities allow you to practice your skills as a parent advocate, while you connect with others in the autism community.

At a more personal level, your role as an educator starts with your family. One of the first things you'll do after receiving the diagnosis is explain the implications to your children and close relatives. In later chapters, we will explore this situation further. It requires both patience and compassion, but it is well worth keeping your family as informed as possible. Few things in life are more valuable than having a loving family on your side.

On the other hand, it is an unfortunate reality that you are likely to run into a number of people who make rude or insensitive remarks. The good news is that this is one of your biggest opportunities to change things for the better. As an advocate, take it on yourself to educate these people whenever possible, rather than either taking offense at ignorant remarks or passively disregarding them. Every person you affect will affect others.

Bring empathy to this role. Never forget your own initial reaction to the diagnosis. Even if they react inappropriately at first, give other people an opportunity to grow and become enlightened, as you did. Ask yourself how you would react—have reacted, perhaps, in the past—when you were ill-informed. If you knew then what you know now, would you have reacted differently? Assume the same is true for others. Empathy can give you hope and patience that other people will change too, if they understand the situation. Give them the chance to react differently when they understand better. Educate them.

Some people, it's true, will remain as bigoted and closed-minded as ever. But if you assume most people are decent at heart, you're probably going to be validated. Take the time to educate those who will listen. Sometimes that will take a lot of patience and exceptional self-restraint.

Occasionally the correct response is anger! With practice, you will begin to determine the balance that is right for you.

A few years ago, my clients Ana and Raul Ponce were at a restaurant with their three children, two of whom have autism. An acquaintance who had recently attended a conference with them, who also had a son with autism, was with them. As the parents ate dinner, the four children sat at another table. Ana and Raul were happy to see their two autistic sons expressing interest in another child, but a couple at a nearby table began staring and making faces as if they were annoyed. Ana was used to these uncomfortable stares and ignored them. Soon, however, the stares turned into snarls and suddenly the couple stood up and demanded that the children be quiet or leave the restaurant. The couple's behavior intimidated their acquaintance. She grabbed her son and left the restaurant in tears.

Ana and Raul had experienced this type of rude behavior before. The first time it happened it caught them off guard, but since then they had developed a strategy. So now, they were prepared to act as advocates and stand up for their children and themselves. When they were finished with dinner, Ana handed the couple a card that said, essentially: Our children have autism. They have a right to be in a public place. The noise they are making is within the bounds of the noise other kids make that we, as a society, have learned to accept. We all have to learn to tolerate those who are different, even if it causes us a little inconvenience.

When the couple read the card, Ana says they looked embarrassed and apologetic. Their actions had clearly been driven by ignorance, not malice. Had Ana reacted with intolerance, judgment and hostility for their actions, she would have provoked them even further. Had she not been willing to stand up at that moment, she would have missed the opportunity to educate these people about children with autism.

Parent advocacy is not always about facing opposition, like Ana and Raul. Sometimes it is about compassion. Family members may lose patience. Friendships may feel the strain. Even children who dearly love their autistic sibling will sometimes reach the limit of their willingness to sacrifice and share. Recognizing the limitations of others and learning to compensate for them is a constant requirement. But we have a powerful motivation: the autistic children we love.

WHAT TO SAY. . .

When People Are Rude

Offensive comments often indicate a lack of knowledge about autism. Parents of autistic children can use these unpleasant remarks to bring maturity, information and insight to the situation.

GRANDPARENT: What's wrong with him? That's not normal!

PARENT: He has autism. Children with autism perceive the world differently than we do, so they learn and behave in unusual ways. It's actually quite remarkable.

NEIGHBOR: People with autism are always screaming or staring into space.

PARENT: You'd be amazed how many people with autism achieve high positions in business and government. They say that Bill Gates has a form of autism. It gives him a great ability to focus.

BYSTANDER: If she's going to act up, you should just keep her at home!

PARENT: We used to keep people out of public buildings because they were in wheelchairs. Then people realized how hard and unfair that was. Now we have special parking and wheelchair ramps. We've all got traits that others have to make allowances for. We can all use a little compassion.

Throughout this book, you will meet parents who've enriched their lives and those of their children by becoming strong and effective advocates using the seven principles outlined above. The evidence of the power of advocacy is overwhelming. From parents living in rural areas to CEOs of Fortune 500 companies, millions of people around the globe have made a difference in their own lives and the lives of others through advocacy.

The concept of advocacy is not about changing who you are. It's about taking specific actions that will help you achieve well-defined results. This kind of engagement is the often unacknowledged key to the achievements of so many of the high-performing people I meet in my legal practice every day. In fact, I'm convinced it's the secret behind each one of us achieving our full potential, not just in our journey to assist our autistic child, but in our careers, our businesses and personal lives.

Stephen R. Covey says that, if a principle is correct, "it is valid and applicable in a wide variety of circumstances."[7] When you see the effectiveness of the principles of advocacy in helping you stand up for your autistic child, you may be emboldened to apply them in your job, in your intimate relationships and in your business affairs. These principles can empower you in so many aspects of your life. That's what happened to me. In my determination to help my son, I discovered principles that profoundly changed my life. I'm willing to bet it will do the same for you.

PUTTING IT INTO ACTION

1. Start a new system of organization for all your child's medical and school files. If you already have a system in place, think of ways to improve it. If you're ready to go paperless, begin by scanning all critical documents. With the massive volume of records you will accumulate over your child's lifetime, having it stored on a computer or flash drives will not only be beneficial to the planet but in the long run will also be a lot more convenient for you than ever-increasing file boxes of paper.

2. Commit to learning about at least two new interventions that have proven to be successful in the treatment of children with autism. Expanding your knowledge base regarding therapies and treatment will enhance your confidence and build your expertise.

3. Find one venue—for example, your church, your social club, or local community market—and start an education campaign. You can disseminate copies of articles, plan to give a brief talk or even host a workshop with local experts.

4. Contact your child's school or therapy venue and volunteer. This is a great way to contribute. Whether it's offering to drive for a field trip or to facilitate an art project, your presence and participation will help you build stronger bonds with key members of your child's team.

PART II

Personal Advocacy: New Ways of Adapting

CHAPTER 4

Family Challenges: Advocating to Your Family

A utism is a family matter. Once it comes into the home, it shapes the lives of every member of the family. Despite the joy and happiness an autistic child can bring, sacrifices must inevitably be made. When a startled autistic child begins to emit a high-pitched squeal, everyone in the house is affected. If she requires an additional thirty minutes to cope with every transition—from a jaunt to the grocery store to a family outing to the park—it affects the rhythm of the whole family. Shopping trips and movies may have to be cut short. Peaceful family gatherings may be interrupted. Even a child rocking quietly in the corner, staring at a fixed point in space, can be unsettling to the family norm.

There is no doubt that a loving family can adjust to all of these changes, but in order to make a smooth adjustment, you must actively advocate for your autistic child within the family itself. Along with you, every member of the family will experience moments of frustration and stress. Knowing that this is inevitable, you can watch out for these moments and be ready to stand together and support one another.

STRIVE FOR BALANCE

The addition of an autistic child does not change the fundamental identity of a family. If you work from the assumption that autism will be a part of your family's life, but not the center of its life, it will make your advocacy easier.

At the time of Marty's diagnosis, Ernest and I had one daughter in preschool and another in elementary school. I ran a law firm and he ran a couple of companies. All of us were scheduled from morning to night. We knew that Marty would need a great deal of time for therapy and possibly have to attend a different school from his sisters. We didn't know what kind of medical treatments or additional interventions we might need to anticipate. And we didn't know what we could expect from Marty himself. We wondered how fully he would be able to participate in our family life.

To get insight into the best approaches we might take, we consulted Dr. B. J. Freeman of the UCLA Autism Evaluation Clinic. She recommended that we make every effort to integrate Marty into our family rituals and routines. Of the thousands of families she saw while heading the clinic, the happiest and most balanced families were those who learned quickly to integrate their autistic child into their ordinary lives. Ironically, those families who did the opposite—giving all their attention to their special-needs child—suffered many more problems as a result.

We took her advice to heart. When Michael and Morgan went to play tennis, Marty went. When our family went to restaurants or church, so did Marty. Rather than change what we did as a family, we worked with Marty's preschool teacher and therapist to help us help Marty tolerate the noises and stimuli in restaurants and other public places. To our surprise, he adapted sooner than we expected. He was soon able to sit still through a ninety-minute church service in a crowded room—even with loud gospel music!

At the same time, of course, we also adapted to him, embracing his differences and giving him the extra time and care he needed whenever possible. But caring for Marty meant first and foremost providing a safe and loving home environment. We could not do that without respecting the needs of every member of our family. A great example was when we tried a wheat-free/gluten-free diet for several months.

Our research had shown that a wheat-free/gluten-free diet could be beneficial for children with autism. The diet was popular in the autism community, based on a theory that in the bodies of many people with autism wheat and gluten form peptides or substances that act as opiates. These peptides then alter their perception and behavior, like a drug.[1] We heard compelling success stories and were eager to try it, but we knew we had to measure its success not just for Marty but for the entire family.

As it turned out, not allowing our girls to have many of the foods they enjoyed in the house was ill-advised—especially when at the same time we were asking them to adjust to the constant imposition of in-home therapists, doctors' appointments and team meetings about Marty.

Although the prospect of improvement was hard to give up, we knew we had to make the best decision for us under the existing circumstances. Remember that thinking critically is **Advocacy Principle 3**:

- Think for yourself
- Examine the pros and cons
- Notice emotional biases—in yourself and others
- Suspend judgment until all the evidence is in
- Remember how much you don't know

We used every aspect of it to make our decision. We examined the pros and cons—not only of the diet itself, but of its impact on our family. Our biases were obvious: We were willing to subject ourselves to such a restrictive diet in the first place because of our emotional investment in its promise. We suspended judgment, until we saw evidence that it wouldn't work for our family. And then we gratefully reminded ourselves of how much we didn't know. It was less painful to walk away when we realized that, despite our hopes, Marty might or might not be one of the children whose symptoms were related to wheat and gluten— even if the theory proved to be correct, and the evidence for that is not yet in. We could not let an uncertain prospect of improvement for our son outweigh the very clear needs of our daughters.

Believe me, I know how hard it is to balance the needs of everyone in the family. It truly is one of the biggest challenges faced by the parents of a special-needs child. When activists like Jim Sinclair say autism is not something an autistic child has but a pervasive "way of being," they might be talking about the change it brings to the family as well. A diagnosis of autism brings a new way of being to the family that is both pervasive and permanent.

When the autism card is dealt, it's dealt to the family unit as a whole, and everyone in it is going to have to make some adjustments. But it's important to remember that every person in the family deserves his own time to be the focus of attention. If one child is always given consideration above everyone else, resentment and conflict are inevitable.

There are going to be times when it just isn't fair to insist that a disruptive autistic child be included, as Sandra Harris, PhD, executive director of the Douglass Developmental Disabilities Center at Rutgers University, points out. When a child with autism cannot sit still during a school play, for instance, it may be better to bring along a sitter who can take her outside, so the parents can give their well-deserved attention to the child who is performing.[2]

When parents become completely preoccupied with an autistic child, the impact on the other siblings can be profound. They may engage in negative acting out, seeking attention by regressing, poor performance in school, accidents, physical illness, psychosomatic symptoms or hostility toward the child who is getting more attention. Other children, when faced with a situation that doesn't address their own needs, may become "parentified" and take on the role of their sibling's caregiver. These kids can grow up feeling like their self-worth depends on how much they sacrifice for others or work to take the strain off their parents.[3]

Each child deserves his own attention and care. Insisting that siblings constantly sacrifice their fair share of attention for another child may teach them that their own needs are invalid and that they can find approval only in subjugating their needs to those of someone else. As adults, they may have difficulty expressing their needs and feel that they do not deserve love or attention. Even knowing this intellectually, you can find the balance difficult to achieve.

As much as you need assistance, resist the temptation to make your child a spare parent. Affirm your appreciation for her willingness to help out, while at the same time letting her know that you don't expect her to assume responsibility for her sibling's care. Tell her, "It's wonderful that you want to help out, but Mommy or Daddy will get your brother ready. In the mornings, I want you to focus on getting yourself ready for school, so you can have a great day." This validates your child's efforts to help, while lifting the parenting burden from her. Maybe she can help out with homework or other activities that are age-appropriate, but be sure her responsibilities are suitable to both her age and temperament.

Most of those who have a special-needs sibling turn out to be more compassionate and caring than their peers. They have seen up close what it's like to have a hard time in life.[4] It changes their view of the world. Often they become strong, compassionate advocates themselves.

BEWARE OF ADVOCACY BURNOUT

Regardless of your deep affection for your child, autism causes a lot of stress. Your child may have poor verbal communication skills, disturbing repetitive behaviors such as tapping and head banging, an aversion to physical contact and an inability to look you in the eye, all of which can make daily life difficult. Add to that the strict routines required by an autistic child and the astonishing number of consultations, treatments and appointments, and you have a disproportionate strain on families.

Compared with parents whose children have other chronic healthcare needs, those with an autistic child are three times more likely to have to quit their jobs or reduce working hours. They pay more for their kids' health and therapeutic needs, spend more time providing or arranging for that care, and are more likely to have financial difficulties.[5]

The chronic stress that raising a child with special needs entails can put pressure on families at their weakest points. It has been widely reported that the divorce rate among parents of children with autism is as high as 80 percent, but this has not been substantiated. (The National Autistic Society is currently conducting a survey on the divorce rate in families with autism.) According to the 2000 U.S. census, 57 percent of *all* marriages end in divorce—and more marital distress is reported among families of children with special needs.[6]

As you might imagine, the diagnosis of autism has a greater negative impact if a family is already under stress for other reasons, such as an illness in the family, a new transition to parenthood or retirement. Young families, in which the parents are still making an adjustment to married life, are especially vulnerable to unexpected stressors.

On the other hand, a challenge of this magnitude can actually bring out the best in each member of the family. The qualities that make family life so rewarding in the first place are the same ones that make it possible for a family to grow stronger and more resilient as you face these challenges together:

- **Strong relationships.** Mutual respect, loyalty, trust, shared values and cooperation.
- **Secure base.** A stable bond between the parents can provide a secure base from which the entire family can confront the world, and buffers the effects of any stressors.

- **Communication skills.** Empathy, reflective listening and supportive feedback are invaluable for effective communication. An open dialogue between family members allows for support, clarification and sharing information more easily.
- **Self-care.** Parents who model appropriate self-soothing behaviors—from taking care of one's health to scheduling relaxation time—improve the coping skills of their children.
- **Social support.** Building a warm, extended family of friends, health-care providers, volunteer organizations and support groups will broaden the foundation on which the family's well-being rests.

When you're faced with a challenge, your natural response is probably to turn your full attention to solving it. (Those of us who are professional problem solvers can have even more trouble in this regard!) If there's a problem, we want to tackle it and fix it. Then we want to put it behind us and move on. But the challenges posed by autism are different. They can't be solved. They aren't met once, but over and over again. They're ongoing.

At the UCLA Medical Center, Dr. Freeman found that some families believed—sometimes consciously but often unconsciously—that if they focused all their efforts on the child, if they just tried hard enough, the disorder would disappear. When they reached their limits and absolutely couldn't go any farther, only to find that the autism was still there, they were more than disappointed; they felt bitter, angry and despairing.

When I met Bianca, she was quickly approaching the danger zone. Bianca was contemplating moving away from her husband, Jon, and her fourteen-year-old son, Ryan, so that her autistic child, Milo, could have access to treatments by out-of-town specialists.

Bianca had worked to develop a strong team of supporters to assist with the intensive level of care her son required. Milo was nonverbal and confined to a wheelchair. He was also a sickly child in regular need of medical attention. Bianca told me she had recently heard of a specialist who might be able to do more, but she would have to move across the country, so Milo would have access to the treatments.

She had already quit her job and literally stopped leaving the house unless it was for a medical, school or therapy appointment for Milo. If she wasn't at one of the appointments, she was researching new treatment options. All of her time was consumed with something related to Milo.

Together, Bianca and Jon had spent hundreds of thousands of dollars on medical care, therapists, lawyers, doctors, tutors and specialized equipment for their home. When Bianca consulted me about a legal matter, I was dismayed to learn that she had become so engulfed in finding "a cure for Milo" that she was prepared to leave her family to pursue it. I gently asked her if she was willing to consider alternatives. Bianca had made such an unqualified commitment to "solving the problem" that it took several discussions before she was willing to shift her perspective and see the bigger picture.

As zealous advocates, of course, we want to get the best help possible for our child, but part of the child's growth and development is inextricably linked to being in a happy and supportive family environment. Furthermore, raising a child with a disability is much easier when there is more than one parent or caregiver around. By moving out of the house, Bianca would have lost the benefit of the assistance her husband and teenage son were ready to give. The increased burden might well have pushed Bianca or her marriage to the breaking point. Not only did she stay put but she decided to stop investing time and money in lawsuits; settling some of the disputes with providers reduced her stress considerably. She began to put more of her time into things she could control, such as enjoyable activities and vacations, that not only made her happier but enhanced the life of every member of the family—including Milo.

Your success as a parent advocate is not measured by the specific tasks you accomplish or the number of service hours you acquire for your child. It is far more valuable to cultivate relationships that celebrate your child's differences and show those around you how to do the same. If you become consumed with the latest technological advances, every promising new treatment, the maximum number of therapy hours, the world's most renowned doctors, you will never catch up. Instead, you'll be doomed to feel as if you are failing, no matter what you do. Preoccupation with external factors like these will inevitably leave you with a nagging feeling that you have not done enough even when you have given more than you should.

If it surprises you to hear that you should not give everything you've got, consider it a red flag, a warning that you are headed for burnout. As a parent you can love unconditionally, with your whole heart, but when it comes to advocacy, you have to keep something in reserve. If you expend all your time and all your resources on your child today, what will you do tomorrow? How will you carry on? Skilled advocates learn to pace themselves. Otherwise, burnout will rapidly bring everything to a halt.

DO YOU HAVE SIGNS OF ADVOCACY BURNOUT?

All of us have felt a fleeting sense of fatigue, stress, anxiety or depression. Emotions like these can be a part of the normal ups and downs of our busy lives. When these emotions become chronic, however, they are a sign of burnout.

When parent advocates try to give more than they can afford—physically, emotionally or even financially—the strain can be immobilizing. It's as if you've been filling up a wheelbarrow, then pushing it up a hill, over and over again. You're willing to do it as many times as you have to, but the reality is, you can go up and down that hill only so many times before you drop. Like it or not, there are limits.

Trying to go beyond your limits is not only futile, it's counterproductive. It takes much longer to recover from burnout than it does to rest, take care of yourself and get help from others in smaller increments along the way. Your passionate sense of commitment and dedication to helping your child are admirable. It's your responsibility to make sure they're sensible as well. Learn to pace yourself. Stay alert to signs of burnout and apply the appropriate solution when you notice them.

It's not uncommon for parents to get so caught up in caring for their child that they lose their perspective and start to feel guilty if they spend any time on themselves. If you notice yourself starting to feel like this, take action. It may be hard at first, but like any new skill it can be learned through repetition! Do not indulge in guilt when you take care of yourself to prevent burnout. If you can do so much for your child, you can do this as well. It will be a benefit for you both.

CLASSIC SIGNS OF ADVOCACY BURNOUT

SIGN: Preoccupation with child's care to the exclusion of your personal needs and the needs of other family members.

SOLUTION: Get help. You cannot single-handedly meet all of your child's needs. Enlist family members, friends and even paid professionals. You cannot give your best if you are not in the best of health, both emotionally and physically.

SIGN: Irritation and frustration with family, friends and coworkers.

SOLUTION: Let go. There are no perfect parents, caregivers or advocates. There is nothing to be angry about. Your anger says more about your own expectations and exhaustion than it does about them. Lighten up.

SIGN: Bitterness toward your team or your child because he is not getting better.

SOLUTION: Stop chasing cures. Focus on nurturing the strengths and intrinsic talents that your child has. Become a champion of your child's abilities and eliminate any grudges you hold about his inabilities.

SIGN: Isolation and withdrawal from your usual routine.

SOLUTION: As much as you may not want to be around other people, it's in our DNA to connect with others. Even if it's only one person, make it a point to connect with someone every day. The experience of being with others will uplift and encourage you. Getting good feedback from others helps all of us become more aware of who we are and what's important to us.

The great thing about burnout is that—unlike so many things—it's completely in your hands. As soon as you recognize the signs, assume your role as an advocate and let it work for you. **Advocacy Principle 1** is to take responsibility. It is the best course of action for burnout.

Over the years, I've come to know Dr. Phil personally and professionally. In doing so, I've come to trust and respect his advice. When Dr. Phil talks about taking responsibility for your life, he begins by saying, "You're getting something from your behavior, or else you wouldn't do it. So define your payoffs; then cut them out."

I know you're not consciously pushing yourself to the point of burnout. As a parent advocate, burnout can creep up on you. The sheer volume of new demands can leave people scrambling to catch up, even when they have professional careers as managers! I can personally attest to the desire to do too much to help my own son. I can still remember the feeling in the pit of my stomach when I stood looking at the towers he'd built all around his bedroom floor and finally let myself realize that something was wrong. I know how that feeling can propel you headlong toward an urge to do whatever it takes—no matter what the cost—to make things right again. But if I had followed that urge, I would've burned out within months.

If something is driving you to go to the limit, at any cost, ask yourself what you're getting out of it. What do you expect to get? Do you feel an overwhelming sense of guilt, even when you know you're not to blame? Are you trying to escape some aspect of the situation that you're afraid to accept? Letting go of these urges can be hard and painful at first. We hold on to them out of fear that letting go will be worse, but it's not. By accepting every aspect of the situation—with all its disappointments, limitations and unknowns—you can experience a greater sense of calm. From that place, you will not only protect yourself from burnout, but accomplish so much more for your child.

SUSTAINING YOUR PRIMARY RELATIONSHIP

Having a child with autism in the family can place such extreme demands on parents that they have very little time left for each other. Even the small things seem to require enormous energy. A child with autism may not express her basic needs in a way that parents can interpret. So they are left to play a guessing game: Is she making that high-pitched shrieking sound because she's thirsty or hungry or simply alarmed? If the parents can't figure it out, everyone is left with a sense of tension and frustration. Struggling with daily activities like getting an autistic child to stay in bed at night or eat something other than white food can add more stress. When one unexpected challenge follows another, it can leave both parents exhausted and emotionally drained. Even if they have time alone together, they may not have the energy left to connect. But it doesn't have to be that way.

My husband and I have been happily married for twenty years. Marty has been in our lives for almost half that time, and our marriage is stronger than ever. From the beginning, the challenge of autism made us pull closer together as a family. Through the years, we've found ways to support each other and maintain our personal connection, even when the competing demands became exhausting.

Although almost every couple struggles to find the balance in the beginning, many do manage to sustain a healthy, loving relationship as spouses while meeting the needs of their child. I saw a great example of this in my clients Virginia and Andres Victorin. Their fourteen-year-old son, Gabriel, had been diagnosed with autism as a toddler. Virginia and Andres have worked very diligently to ensure that Gabe had consistent interventions and opportunities to participate in sports and other social activities. Virginia is very active in the disability community and was serving on a number of boards, including the Mayor's Disability Council.

Not only have these busy professionals dealt with the demands of raising an autistic child; they had also been through the deaths of parents, the illness of relatives, the downsizing of Andres's firm, and the difficult transition of their son from elementary to high school. Through it all, this couple maintained a very close relationship. One factor was that, from the beginning, they agreed to share the responsibility of attending Gabe's medical and school appointments. They also communicate constantly and make joint decisions about Gabe's treatment, education and care. Another great strategy has been to focus much of Gabe's therapy on facilitating his involvement in social and recreational activities that the entire family enjoys.

Although Andres is more involved with the long-term issues of providing financial care for Gabe, and Virginia spends more time on the day-to-day management of his schedule, they share information and decisions with respect to both. Virginia and Andres's shared responsibility is the key to their enduring relationship.

Take responsibility for your own behavior; then, as Dr. Phil says, "Behave your way to success. Your past easily becomes your future because what you fear, you create. If you feel deprived of some experience, or emotion from someone else, give yourself emotional closure.

Give yourself what you didn't get from someone else *now*."[7] You have the
responsibility—and the power—to create what you want from your life
together.

10 THINGS COUPLES CAN DO
TO KEEP THEIR RELATIONSHIP STRONG

1. **Reaffirm your priorities.** With so many demands on your
    time and attention, it can be easy for one or both of you to
    feel your relationship is losing its importance. Remind
    yourself and each other to make it a priority.

2. **Talk, talk, talk!** Communicate your feelings. Remember
    that men and women process and express emotions
    differently.

3. **Make time.** Date night has become a cliché, but it works!
    Set a time every week to focus only on each other. Do not
    spend it talking about the kids.

4. **Let the small things slide.** Notice the kinds of things you
    say to each other in passing. Be sure your comments aren't
    always instructions or complaints. Praise and affection go a
    lot farther.

5. **Share responsibilities.** Make mutual choices about
    sharing the load. Don't assume your spouse knows what
    you're thinking and wishing he would do. If you want
    something, ask!

6. **Stay intimate.** Not only is sex one of the best things you
    can do to relieve stress, but it creates an important physical
    bond. You can help sustain that bond every day with a kiss,
    hug or pat on the shoulder to make your partner feel loved.

7. **Be generous.** Give to each other every day. It takes a few
    seconds to share a private smile across a room or offer a
    word of appreciation and encouragement. Generosity will
    not only benefit your partner; it will warm your own heart.

8. **Spend time apart.** It may be counterintuitive, but the truth is, you can't make another person happy if you're not happy yourself. Both of you need personal time away that is not spent at work or with your child. It will help prevent burnout and make you a more fulfilled, better-rounded person and companion.[8]

9. **Be honest about your limits.** If you are struggling to make time for the relationship or worry that it's being placed under too much strain, share your concerns with your partner. Discuss your limits, inquire about his and learn how to help each other keep your balance.

10. **Remember you're in this together.** When the pressure mounts, look for new ways to tackle every challenge as a team. Having someone to share your burdens is something to constantly be grateful for. Express your appreciation to each other and stand together.

HELPING SIBLINGS ADJUST

If you have other children, spend time talking to them about what it means for their sibling to have autism. Through their sibling, autism has become a permanent addition to the family. It is of direct importance to them. In many cases, siblings become caregivers for their autistic brother or sister in later life.

Listen to their concerns without judgment or censure. Establish the groundwork for open communication about this sensitive subject. Let them know it's always okay to ask you questions or tell you their concerns. Do not expect them to be politically correct or sensitive from the start. You can teach them the preferred way of framing statements about autism for the outside world later. In your early conversations with them, allow them to say what they really feel. And recognize that it's perfectly normal for siblings to:

- wish their autistic sibling were "normal"
- worry that their autistic sibling will die
- fear that they will catch autism

- feel guilty because they can enjoy activities that their autistic sibling cannot
- express anger because parents are devoting so much time to their autistic sibling
- resent the autistic sibling because they never have to do chores
- hope things will one day be like they were before

Explaining what autism means in age-appropriate terms can help them adjust. Let them know what they can expect in terms of behavior, such as vocalizations, lining things up, biting, and aggression. Acknowledge the unusual behavior they have observed and help them recognize that the behavior is caused by the condition, not from being "naughty." You may even explain the types of medication and therapies their sibling will be receiving and how you hope it will help.

Obviously, the age of your other children will dictate to a great degree when and what you discuss. But know that even toddlers will notice some of the behaviors of a child with autism. For example, a sibling might recognize that his sister or brother doesn't talk, or talks only when asked specific questions. He might be aware that his brother or sister doesn't respond when called by name, cries for no apparent reason, eats only certain foods, or does unusual things with toys, like lining up the crayons instead of coloring.

You may fear that talking to your child about his sibling's autism will somehow "taint" or harm their positive relationship. In fact, the opposite is true. Your child can come to dislike or resent his sibling when he doesn't understand her behavior. Be honest about autism's challenges while emphasizing the positive steps you are taking to meet them. Talk about the autistic child's strengths, likes and endearing qualities so siblings learn to focus on the positive and minimize the negative. Above all, reassure your child of how much you love his sibling despite the disability and help him see how he too can love her for who she is.

We've always pointed out to our daughters that Marty has great motor skills and the makings of a good athlete. He now loves to swim, play basketball, ride bicycles or scooters, and do just about anything sports-related. Although he doesn't play organized sports, my girls often boast about what a great swimmer he is; how fast he learned to ride a bicycle without training wheels; and how he is an excellent catcher. It is clear that focusing on these attributes helps them, particularly when they think about the things he has more trouble with, like holding a conversation, doing schoolwork and initiating games with friends.

WHAT TO SAY. . .

When Explaining Autism to Siblings

Eventually, siblings of autistic children come to understand this disorder intimately. As a parent, your explanations can help spare them unnecessary anxiety and increase their ability to deal with the unusual challenges they face when their brother or sister is autistic. When you talk to them, use very clear terms to explain the facts.

If they do not ask the questions below, you can bring up these subjects yourself. Many children wonder about these things, whether they ask or not.

QUESTION: Why is my brother different?

ANSWER: He has autism. This condition makes it difficult for him to talk, to play with others and to learn some things. Your brother is smart, but he learns differently. It's important for all of us to help him. He will be okay, but he will be even more okay with your help!

QUESTION: Why did this happen to him?

ANSWER: We don't know what causes it and currently there is no cure. Your brother is not alone. There are many children who have autism.

QUESTION: Will I become autistic?

ANSWER: You don't have to worry. Autism isn't something you can catch from him—it's not like a cold or sore throat.

QUESTION: Will he ever learn to talk?

ANSWER: Your brother will probably learn how to talk. It's just going to take him longer and he is going to need extra help from someone trained to teach children how to talk.

QUESTION: Why does he have to act like that? I don't like it.

ANSWER: Sometimes your brother will do things such as cry, kick or scream. Remember: this kind of behavior isn't directed at you. He loves you. When he does these things, it is because of his autism.

Parents play a major role in creating an environment that is conducive to bonding and positive sibling relationships. Making your other children feel a part of the journey by getting them involved, when appropriate, in medical and therapy appointments will alleviate some of the issues. Both of our daughters—particularly Morgan, who is only two years older—frequently participate in therapy with Marty. On Saturdays when Marty has social/community therapy, Morgan tags along. She looks forward to trips to the skating rink, bowling alley, park and the local outdoor mall with Marty and his therapist. The therapist likes having her because it's good for Marty; it gives him more opportunities to practice interacting with a peer in a social setting. And it's good for Morgan too; it helps minimize the tension and resentment she might otherwise feel about Marty getting extra attention from so many different adults—and so many fun outings!

When a sibling does show signs of resentment or starts acting out, intervene on her behalf, just as you would for your autistic child. Meet with her teachers, coaches and any other adults in her daily life to let them know about the adjustments she is having to make at home. Let them know that there may be days when her autistic brother decides to color on her homework, write in her textbook or disassemble her science project. Ask for their support and understanding.

Use **Advocacy Principle 4** in these meetings: Speak with authority. Explain that it is not unusual for other children in the family to respond to the stress by exhibiting uncharacteristic behavior, such as picking fights, bullying others or falling behind in schoolwork.

Don't wait for the teachers or coaches to call you about this behavior. Go to them first. Be proactive. Your explanation will give them a better understanding of why she seems to have changed. By standing up for her and showing compassion for the stress she's under, it will make her feel acknowledged and reassured that her needs are important too.

COMMON QUESTIONS
FROM SIBLINGS' FRIENDS

Be aware that siblings will often encounter questions, stares and comments from their friends. Rest assured that every time you answer such a comment yourself, your children are listening and learning how to re-

spond. Beyond that modeling, you can teach them more directly what to say when friends ask them about their autistic sibling.

FRIEND: Why does your sister talk like that?

SIBLING: My sister has her own special way of communicating. It may be difficult for you to understand, so if you want to say something to her, let me know and I will try to help.

FRIEND: Is your brother a *retard*?

SIBLING: No. He has a condition called autism. He learns differently, but he is really good at a lot of things.

FRIEND: Why doesn't your brother go to regular school?

SIBLING: My brother needs special classes that our school doesn't have.

FRIEND: Why does your sister always play by herself?

SIBLING: My sister is a little slow getting started, but she can play with us.

COPING WITH SIBLING REACTIONS

Even children who are protective of their autistic sibling at school can experience very conflicted emotions at home. Anger, jealousy and embarrassment are three of the most common initial reactions among siblings of an autistic child. Each one must be addressed.

Anger

A diagnosis of autism means a lot of changes to your family's lifestyle and routines. I often meet parents who cancel summer vacations and trips to amusement parks for fear that their autistic child will not be able to adapt to the environments. Other children in the family are sure to resent these restrictions. Anger is an understandable response.

Canceling vacations and completely altering family traditions and holidays is not the answer. There are activities that your autistic child can participate in even if it means getting additional help for the outing. For example, amusement parks are less crowded in the mornings when they first open. You can take your entire family, along with an extra adult to care for your autistic child in the event he has a tantrum and needs to retreat to a quiet zone or becomes fascinated with one attraction and wants to spend the entire day with that activity. Being together and maintaining those activities that your other children value is important for the happiness of your family.

Jealousy

Dr. Lynn Koegel, head of the autism program at the University of California–Santa Barbara, once told me that children often report that they feel resentment and jealousy because their autistic sibling gets all the attention. If, despite your best attempts to meet each of your children's needs for attention, you are still faced with this reaction from one of your children, try setting aside special personal time every week to do something that child cares about. Let her know how much she means to you.

Teach her to speak up for her own needs, to be her own advocate, rather than acting out if she feels neglected. Assure her that you understand her feelings and will be ready to take her complaints seriously, if she will communicate them to you.

Embarrassment

Whether they mention it or not, children may feel embarrassed by an autistic sibling's behavior. You may notice that they seem reluctant to bring friends home.

You can defuse most of the tension around this embarrassment by admitting that you agree—your autistic child's behavior *is* weird at times. It would be unnatural to deny it. Without laughing at your autistic child, it's possible to develop a special response that acknowledges that weirdness. Some families say, "Oh, my God . . ." or, "Oh, well, that's autism," or, "That's just Sarah being Sarah." It may take time, but gradually, your children will adjust and their embarrassment will diminish.

When that happens, they will be ready to speak up in defense of their autistic sibling. There may be situations where they will have to educate a friend or stranger: "My brother is not being bad; he has autism and this is one of the symptoms." In other situations, they may need to be even more assertive and say, "Your laughing is rude and insensitive. My brother has autism."

In many cases, they will become responsible for their autistic sibling's care in years to come. My friend Miranda is a good example. Her sister Darla was diagnosed with Down syndrome as a small child and later with autism. Darla is now forty-six years old. She is nonverbal and incapable of living independently. When their mother passed away, there was no question about whether Miranda would assume guardianship and care for Darla. As the oldest of four children, she had known at a young age that she might ultimately become Darla's primary caregiver.

Although she is a successful attorney and nonprofit director, Miranda didn't hesitate. She had built this contingency into her personal and professional plans from the beginning. "I knew that anyone I married would have to take this possibility into account," Miranda said. "I love my sister, and my mother taught us early on that, as a family, Darla's care was our collective responsibility—just as the care of any one of us would be. End of story."

As your children mature, be sure to engage in regular dialogue with them about the care of their autistic sibling later in life. There are many options, including residential-care homes, assisted-living facilities, special housing for the disabled and shared living arrangements. Even families who decide that a sibling will be the primary caregiver can make use of numerous day programs, supportive employment opportunities and social or recreational activities. As you discuss these possibilities, never lose sight of the fact that your children have a right to make decisions about their own lives and the level of involvement they will, or will not, have in the care of their adult autistic sibling.

GETTING OTHER FAMILY MEMBERS INVOLVED

Talk with your immediate family members about your child's diagnosis as soon as possible. Get them involved. Don't stop at simply telling relatives that your child has autism. Take advantage of the opportunity to educate them (**Advocacy Principle 7**) about how it affects your child. Describe the specific symptoms, proposed treatments and expected outcomes.

Be creative. You can send a family letter to all of your relatives by post or e-mail. Many parents set up a blog to share daily or weekly events. Others use the Internet to set up a page for their child on Facebook, MySpace or Twitter to share updates. The idea is to provide your family with comprehensive information and demystify the label. It's an important part of your role as an advocate.

Consider providing practical information about how the diagnosis may affect family outings or gatherings. For example, if your child has food allergies or is on a restricted diet, don't wait until you pull up in the driveway on Thanksgiving Day to tell your parents. Provide this information in your blog or e-mail. Suggest alternative dishes. Offer to bring special meals.

The more you educate your immediate family so they can understand the disorder, the more likely that you will reduce tension that can occur from surprises and disappointments. Suggest ways your relatives can develop a close relationship with your child despite any challenges she may have with communication. Without creating unrealistic expectations, it may be helpful to tell your relatives that, although your child may have limited language now, you expect her speech to improve after intensive therapy. Educate all your relatives about alternative ways that they can communicate more successfully with your child.

Make sure that your relatives understand the limits of your child's tolerance for certain activities, and that when those limits are exceeded his reactions cannot be compared to a typical child's tantrums or acting out. Some older family members may misinterpret your child's behavior as deliberate defiance. They may even believe that spanking or other forms of discipline might be the solution. As your child's advocate, it is your responsibility to educate your loved ones so they can understand the difference. Then you can teach them useful strategies to redirect your child, offer positive reinforcement and enjoy the time they spend with him.

Because you know what your child responds to best, offer relatives suggestions for ways they can bond with him. For example, if he loves numbers and math, invite grandparents to participate in homework assignments. Suggest they visit a bookstore together and look through math books or play simple games involving counting or number recognition.

Most family members will take their cues from you. So it's important to convey that you are not the only one capable of spending time with him or addressing his needs. There is no reason for him to be isolated from the rest of the family. Letting go and accepting the different parenting styles of grandparents, aunts and uncles will give you a much-needed respite and allow your child to become a beloved, integral member of your family.

Relying on Your Loved Ones

According to Seth Godin in *Tribes*,[9] when we connect to one another, we each become capable of accomplishing more than we can alone. It is our infrastructure of support and deep relationships that help us recognize our unique strength and power. I am grateful to know I can face autism with the people I love by my side.

My own experience has convinced me that the key to finding sustainable strength lies in connecting with loved ones who can provide honest support when big and small issues arise. One of the most important things about a strong family network is that it gives us a safe haven—a place where we can allow ourselves to be vulnerable, to express our own pain, our dashed hopes and our fears. In turn, we are opening ourselves up and readying ourselves to receive assistance, feedback, encouragement and support—knowing that it comes from a caring place, from the family we know and trust.

PUTTING IT INTO ACTION

1. Make a list of the activities that your child enjoys the most that you can share with a grandparent, aunt or uncle. Think of ways your relative can use these activities to interact with your child.

2. Keep a record of the way you spend your time over the next two weeks. Then tally the hours and consider whether you have spent a disproportionate amount of time on concerns related to your autistic child versus your other children, your spouse and yourself. If 60 to 70 percent of your available time is spent on your autistic child, things are out of balance and you may want to look for ways to reallocate your time. This may mean delegating certain tasks associated with your autistic child to someone else, or it may require giving up something you've been doing. Neither one is easy, but in the long run, your life will be more sustainable.

3. Share **Advocacy Principle 7**—educate—with other family members. Explain the value of educating the people around them. Help them identify ways they can educate close friends and extended family members about autism and how it affects your child. Encourage them to involve others in the process of education. Every person who shares this connection to autism helps defuse any stigma and creates greater understanding in society.

4. Reread the "Signs of Advocate Burnout." Ask yourself if any of these signs apply to you. If they do, come up with a specific plan to alleviate burnout. Keep in mind that burnout does not resolve itself. The very word "burnout" means something charred and spent that cannot spring back to life on its own. You have to do something to renew your energy and give yourself the break you need. The parent advocates who thrive are always finding new ways to lift themselves back up and refresh their spirits, even in tiny moments. Find moments like that for yourself every day.

5. Commit to writing a blog, a periodic family letter or a journal on your child's progress. Be sure to make note of his special strengths. Include anecdotes and photos that others would enjoy. Sharing this information will not only help other family members understand your child, but their response will also help remind you why your work as an advocate is so important.

CHAPTER 5

Family Challenges:
Advocating to Your Growing Child

n the beginning, you may need to advocate not just *for* your autistic child but *to* him, in order to keep him engaged with the family and the world around him. It is vital for his well-being, and for the family he loves, that you do everything possible to prevent your child from shutting off the outside stimuli and retreating out of reach. As he grows, you may find your role changing; you may start by advocating that your child master daily skills like dressing and going to the bathroom by himself, and later to make new friends, learn social skills, form a habit of role-playing before going into unfamiliar situations, and gradually acquire the skills he needs to be independent.

Of course, an autistic child's abilities vary depending on where she is on the spectrum, and those abilities will increase as she grows up. With a nonverbal child or one with more disruptive behavior, your advocacy may need to involve direct intervention to keep his attention and engagement. If your child has strong verbal and functional skills but difficulty with social interactions, you will have to take a more significant role in helping him to initiate playdates and social activities that will keep him involved with others.

In his article "Building a Bridge: Breakthrough Strategies for Our Children," Raun K. Kaufman points out that children with autism are "continually asked to stop doing what they want (their repetitive or unusual behaviors) and start doing what someone else wants (sit down at a table, play a specific game, use the toilet, write their name, etc.). We are then baffled when it appears to be such a struggle to engage these children. But, really, are we any different?"[1] It is hard to motivate a child to leave his comfort zone and stay engaged with the world if the world won't meet him halfway.

Advocacy to your child involves more than containing her behavior and including her in activities. It extends to teaching her self-determination skills that can empower her and make her feel that the world is worth engaging. Your own home is the ideal environment to provide your child with safe opportunities to explore her world by making choices, taking appropriate risks, accepting consequences, experimenting with control and expressing opinions.[2]

WHAT TO SAY. . .

When Your Child Asks about Autism

Inevitably, your child with mild to moderate to high-functioning autism will ask questions about his disorder. He will want to know why he is different from other children at school, in the neighborhood, or on the playground. If you can offer him reassurance, it will help him feel better about himself and his condition.

- You are very special and we all love you very much. You have a condition called autism. There are lots of people like you and doctors are learning more about it every day.
- You have both strengths and weaknesses. We all do. You have very special strengths [mention them specifically] and challenges [mention these too]. But your strengths are the most important thing, and we will help you with any challenges you face.
- You can make friends. You just have to work harder at it than your brothers and sisters do. We are going to get you special tutors to help you learn how to do it.

ADVOCATE OPENNESS

Initiating a conversation with your child about his disorder is an important part of being a proactive advocate to him. Assuming your child has the cognitive ability to understand, talk to him about autism. Be honest and vulnerable. The more comfortable you are with it, the more comfortable your child will be. It may not always be easy, but your candor will build trust for future discussions.

As an advocate, it is important that you initiate this conversation. You may prefer to wait until your child starts asking questions, but that's not advisable. While you wait, you run the risk of him first noticing his condition because of another child's cruel remark or a pointed question from an inquisitive relative. It is far better to apply **Advocacy Principle 4**: Speak with authority. Stay calm and grounded. Don't downplay the seriousness of the condition, but focus on his strengths and all the progress he has made. Assure your child that you and the entire family are there to support him and to provide assistance with his care, education and every other aspect of his life.

When you talk with him about autism, be prepared for different responses. He may assume at first that this is a punishment for being "bad." He may be sad or angry at the unfairness of it, or even become angry with you or the doctors for not being able to cure him. Relieving your child of any sense of guilt is an important step that will also help him understand the need for treatment. Tell him what he can expect in terms of treatment and, depending on his age, give him choices. Uncomfortable treatments or restrictions in diet and activity may make him feel withdrawn or even bitter. Allowing him to discuss or give input on his diet and treatment options, as much as possible, will help give him a reassuring sense of control.

Don't make promises about what the treatment will do for him, but prepare your child for what to expect from various interventions. This will minimize his anxiety, which is often based on the unknown or incorrect assumptions about the future. With each therapy or training, it is important to talk about why you chose it, what it is designed to do and who else will be involved. If possible, let him meet other children who have had that particular therapy. To increase his level of comfort, you may even want to take a little time to rehearse the first visit to a new doctor or therapist.

Most important, establish a shame-free environment, where even the potentially embarrassing topics are safe to discuss. If nothing else, autism generates an exceptional number of awkward moments. Make sure your autistic child—and, indeed, every member of your family—knows that they can mention those awkward moments to you. If you are able to take responsibility (**Advocacy Principle 1**) for staying calm and refusing to give in to embarrassment yourself, you will set the tone for the people around you—particularly your autistic child.

Imagine the security such an unflinching stance of support will offer your child! If you advocate an atmosphere of openness, then every new challenge will provide you with an opportunity to prove you can be trusted, no matter what.

ADVOCATE DAILY LIFE SKILLS

Despite what many people think, children with autism can learn most skills for daily life—such as using the toilet, bathing themselves, brushing their teeth, dressing themselves, preparing simple meals and cleaning their own room. Dr. Lynn Koegel—whose advice our family has relied on over the years—has written several books on how to teach basic self-care skills to children with autism. Some children really benefit from professional instruction; you might consider hiring a behavioral therapist with expertise in teaching children self-care skills (and teaching parents ways to reinforce those skills).

Don't be afraid to set goals, expectations and limits for your child. A child with autism has an enormous capacity for learning. Parents often tell me that they find it difficult to imagine that a child who doesn't speak a word at the age of four will ever be able to talk, but they can! I've seen it many times. So don't be afraid to dream and set high standards for your child. Likewise, don't be afraid to set limits.

Even though your child may acquire the skill later than children without autism, Dr. Koegel recommends introducing the skill at the same age. So, for example, if your other children started learning to brush their own teeth at three years old, introduce this skill to your autistic child at the same age. Likewise with going to the toilet, getting dressed and other skills. Then build on these skills to teach new skills that promote independence.

APPLY ADVOCACY PRINCIPLE 7

Educate Your Child About Going out in Public

Children with autism typically have trouble telling the difference between what should be done in private and what can be done in public. This confusion is caused by a cognitive impairment, but since most children with autism have virtually no privacy themselves, the concept may be even harder to convey! Children who struggle with how to behave in public versus private are also likely to have trouble recognizing the difference in how we treat friends versus strangers. But don't worry; even if their (in)ability to perceive the nuances stays the same, you can teach these things just like other practical skills. The key is to start when they are young.[3]

As you teach your child the rules about what is appropriate in private and in public, think about what he knows of privacy. The constantly evolving team of people around him give him an unusual experience of this issue. While you're explaining, be sure to let him know that he has a right to his own boundaries as well.

Let's face it, you don't need an Advocacy Principle to remind you to teach your child how to live. It's an implicit part of good parenting. But when you teach him how to handle himself in public, to speak up for himself and maintain his own boundaries, you are preparing him to be an advocate for himself in the world. It is an important concept that we'll return to later in this chapter.

While your child may not be able to perceive all the social nuances himself, most children can learn some of the basic rules, if you spell them out. *The Hidden Curriculum: Practical Solutions for Understanding Unstated Rules in Social Situations* is filled with practical ways to help the daily life of your autistic child run more smoothly. These are only a few of the social rules for going out in public.

- Zip up your pants before leaving the restroom.
- Avoid placing any part of your body over the armrest into someone else's seat.
- Sing quietly to yourself, not out loud.
- Stand facing the doors in an elevator, not the back or side.
- Do not stare at other people.[4]

All children need to be taught these rules at some point, but for most of them, the lessons are relatively easy, particularly because they get reinforced daily through the reactions of other people. Since that will not be the case for your autistic child, he will need specific reinforcement from you. It may take a combination of explanation, modeling and persistence.

ADVOCATE LANGUAGE SKILLS

According to speech pathologist Kathie Harrington, MA, many of the most common areas that autistic children find challenging fall under the heading of language skills, such as vocabulary, predicting, sequencing, turn taking and memorizing. She also considers reading phone books and maps to be language skills.

As the mother of an autistic child herself, she knows firsthand that, with patience and determination, these skills can be taught. Any or all of them are likely to be difficult for your child, but they are crucial; he needs these skills whenever he goes into unfamiliar territory at school or in a social setting. You need to help him prepare. Giving attention to each category will improve his ability to cope with the new situation.

- **Vocabulary.** Make a list of terms and vocabulary words that will be used. Help your child understand and remember these words.
- **Predicting.** What comes next, what is missing, and "what if . . . ?" situations are especially hard for autistic children. Imagine situations your child may encounter in the new setting and help her anticipate what may happen next.
- **Sequencing.** The inability to envision a sequence is especially challenging when reading a map or following directions. Help your child practice this skill using both visual and auditory feedback for reinforcement.
- **Memorizing.** School lessons that rely on memorization will help your child acquire this skill, but all it really takes is repetition. Teaching him his own home address and phone number is a good place to start.
- **Telephoning.** Work consistently to teach your child how to use the telephone, call 911, get directions and find a phone number.[5]

ADVOCATE SOCIAL SKILLS

Your advocacy will play an important role in helping your child learn the social skills necessary to make friends. And believe me, even when a child has limited speech or is entirely nonverbal, he *can* make friends. Many nonverbal children use gestures, photos, drawings or computers to communicate. With a little creativity, you may be able to find unusual ways to help your child connect with others.

Every child needs friends. The ability to connect and share with understanding people is one of our most basic human needs. Friends also help shape a child's identity in ways a parent cannot do. Drawing on the skills he has learned at home, your child can make friends within his own peer group, where he will soon learn new social skills that will grow and mature with him.[6] As you advocate social skills to your child, you lay the foundation for these important bonds with others.

Role-playing is a good way to teach these skills. Demonstrate a social situation, such as making a phone call or meeting a new person. Model the skills your child needs; then let him play the same role. Teach him how to answer the telephone, ask about someone else's interests or share toys. If you have other children, encourage them to participate in this role-playing game. When you entertain at home, do not tuck your child into bed before the guests arrive. Allow him to take part. If you help him practice beforehand, he may be able to greet the guests at the door and take their coats. The occasion can give you a chance to teach him how and when to shake hands, which way to pass the food at the table and how to be polite to company.[7]

In addition to modeling, you may want to directly explain some of the basic elements of holding a conversation, such as asking questions and making eye contact. Then gently remind him of those skills in your daily conversations, until they become a habit.

Social isolation can be a problem for children with autism, even more than it is for their parents. The National Dissemination Center for Children with Disabilities (which goes by its former acronym, NICHCY)[8] suggests scheduling activities that offer healthy outlets for your child's energy, build his self-esteem and allow him to interact with other kids his age. While you are teaching social skills at home, use these suggestions from NICHCY to give your child a chance to be rewarded for those skills in the outside world.

- **Hobbies.** Help your child develop hobbies. Apart from the satisfaction of the hobby itself, shared hobbies can be a great meeting ground for new friends.
- **Community groups.** Encourage your child to join groups like the Scouts, the 4-H club, a church youth group or the YMCA, whenever it's appropriate.
- **Extracurricular activities.** Special-interest clubs for sports, chess, science, music or other activities are available at most schools. After-school day-care programs may even be an option.
- **Volunteering.** Your child may be able to participate in volunteer groups either directly or indirectly by offering to help in a special role suited to his abilities.

According to NICHCY, it is natural to want to shield your child from the possibility of rejection, failure and hurt feelings. But the truth is, all children have to go through a social learning curve with their peers. There may be more obstacles in the road for an autistic child, but the process is the same. Rather than protecting him from the risk of negative experiences, teach him to be resilient. Support him by being available to talk about his fears, uncertainties and experiences. When an attempt to form a friendship doesn't work, encourage him to try again.[9]

Social skills are learned every day. They are built on your child's experiences with all the people he encounters. Give him as many opportunities as possible to participate with others in a positive way.

ADVOCATE TO YOUR TEEN

Autistic teens must wrestle with even more complicated issues than ordinary teens. Adolescence is a time when, according to the National Institute of Mental Health, autistic children "may become painfully aware that they are different from their peers."[10] To cope with this realization, many teens have moments when they regress—reverting to the hitting, rocking or other behavior they may have conquered long ago. It may make things more difficult, but it's a very normal reaction to stress.

As you know only too well, autistic children are especially challenged by transitions and change. Well, consider how many changes adolescence brings! Not only are there dramatic outward changes to the body; there are also hormonal changes that can cause mood swings, body odors, menstruation and sexual urges. It is a lot for an autistic child to contend with. When these dramatic changes are accompanied by a growing desire for independence, the high school years of an autistic child can be daunting for parents and siblings as well. While every member in the family plays a vital role and can help your growing child navigate his teen years, parents have a special responsibility to tackle the issues of teen friendships, sexuality and independence with their autistic teenager.

TEEN FRIENDSHIPS

Perhaps the most significant issue that teens with autism face is difficulty in making friends. UCLA professor Elizabeth Laugeson, PsyD, says that making friends can be harder for adolescents with autism because "they typically lack the ability to pick up on all the social cues most of us take for granted—things like body language, hand gestures and facial expressions, along with speech inflections like warmth, sarcasm or hostility. Lack of these basic social skills may lead to rejection, isolation or bullying from their peers. And sadly, that isolation can carry into their adult life." At UCLA, Dr. Laugeson and her colleagues conducted a special social-skills program for high-functioning teens with autism. This twelve-week program consisted of weekly ninety-minute sessions where teens gathered together to learn how to engage in age- and peer-appropriate conversations and social activities. The teens focused on increasing language and communication skills with an emphasis on generalizing it to typical teen settings such as the mall, the movies and restaurants. This interactive program also included substantial parent participation in order to provide for opportunities to practice in the home setting. "A lot of our kids came into the program with virtually no social contact outside of school," Dr. Laugeson says. "We saw a dramatic increase in the amount of get-togethers with friends. They weren't so socially isolated anymore."[11]

Many cities have their own social-skills training programs for autistic teens. Ask your pediatrician or contact your local university to find an appropriate program. If you live in a small town or city where such programs don't exist, take responsibility for creating one (**Advocacy Principle 1**). The benefits will extend to other participating children and their parents. The community and warm connections that result will amply reward your efforts.

If you know other teens with autism or related disabilities, begin by contacting their parents to see if they would be interested in having their children participate. Next you'll want to find a professional to lead the group. Contact a professor, psychologist or therapist who works with autistic students and share information about the UCLA program and its positive outcomes. Dr. Laugeson and her group are working on creating models that can be used in schools, a guide for mental-health professionals and a do-it-yourself guide for parents. If necessary, don't be afraid to lead such a group yourself! Research institutions like UCLA and others throughout the country have a wealth of information and self-help guides for parents on facilitating communication and social relations for children and teens with autism.

To help friendships develop, look for social activities that are geared for individuals with disabilities, but also provide interaction with children without autism. For example, my own nonprofit organization, Special Needs Network, sponsors a community health fair and carnival each year for special-needs children and their siblings and peers without autism. This event provides children and teens with autism an opportunity to interact in a safe environment with the assistance of trained therapists. All of the kids play games, do arts and crafts and even dance with age-appropriate peers. Don't forget about siblings, cousins and neighbors; they're often the best training ground for peer relationships in your child's life.

Although a teen without autism doesn't want his parents picking out friends or planning outings for him, an autistic teen needs more parental involvement to smooth the way. You can still encourage his developing independence and self-confidence, as you would with a teen without autism. The difference is, an autistic teen may need you to initiate the situation for him. Planning a movie night and inviting one or two peers over is a good way to start. You or your child's therapist can practice role-playing the situation in advance. The therapist can even be present to assist with initial visits. Family gatherings also offer chances for your autistic child to practice initiating discussions and interacting with peers.

No teen learns social skills overnight. The stakes are high and adolescent peers can be unforgiving of faux pas. Think back on your own adolescence; you can probably remember only too vividly the trial and error involved in that stage of life. As adults, we have the advantage of hindsight: We know that it's a temporary phase. Children—and especially teens—can feel that everything rests on the moment. It makes every slight embarrassment and misstep harder to bear. But keep reminding yourself that this too shall pass. If you can stand by your child with patience—stepping in as an advocate, when necessary—you will see her through.

TEEN SEXUALITY

Being liked and accepted, displaying and receiving affection, feeling that we are worthwhile, doing what we can to be attractive, having a friend to share our experiences—these are among our deepest human needs. Sexuality is intimately connected with those needs. It goes far beyond the physical sensations and sexual urges that our bodies begin to experience so strongly in adolescence. It is also about how we see ourselves—whether we like ourselves, what we understand about ourselves as men and women and how we share with others.[12]

When you think about how you're going to approach the topic, keep in mind that it's not necessary to sit your child down to have "the Talk" about sex. In fact, that's not even recommended. It's much easier and more effective to use the many daily "teachable moments" that will occur to initiate an informal and relaxed discussion. The subject may come up through a television show, the pregnancy of a friend or relative, or a question about sex that your child asks.

If you would rather open the conversation yourself, you might consider bringing home books about sexuality to share with your child, much as you would any other book. If your child is young, you can curl up together and read, looking at the illustrations and talking about the content in a relaxed way. An older child may prefer to read the books alone. If that's the case, offer to answer any questions later—and make it easy for her to ask. Most adolescents are nervous about sex in the beginning. You can take up the slack, compensating for their embarrassment by treating this natural, healthy topic in a matter-of-fact way, even if you feel a bit nervous yourself.

Whatever your child's age, be sure to use accurate words when talking about sex. Using coy or silly names for body parts and sexual acts sends the wrong message to your child. Be sure to share your feelings about different common terms people use and tell your child the language you prefer. You can explain that alternate terms may be used in public—not because the accurate words are wrong, but because these body parts and sexual acts are private.

In some of your discussions about sex with your child, take the time to explain your own values, what made you choose these values and why they are important to you. With teens, it is important to convey your views and expectations regarding teenage sex. Although they may not show it, they are listening! Studies show that parental attitudes toward sex are quite important to teens.[13]

Information about birth control is essential for teens to have *before* they become sexually active. They need to know that many methods of birth control do not provide protection against disease and few provide absolute protection against pregnancy. Let them know which methods do offer protection, as well as how to obtain and use these methods.

Do not worry that, by discussing sex with your teen, you will encourage his sexual feelings. Those feelings are already there, because sexuality is a part of each human being throughout the entire life cycle. By explaining your own expectations, you can also avoid giving him the impression that you are encouraging him to engage in sex anytime soon.

APPLY ADVOCACY PRINCIPLE 3

Be Discerning about Your Child's Needs

*Children on the autism spectrum may have a wide range of sensory, orthopedic, mental, emotional or learning disabilities. Each of them needs information about sexuality, but the best way to present that information may vary. This is where **Advocacy Principle 3** becomes a vital part of your advocacy to your child.*

If you are nervous about sex, as many parents are, you may be tempted to rush through your explanations or do whatever seems standard. That may not be adequate for your special-needs child, and the subject is too important to treat it carelessly.

Think critically about the nature of your child's limitations and how these may affect his experience of sexuality. While some low-functioning people with autism may never engage in sexual activity, their bodies will mature regardless. If you do not explain the nature of their urges, they will be left to glean this information from other sources.

Tailoring your explanations to their capacities is crucial. For example, any books about sexuality you share with a teen who has a visual impairment may need to be presented via audio, Braille or large print. A teen with a significant physical disability may need to be told how it will affect his sexual relationships. Teens with learning disabilities do not generally require special materials to learn about sexuality. They may need only some modification to the pace and manner in which information is presented and an increased emphasis on social skills.[14]

There are many misconceptions about the sexuality of people with disabilities. The most common myth is that teens and adults with disabilities are asexual. It's easy to assume that people with disabilities cannot marry or have children. Historically, some societies have gone so far as to try to prevent it.

Thanks to the work of advocates for almost sixty years, more people are beginning to understand that those who are disabled have the same rights as others. These rights include education, employment, self-determination, independence and sexuality.[15] As with all rights, this right brings with it responsibilities, not only for the person with a disability but also for that individual's parents and caregivers. Adequately preparing a child for adulthood, with its many choices and responsibilities, is certainly one of the greatest challenges that parents face.

All teens need complete information about your values and the subtleties of friendship, dating, love and intimacy. They also need to know how to protect themselves against unwanted pregnancies, sexually transmitted diseases and sexual exploitation.

Sexual education can be an important element of personal and sexual safety.

Teens with special needs are sexual beings just like the rest of us. Respecting each child's dignity, teaching healthy attitudes and expression and maintaining safety is the job of all parents, as well as teachers and health-care professionals—whether a child has a disability or not.

Depending on the nature of the disability, emotional maturity may not develop in some adolescents at the same rate as physical maturity. This does not mean that physical development won't occur. It will. You can help your child cope with physical and emotional development by anticipating it. Talking openly with your child about sexuality, as well as the values and choices surrounding sexual expression, will help prepare him to deal with his feelings in a safe, healthy and responsible way.

TEEN INDEPENDENCE

As a mother of a teen and a tween, I am constantly challenged by the need to keep up with the latest fashion, music and technology. Twitter, Facebook, MySpace, IM and the endless string of text messages help me stay current and better able to communicate and connect with them. My fashion-conscious twelve-year-old has banished my input from her wardrobe. (And she wants to pick out Marty's clothes, as well. She says my choices make him stick out like a sore thumb and just increase his chances of being picked on. Now that's harsh!) Teens with autism are no different. In their own way, they are just as eager to keep up with their peers. Learning to let go and allow our kids to gain independence as they reach their teen years is something all parents must do, even when autism is involved.

Knowing when and how to let go can be tough. If you are concerned about your child's ability to cope, experiment by taking little steps. Give him time to learn and get used to new levels of freedom. Enlist his siblings or peers to introduce him to age-appropriate music, computer games, popular movies, texting and cooking simple meals.

When necessary, consult with his doctors, teachers or therapists for advice. Adopt the use of visual schedules and choice charts to help your teen manage his day or week. Providing assistance does not mean inhibiting independence. Watch for signs from your child that he is able to assume greater responsibilities—both at home and at school. Be ready to teach him how to perform daily tasks rather than relying on you. Do not deprive him of the important and rewarding experience of mastering day-to-day tasks; it can instill pride and self-confidence that can prepare him for adult life. Praise his efforts at assuming responsibility (and applaud yourself for having the wisdom and courage to let him take these vital steps!).

The best thing you can do to cultivate independence in your child is to treat him as normally as possible. Avoid coddling and overindulging. Discipline shows your child you love him enough to give him security and structure. Use positive reinforcement to praise his conduct, but don't be afraid to use age-appropriate time-outs and to make him earn privileges, as your other children do. As your child matures, increase his responsibilities accordingly. Every time he rises to the challenge, he has taken a healthy step toward becoming an independent adult.

DRIVING AND YOUR AUTISTIC CHILD

Many teens and adults with autism spectrum disorders learn to drive. Evaluate your child's strengths and limitations carefully. Consider the fact that autism can make it hard to process more than one thing at a time. Driving requires continual processing. A driver must not only take the information in, but evaluate which parts of it should be given the most priority. This cognitive ability can be very difficult for someone with autism.

Unexpected noises are commonplace on the road. A driver must constantly monitor the road ahead of him as well as in the side- and rearview mirrors. Decisions on the road must be made instantaneously. In this setting a good decision arrived at too late is often just as ineffective as a wrong decision. Quick decisions also have to be made in conjunction with physical responses, such as braking, honking, accelerating, choosing a lane or making a turn.

With practice, your child may be able to adapt to these driving situations. Video games that allow players to simulate driving situations can help him develop a skill set that makes driving possible.

Kathie Harrington, the speech pathologist mentioned earlier, says of her autistic son, "He doesn't go over thirty-five miles per hour most of the time. He doesn't go in reverse unless he is forced to. He plans every lane change and turn before he leaves the house. He checks his seat with a ruler every time he gets in to make sure that it is the same distance from the steering wheel. He turns on his radio at stoplights only. If he has a passenger, he talks at stoplights/signs only. He drives himself to work, the athletic club and the mall. I don't ride with him too much, but I can smile about it because my son is independent. Doug drives."[16]

Driving represents a solid achievement in independence for teens and adults with autism. If your child is high-functioning and you can provide him with enough time and support, it may be possible for him to become a good driver. Begin with individual skills and build on them in safe environments until both of you are confident of his skills. The results will speak for themselves.

TEACHING YOUR CHILD ADVOCACY

As your autistic child grows up, the reins of advocacy will begin to shift gradually from your hands to his. In order to make that transition, you will need to teach your child to advocate for himself. As you patiently help him learn the principles of advocacy, he will be better able to stand up for himself and, in the process, gain a greater sense of safety, confidence and self-esteem.

As an advocate, you can not only meet him halfway, but you can collaborate with your child to lay the groundwork for his future place in life. Autistic children may need to advocate for appropriate boundaries at the simplest level (**Advocacy Principle 7**). Learning to close the door when they use the bathroom, to cover their private parts after showering, to say "no" or "don't touch me," to avoid staring at other people or invading the physical space of others by swinging their arms, are just a few examples. Like all children, they must be taught to provide their name, address, phone number, parents' names and school names in the event they are ever separated from their parents or caregivers.

Children with autism also need to learn how to talk about autism! There will certainly come a time when they have to disclose their condition to individuals outside of their immediate circle. Children in elementary school may be asked why they are in a special class or why they have their own assistant with them in the classroom. All of the questions that may be asked of siblings ("What's wrong with you?" "Are you re-tarded?" "Why do you talk like that?") will be asked of your autistic children and teens too. You will need to prepare them to answer these questions. (Nonverbal children may be taught to let others know they have autism by using sign language, pictures or writings.)

One of my clients is a boy named Robert Vasquez, who attends a charter school in a general-education class. Although he was diagnosed with autism when he was two, he has attended public school since kindergarten. There were very few children with autism or other disabilities at Robert's school. Most of the other children didn't even know that he had autism.

Robert's mother was upset that a group of boys had been calling him names and teasing him because he didn't play with them on the playground and spent most of his time alone. Robert complained that the boys were frightening him and he didn't want to go to school anymore. His mother, Diana, notified the school and worked with them on a plan to have teachers monitor the situation, but she isn't always going to be there to advocate for him. In fact, Robert will be entering middle school next year and the social dynamics will change. In middle school, students are expected to resolve conflicts with minimal adult participation, especially parental participation. By teaching Robert advocacy skills, we can give him the means to stand up for himself on the new campus and in the years ahead, as he moves toward becoming an independent adult.

Advocating to your child with autism and teaching him to advocate for himself are every bit as crucial as your advocacy to the world on his behalf. As you model the skills you use on his behalf, he will be watching you and learning. Then, if you take the time to actively teach him these advocacy principles, over the years he will become a stronger individual, with a solid foundation to stand on. Learning how to advocate for himself will allow him to gain independence and learn the life skills he needs to continue his education, have sustained employment, live independently and enjoy a better quality of life.

THE 7 ADVOCACY PRINCIPLES
FOR YOUR CHILD

As these examples demonstrate, many of the principles you are using to hone your abilities as an advocate can be adapted to your child.

1. **Take Responsibility.** Do not wait passively for someone to notice when you need something. If you need help, ask for it.

2. **Learn.** Practicing can help you do things that would have seemed too hard before, such as participating in individual education program meetings or going to the counselor's office in high school.

3. **Think Critically.** Know your own limits. Think carefully about what to do in situations that challenge you. If you prepare beforehand, you can make things easier.

4. **Speak with Authority.** You have the same rights as your peers. It's okay to ask for special accommodations in class or request a change of cubicles at work because of the noise level. Speak up.

5. **Document.** Keep files of your important papers and make notes about what you have learned in therapy or class, so you can review them later.

6. **Collaborate.** Learn to rely on your team and seek intervention when you need it.

7. **Educate.** Sometimes it will be up to you to tell people you have autism and explain its characteristics. In these cases, you can be the teacher.

PUTTING IT INTO ACTION

1. Make it a point to actively teach your child the advocacy skills you have learned. Help him identify situations in his own life

where he can begin to apply these skills. Your everyday advocacy is laying the groundwork for the advocacy your child will use to stand up for himself in the future.

2. Think of five important but age-appropriate skills—anything from crossing the street only at a red light or dialing 911 to cooking a meal or texting on his phone. Start working on these skills *today*, with either the help of other family members or a trained professional.

3. Help your child set up a filing system for his own notes and papers. Identify three ways that he can use these files to review the skills he's learned, remember important details or keep appointments. Follow up on a regular basis until he has developed the habit of using the system for his own benefit.

CHAPTER 6

Empowerment Circles: Avoiding Isolation

Empowerment circles have been a part of my life ever since I can remember. When I was growing up on the streets of St. Louis, I was fortunate to be surrounded by loving women. My grandmother, my godmother, my mother and the other women in the housing project where I grew up nurtured and supported me every step of the way. The course of my life would have been completely different without their wisdom and insight.

As a child, I didn't have a formal name for this group of supporters. They were simply a part of my life. I just wanted to get into a good college that could help me build a better life for myself. In order to do that, I made a conscious effort to find career counselors and academic advisers who could show me the way. After graduation, I wanted to build a legal career that allowed me control over which clients I represented. Aware of my inexperience, I knew it would be wise to surround myself with individuals with the technical expertise, advice and information I needed to navigate the legal profession. Drawing on the lawyers, businesspeople and classmates from college and law school with whom I had developed trusting relationships, I soon formed a close-knit group that was invaluable in guiding me.

With these inner circles of friends and family—offering expertise, wisdom, honesty and support—I achieved far more than I could ever have imagined possible. I discovered firsthand what the great leaders and peak performers throughout history have always known: Exceptional achievement in work and life is a collaborative process. Supportive relationships can make the pivotal difference in why some people succeed more than others. These relationships planted the first seeds in my mind for what would later become empowerment circles.

By the time we learned of Marty's autism, I knew I needed a strong, knowledgeable circle of people with candor, insight and experience to share. But I was at a loss. I didn't happen to have many existing relationships with experts on special-needs children. And what would I give them in return?

When I was a young girl in a loving community or an up-and-coming attorney finding my way in a new career, there were people ready to help. As a successful attorney with a husband and three children, I needed to expand the model that had worked so well for me in the past.

My first call was to Cheryl Gully, a dear family friend who is also a licensed social worker. I knew she was connected to social service agencies and the entire system of care for children with special needs. She had even taught classes to foster-care parents of children with special needs. Talking openly to her about Marty made me feel like a tremendous burden had been lifted. Until that call, I had not spoken to anyone about Marty's diagnosis other than my husband and one of my closest friends, Terri Hamilton Brown, who lived far away. The conversation went so well, I quickly invited others to join my empowerment circle. A beloved pastor of my church, one of the doctors who evaluated Marty at UCLA and several well-informed parents of children with autism soon became part of my team. Because most of my trusted advisers live in different parts of the community, we have never met as a group. Instead, we often talk by e-mail or in conference calls. You'd be surprised by how much difference a ten-minute call at just the right moment can make!

The support of this close circle of friends and peers continues to define, enrich and encourage my development as an advocate for Marty. I feel happier and more purposeful. After I'd been working with my group for several months, my anxiety and sadness lifted. Autism no longer had a choke hold on my emotions. My relationships with my family and everyone around me—including the staff at my law firm—improved. The ability to vent, talk, learn, grow and give back to others in my empowerment circle—my safe place—was even more essential than it had been in the past. Because I no longer felt overwhelmed, I could put my son's autism in perspective and restore the balance to my life, allowing myself to focus some of my energies on my other commitments to my family members and coworkers. New challenges and conflicts constantly come up, as Marty grows and aspects of his program change, but now I can address them with more confidence because of the long-standing support of my team.

It's clear to me that empowerment circles are not only critical to success in business or a professional career; they are critical to a parent with a special-needs child. We can't know everything, be everywhere or do it all. A group of confidants and advisers can not only provide emotional support, but, if you choose carefully, your group will be made up of people who come armed with practical ideas, suggestions and contacts.

Whether you are trying to obtain a diagnosis, decide which medication is best, deal with difficult behaviors, find the best school for your child or identify an appropriate social group for your teenager, having empathetic, conscientious and resourceful people in your inner circle is critical. At its best, an empowerment circle can help minimize the emotional force of the blow when things go wrong and provide tangible assistance that can help you cope with—or even prevent—a crisis.

Successful businesses have been using a form of empowerment circles for years. A recent *Harvard Business Review* article, "Eight Ways to Build Collaborative Teams," reported that deep social bonds were the major predictor of success in a study of fifty-five high-performing teams.[1] In his book *Who's Got Your Back, New York Times* bestselling author Keith Ferrazzi calls these bonds "lifeline relationships" and says that they are the reason some people succeed more than others. He tripled his company's earnings in one year by creating "lifeline" relationships to guide, encourage and help him be accountable to his personal and professional goals.[2]

Mentors and personal coaches can be invaluable too, but in those relationships, there is a one-way flow of information and advice—from your mentor or coach to you. They share their knowledge, wisdom and experience with you; but you don't give them advice and feedback. Empowerment circles thrive on reciprocity. Although someone in the circle may have superior knowledge on a specific topic or a particular expertise, this doesn't elevate her status in the circle or give her greater authority on other issues.

Initially, sharing with other parents can seem daunting. One of the focuses of my workshops is helping parents make connections to others who might be good candidates for an empowerment circle. Using **Advocacy Principle 4**, in an exercise I call Parent 2 Parent, each participant stands up and speaks about his situation, describing his autistic or other special-needs child and explaining some of the most pressing challenges he faces. After everyone has had a turn to speak, I ask parents to pick partners, based on the struggles people have shared about their health, finances, personal relationships or careers.

The partners come together to share personal experience and sage advice. Imagine a roomful of parents—who are initially strangers—talking openly about the strategies they have used to deal with the familiar obstacles and encounters every parent faces with an autistic child. It is immediately obvious that, by establishing close relationships with other people, sharing your challenges and offering your expertise, you can build a foundation that can help you face seemingly insurmountable odds.

When I first met Luana Garrison, she was starting over after a difficult divorce. She had just relocated to Los Angeles and changed jobs. Her son, Christopher, had been diagnosed with epilepsy and developmental delays a little after his second birthday and had been in and out of hospitals his whole life. He had changed schools a number of times and had taken just about every medication on the market that could even remotely help him, but he was still struggling.

Luana had encountered one roadblock after another. Even her husband, who might have been her one ally, was gone. When she turned to her church, she was met with awkward stares and prejudice against disabled children. She had hoped to attend services, but knew she would need assistance from the staff to do so, and the church leaders declined to help. She was beginning to discover that sharing the nature of her child's condition could actually make people *less* sympathetic. Their responses made her isolation seem even more stifling.

By the time Luana consulted me, she was exhausted and frustrated, at her wits' end—in urgent need of encouragement and support. I told her about the many workshops that my law firm and Special Needs Network sponsored. At these meetings, I explained, she would have an opportunity to meet other parents with similar issues and form the kind of bonds that could be the beginning of her own empowerment circle.

Luana eagerly attended the next workshop. She said afterward that it gave her the courage to confront her feelings and the strength to see that she had a bigger purpose. After attending workshops for a year, she called me excitedly to report that her life had improved by leaps and bounds. Rather than suffering alone, against seemingly insurmountable roadblocks, she had begun to share with others. As she opened up and became more vulnerable, she relaxed and found herself to be more giving and trusting. She was so energized by her interactions with people who truly understood what she was going through that she had more energy to focus on her son.

Once she understood how empowering a group can be, she formed a vibrant support group for parents of children with epilepsy in Corona, California.

FIVE WAYS YOUR EMPOWERMENT CIRCLE CAN HELP

Your empowerment circle should be tailor-made to suit your needs. Start thinking now about what you would want and need most from your own circle of helpers, advisers and confidants. Don't even begin to look for members until you know exactly what you want. In the meantime, here are a few ways your empowerment circle can help.

1. **Serving as Your Sounding Board.** Haven't you sometimes wished you had someone to bounce an idea off of before you made a decision? Certainly friends and relatives can be there for you in most cases, but when it comes to autism they can't always help. They just may not have the experience to give you the feedback you need.

2. **Sharing Your Practical Chores.** Believe it or not, the thousand little chores of your everyday life can sometimes be shared. Members of your circle can help with everything from carpooling to playdates.

3. **Broadening Your Information Network.** No matter how well you stay abreast of the latest research, there is always more to learn. It's impossible for any one person to keep up. Your circle can broaden your scope immediately, to help keep you informed about critical treatments, educational opportunities and new care options available.

4. **Bringing You Accountability.** None of us can cope with the constant challenges we face while simultaneously watching our own backs. Your empowerment circle can offer valuable

objectivity, drawing your attention to everything from potential problems with caregivers or treatments to areas you are neglecting in your own life. Accountability isn't always pleasant, but it's priceless.

5. **Giving You Community.** Along with your existing social networks, your empowerment circle can give you a strong sense of community that specifically offers encouragement and support to you as the parent of an autistic child.

AVOID THE TRAP

Like Luana, many parents find that their initial attempts to reach out to others for support are met with rejection, misunderstanding and prejudice. The situation may be compounded when they take their children out in public. People may stare or make rude comments.

"As my son gets older, his odd mannerisms stick out more," Patricia Johnson says of her eighteen-year-old. "He claps and flaps and jumps. Sometimes he will sing loudly. Even younger children are now looking at him like he is odd. It breaks my heart but I do the best I can to ignore it. When he has a crying fit in public, I walk by the other parents and do my best to ignore them too. I stand tall, put on my strong face and walk by. I have better things to worry about."

Even when a parent is prepared for these situations and handles them calmly, the experience is stressful. The danger is that over time, in little increments, a parent can begin to withdraw. It may simply seem easier to stay home than to take the child with difficult behavior out in public. Before long, parents can find themselves avoiding even friends or relatives. But they don't realize that the isolation itself makes everything more difficult—in emotional but also very practical ways.

I'll never forget meeting Diane Murphy at our first town hall meeting of Special Needs Network in Los Angeles. A thousand families attended, along with elected officials, doctors and community leaders. We had invited them all to discuss the impact of autism on communities of color. The meeting was filled with African-American, Latino and Asian families, who shared many of the same fears and frustrations.

Diane and James, who was her husband at the time, sat quietly throughout the day. They had never attended a public meeting and were far too private to stand up in a crowd of people to talk about their autistic daughter. Shiane had first been diagnosed with autism when she was four years old. At the time, the school administrators had said, "Don't worry. She is high-functioning. She'll be fine." By the time Shiane was twelve, her behavior had escalated to the point that Diane had to keep her confined to the house, except for her daily trip to school.

Initially, the family had maintained their normal routine of social outings with family and friends, but as soon as Shiane's behavior began to draw attention to itself, they found the barrage of questions too much to handle. Questions about whether she was "retarded" struck Diane to the core and served only to remind her of the intense sadness she felt when she first learned of her daughter's diagnosis.

When Shiane got older, things became even more difficult. If the family had been able to find a school and services better suited to Shiane's needs, the problems might not have developed. But without those services, Shiane's behavior escalated. Whenever she encountered strangers, she would pull their hair and grab their earrings, necklaces or anything shiny that she could reach. On one of the rare occasions that the family left the house to have dinner at a local restaurant, Shiane spit on a man at an adjoining table. His violent reaction caused Shiane to have a meltdown. Before their dinner arrived, Diane, James and Shiane were all in tears. "No more," Diane said. After that, the family retreated into isolation. Little did she know that that isolation would make it much easier for her daughter to regress.

As they listened to other parents at our town hall meeting, Diane and James began to realize that they were not alone. Their feeling of relief persuaded them of the value of having understanding people in their lives. Not only would they benefit from the experience of other parents, but they could share the lessons they had learned as well.

When I spoke to them afterward, they said the meeting was an awakening for them, like the dawning of a new day. Diane said she had come to the meeting with a sense of despair, but connecting with other families had renewed her sense of hope. I encouraged her to make friends in this community and get more involved.

When parents feel overwhelmed, it can seem impossible to volunteer their time. "What time?" they may wonder. It already feels like there are too few hours in a day. But I assure you that every minute you devote to others—whether in your empowerment circle or in the autistic community—will come back to you in ways more wonderful than you can imagine.

Diane was so motivated by the experience that she increased her involvement dramatically. She devoted herself to becoming more knowledgeable and sharpening her advocacy skills. With the support of her new friends, she found better help for her daughter, so her family could start going back out into the world. At every workshop she attends, she broadens the scope of families with similar issues, and life doesn't look so bleak anymore.

Looking back on those years of isolation, Diane realizes now that, if she and her husband had known how to respond to the rude reactions of others, they might not have been tempted to isolate themselves and avoid contact with other people. But how were they to know? The lessons in good manners their own parents had taught them when they were growing up were of no help at all in situations like these. At our workshops, we help parents connect with one another to provide much-needed support in these difficult situations.

Ordinary parenting skills are simply not enough to cover the challenges presented by autism. It takes a special kind of strength and advocacy to stand up for an autistic child. As a parent advocate, you can apply **Advocacy Principle 2**. When you learn to be an expert at the communication skills you need when dealing with the public, much of your fear and anxiety will subside. Even though a confrontation with a rude stranger may always be stressful, knowing exactly what to do about it is empowering.

- Explain the situation to others in ways that respect your privacy.
- Request that people not get involved.
- Express your feelings of anger, but calmly.
- Apologize, if the situation calls for it.
- Rely on a script of ready answers.

If, for example, you are in a mall and a nice old lady tries to prompt your nonverbal child to talk, you can say, "He doesn't talk to strangers." If your child is having a tantrum because he wants something that you are not going to buy him and a stranger says, "What a brat! He's so spoiled," you can say, "This is not a disciplinary issue. He has autism. Praise is much more effective than hurtful words."

Going out in public can feel so overwhelming that you don't even want to think about what has happened. That's understandable, but it's a mistake. Use **Advocacy Principle 3** to think critically about the situations that are the most upsetting. It's likely that a handful of things upset you the most about going out in public, whether it's the reactions of other people or certain behaviors of your child. Isolate those situations (rather than your family) and be proactive about finding ways to deal with them.

Some parents, for instance, are truly embarrassed if they have to physically chase after their child in order to contain her in a public space. It's one thing to find more discreet tactics to keep her from shouting inappropriately, but if they have to run around themselves, they feel foolish and exposed.

Other parents think nothing of that, since it could happen to any parent, but they are really uncomfortable if their child demonstrates behavior that seems "odd" to others—such as head banging, high-pitched screams or walking rapidly in circles. For some, it is not the autistic behaviors themselves that make going out in public a chore; it is the extra time that everything takes. A child with autism often requires longer transition time. Parents can easily fall into the habit of avoiding taking their child out in public for the sake of speed and efficiency. While that may be a practical solution in many cases, experience can help speed up the transition time for a child, while avoiding it altogether may serve to reinforce the problem.

On any public outing, your autistic child may engage in a number of behaviors that make you prone to isolate. Notice which ones bother you most. If your child running through a store embarrasses you, work to reduce or eliminate that behavior in particular, and let the other things slide. If you aren't sure how to effectively work on the behavior, consult a therapist.

Beyond that, give yourself a break. When emotions are running high, do not expect yourself to always react in a politically correct way. There are rude, uninformed people out there who will hurt, embarrass and anger you. If you react too harshly this time, don't worry. You'll certainly have occasion to practice until you come up with a better response. Many of these people are so far out of line that you can certainly afford yourself a margin of error. You are on a learning curve. And in the meantime, these rude people are not worth isolating yourself.

There are always far more kind, compassionate people in the world than not. Use your advocacy skills to find those people. Surround yourself with the ones of the very highest caliber by inviting them into your empowerment circle.

WHAT TO LOOK FOR

In developing your empowerment circle, look beyond your immediate family, friends and business associates. Hopefully, your family members and friends will always be there for you, ready to support and encourage you along the way. However, especially with family members, there are often unresolved issues and emotional baggage that can make it difficult for them to be objective, and they may not be especially knowledgeable about autism.

Family and friends will be an important part of your child's life and can play a critical role in helping you and your child. But the best empowerment circles offer more than support. They also challenge you and bring in new information and resources that can help you make better progress toward your goals—whether they are goals for moving forward in your career or for getting the best care possible for your autistic child. Experts in the field—such as doctors, therapists and educators—and other parents with special-needs children are ideal candidates for your empowerment group.

In 2000 a study in Scotland explored the impact of parent-to-parent support and found that parents of special-needs children most often got answers to their questions, referrals for health-care professionals, and a host of other supportive services and resources from other parents of special-needs children. It concluded that parents of children with special needs were "uniquely qualified" to help one another.[3]

Above all, your empowerment circle should be tailor-made to meet your needs and suit your tastes. It's up to you to bring your own personal criteria to your choices.

As you develop a list of prospects to invite into your empowerment circle, include only reliable people whose advice and insight you know you can trust. Begin by defining the areas where you need the most help, such as driving to appointments, understanding medical terms, creating calm, learning how to respond to strangers, building your list of service contacts, getting recommendations for caregivers, etc. Start with people you already know who may have the ability and resources to help. Beyond that, include these considerations in your search as well:

Concentric Circles of Empowerment. Think in terms of concentric circles. In the inner circles are those who play an important role in your everyday life. In the outer circles are the professionals who can help on a more limited basis, such as accepting a ten-minute call or e-mail now and then.

Keep in mind that empowerment circles tend to evolve and expand over the years. In the beginning, you may gather only a handful of trusted allies around you in your local area, and that will be sufficient. As time goes on, you may wish to add people farther afield, including carefully selected contacts made online; parents you meet at workshops; experts you contact as a result of reading their books and articles or seeing them in the media; and former therapists and care workers who know your child but are not currently treating him. Not all of these people will live in your local community, but they can still serve an important function as a part of your concentric circles of empowerment.

Willingness and Availability. All of us have such busy schedules, it is important to consider whether a person you have invited to join your empowerment circle will have time for meetings, phone calls and e-mails. Those in your inner circle must be willing to be generous with their time. It is hard to anticipate how long it will take to work through complicated emotions and issues that come up. Commitment to one another is vital. Anyone in your inner circle must be willing to get together with you for a couple of hours at least once a month.

Everyday Assistance. Certain members of your empowerment circle may be included for the sake of managing day-to-day errands. The constant demand of taking your child to medical, school and therapy appointments can take a toll. Other parents of autistic children may welcome the chance to unite their efforts with yours. Driving to appointments, arranging playdates, attending birthday parties and going to school events can all be shared with members of your empowerment circle.

The women who attend my workshops at Special Needs Network always embrace the idea of setting up a regular playdate for several autistic children every week. The parents take turns supervising while the others get a respite. When you meet the parents of children who attend the same school or therapy clinics, use your advocacy skills to speak up and be proactive (**Advocacy Principle 4**)! Suggest a rotating playdate or carpooling. Few beleaguered parents of autistic children will turn down the offer. Among those who prove to be the best match for you and your children, consider inviting them to be a part of your empowerment circle as well.

Confirmed Expertise. Having someone in your empowerment circle with true expertise in autism is also important. You are entering an entirely new world. Despite my fifteen years' legal experience with disability rights, when Marty was diagnosed with autism I felt like I was thrust into an entirely new world with unfamiliar terms, processes and procedures. Look for someone more knowledgeable than you are, who has experience in the specific areas you need to explore. A special-education teacher, a speech therapist, a special-needs attorney, a counselor, a doctor or even a parent with an older child with a similar diagnosis are all good options. Those you invite must be able to understand your concerns and be sufficiently well versed, so you can trust their advice.

Genuine Interest. It's a fact of human nature that sometimes all of us say "yes" because we're too polite to say "no." In your eager search for good candidates, be aware that some of the people you invite may recognize that they could be helpful and may even agree to participate even though they're not actually interested. It's not always easy to tell, but try to be objective. Don't let your own eagerness to hear "yes" override the clues that they don't really want to be involved.

The people in your empowerment circle must have a genuine interest in autism and in your child. Otherwise, you are wasting your time and theirs. People who agree to help but have a low level of interest tend to be chronically unreliable. Your expectation of support is likely to be met with disappointment. Trust me. I have learned to limit any discussions about Marty to those people who know him well or those in the disability community who have already shown real interest. No one wants to go to a girls' night out and be bombarded with tales of your child's therapies any more than they want to hear the next person's incessant bragging about their child's cute remarks or stellar grades. It's the quickest way to get uninvited to the next soiree. Everyone in your empowerment circles, at every level, must have more than a passing interest in order to add value to the group and sustain their commitment.

Shared Philosophy. Finding others who support your approach is vital. A good fit will alleviate potential conflict and tension. Although you don't want to find someone who will coddle you or parrot your every opinion, you do need to have a compatible philosophy. A parent who is fundamentally unwilling to accept his child's diagnosis or an expert who is adamantly opposed to your primary treatment plan should not be invited to join your group.

Candid Opinions. Ideal members of your empowerment circle will be able to share their opinions candidly with you. With so many distractions and difficult choices, there will be times when you lose sight of the forest for the trees. Maybe you start focusing too obsessively on getting a particular treatment and don't notice that it's time to look for new options. Maybe you become so emotionally caught up in a situation that you can't see that your response is making things worse. Maybe you've become so overwhelmed that you start feeling sorry for yourself or you fail to give yourself the acknowledgment you deserve. Losing perspective from time to time is inevitable. That's why you need people in your empowerment circle who have the courage to tell you a few home truths when you need to hear them.

When you choose your people well and encourage a tone of candor, it will allow you to be more open and honest with them in return. When you speak your truth, your circle of empowerment will be better able to understand your fears and struggles, be ready to hold you accountable to help you achieve your goals, and provide you with the gentle, loving support you need.

MAKE IT A COURTSHIP

An empowerment group has to be mutual. In any relationship, when you ask a lot, you have to be prepared to give a lot. An empowerment group asks a lot of its members. Each one should be ready to pitch in and help the others, within reason, whenever they can. A group like this can be incredibly powerful and useful, but it will work only if you are also willing to give 110 percent.

Doing so will sustain your group, but it will also make you feel better about yourself. When you make a substantial contribution, you will feel more valuable to the group as well. Your opinion will count more. Your bonds with the other members will strengthen and grow. Everything about the interaction changes when you meet people with reciprocity.

Unfortunately, many parents feel so overwhelmed by their situation that their emotions threaten to burden others who would otherwise be willing to help. It's easy to get lost in your own struggles and assume that everyone else has the same gut-wrenching feeling you have about your situation.

If you would like to sustain the support of others, you have to keep your emotions in check. I'm not suggesting that you suppress all your feelings and pretend things are fine when they're not. Rather, I'm proposing that you protect the important boundaries that exist between all of us. It's not a matter of suffering in silence, but of finding a more appropriate and effective way of sharing.

If you have trouble striking the right balance between holding back when you need help and overburdening other people with your emotions, turn to a friend for advice. Ask her to help you recognize when you are sharing too much.

Most people are deeply decent. If they heard your story, in all of its detail, they would very likely be moved and empathetic. But they have their own needs as well. Never forget that their first responsibility is to their own lives, not yours.

The only sustainable relationships are those that are mutual, where each person has something they can take away from the encounter. An empowered person empowers others. When you offer something to someone in your group, they will immediately recognize that you're coming to the relationship with their interests at heart, as well. And they will be much more inclined to give back to you in return.

Among your closest friends, you have already established a natural give-and-take that keeps the relationship going. When you approach other people about joining your empowerment circle, you need to let them know right away that the group is reciprocal and you expect them to benefit as well.

Ideally, you can be specific. Suppose you'd like to invite your child's speech therapist to join your empowerment group. You've gotten to know her, as she's worked with your child, and have joked together about how hard it can be to find a reliable babysitter. As you explain the function of the group to her, you can use babysitting as an example of how the group might be reciprocal for her too. Experts in the group may be able to offer advice or exchange services that will be useful to her. Others may be available for babysitting, carpooling or cooking.

It is not a tit-for-tat mentality, but the entire premise of the empowerment group is based on sharing. Each member will always be free to let the others know what they could use help with. At its best—and most sustainable—it will be a balanced exchange. If you ask someone for something, without making it clear that you are offering something they want in return, it can put them off.

The thing is, when you don't know them well enough, you don't know what to offer. And if you ask, "What can I do for you?" most people will say nothing. It makes them uncomfortable. That's why there has to be a period of courtship, where you casually talk and get to know one another.

Take the time to build these relationships and they will be long-lasting. Listen carefully to what they say. Be on the lookout for ways to make a contribution to their lives. In the courtship period, you can consciously cultivate that give-and-take. This is the kind of mutuality that exists naturally in friendships.

Be very careful not to exploit these relationships. Feigned interest in their needs is not a fair exchange. If your only real interest is in getting your own needs met, hire the person to provide the service you want in exchange for payment.

Otherwise, be generous as you volunteer your contribution to their lives. Apart from any specific thing they give you in return, the mutual reciprocity will create a warm, supportive environment that is beyond measure.

In your courtship, as you get to know them better, you'll come to know what they like or need. And then you can offer specific help: "I know your kids play basketball and you have a hard time picking them up. I can bring them home for you on Thursday." "I know you have a nonprofit. I have some contacts that may be able to help you."

The beauty of a good friendship is that friends don't need to ask. They listen, they care and they instinctively act to help one another. If I'm having guests from out of town, you'll volunteer to bring food over. And I would do the same for you. If I'm going through a difficult time, you will know the kinds of things that might help.

In some cases, the relationships with people in your empowerment group will be less personal. If you ask a school administrator to join the group, for instance, you may specifically offer to head up her next bake sale or volunteer to participate in her music workshop or art class. But the courtship period is still vital. Remember, "What can I do for you?" is the least effective way of finding the contribution that will be most appealing to them. Yet, after only a few conversations in which you show interest in the principal's activities, you may find out what school activities matter to her most. Then you can volunteer to do something truly valuable in exchange for her involvement in your group.

When you turn to an expert who is less accessible to you, you can be even more direct. Take, for example, the professional who has developed the therapy your child uses. She is unlikely to be available to come to a group meeting at your house every month, though she may agree to a limited, ten-minute consultation (many people will agree to a quick consultation free of charge). If you want to be able to speak to her on an ongoing basis, you'll need to offer her something in return.

In this case, a little research may take the place of the casual conversations in the hall that you could have with the principal. Check the professional's Web site, for example, and you may find that she supports a certain charity. If so, you can volunteer to participate or recruit people to participate in a fund-raising walk for that charity. Or you may be able to offer your own specific expertise in return. As an attorney, I once offered legal advice in exchange for services from the dentist in my empowerment group.

Regardless of the nature of the exchange, be sure to follow up with a thank-you note and an expression of gratitude for their support. A mentality that says, "I don't need to thank them; I'm giving them something in return," misses the point. No one has to give you anything. Stinginess will poison your efforts. And thanks are free. You can surely afford to show your appreciation. Always remember, this is an empowerment circle, not an entitlement circle.

WHERE TO LOOK

Start at your child's doctor's office, school, therapy centers, recreational activities and playgrounds. You may even find appropriate people to invite into your empowerment circle at work or at autism conferences and workshops. Go out of your way to interact with the people you meet there. In order to evaluate whether or not they would be appropriate for your circle, take the time to share your experiences and talk openly about your challenges, as well as your successes. Listen carefully to what they say and the way they respond. Ask yourself whether they are offering the kind of feedback and support you are looking for in your group.

Use good judgment. You are looking for people to build long-lasting, trusting relationships with. That is not going to happen with everyone you meet. Just because someone has a child with autism doesn't mean that she is right for your circle. Building your empowerment circles— even on the outer rings—is a serious endeavor and requires a serious search and recruitment effort.

Don't be afraid to ask your child's doctors or teachers to introduce you to other parents with children on the spectrum. Many of the parents who are closest to me today are those I have met through my son's teachers and doctors. I always make it clear to his support team that I am interested in connecting with other parents, because I have learned the value of collaboration and sharing information. Not everyone you meet through such encounters will be an ideal candidate for your empowerment circle, but one or two might develop into great support partners.

Stay open to possibilities. The people who become our closest friends can crop up in the most unexpected places! Parents often tell me that, once they started telling coworkers that they have a child with autism, they suddenly discovered that a surprising number of them had their own experiences with special-needs family members. The same thing can happen in discussions with total strangers you meet at the grocery store, the dry cleaner's or at church.

The mutual need for support among parents with autistic children is so great that the chat rooms and blogs of national and international autism spectrum organizations have experienced exponential growth. Discernment is an absolute necessity, however. Without it, you risk spending what little time you have following dead ends because of remarks made by people unqualified to give advice.

So be sure to apply critical thinking (**Advocacy Principle 3**) before accepting what you hear online, while enjoying the 24/7 companionship they offer. Bring to online chats the same discernment you use in the friendships you have face-to-face. Rather than assuming anyone who happens to be online in a particular chat room has the same level of credibility, work to identify a few people whose advice and support seem the most viable; then strike up friendships with them that can be continued in private.

MAKING CONNECTIONS ONLINE

AUTISM SOCIETY OF AMERICA

http://www.autismsource.org

Experts in almost every region of the country can be found at organizations affiliated with your local Autism Society of America (ASA).

AUTISM SPEAKS

http://autismspeaksnetwork.ning.com

The Autism Speaks network has fifteen active chat rooms online for parents and others to support one another with advice and resources, including rooms especially for parents coping with autism, newly diagnosed, single parents, moms, dads, siblings, relatives, teachers, scientists, caregivers and those who have autism. (*See* Groups.)

BEST BUDDIES

http://www.bestbuddies.org

Best Buddies is a nonprofit, global volunteer organization that creates opportunities for one-to-one friendships, integrated employment and leadership development for people with intellectual and developmental disabilities.

CARECENTRAL

http://www.carecentral.com

CareCentral allows caregivers to keep family and friends informed of their needs and of the progress their autistic child is making. It provides parents with private Web sites for their circle of friends and family only.

MEETUP.COM / GATHER.COM

http://www.meetup.com / http://www.gather.com

Meetup and Gather both provide online venues for support groups related to autism. Parents can search for existing groups or form their own.

AUTISM CONNECTS

http://www.autismconnects.com

Autism Connects is a virtual community where those connected to autism spectrum disorder can share images and stories, post events, participate in surveys, ask questions and provide answers.

ASD FRIENDLY

http://www.asdfriendly.org

ASD Friendly is a UK Web site that attracts tens of thousands of ASD parents and caregivers to many chat rooms. It also provides a free, friendly, confidential help line for parents and others seeking clarification, help and advice related to special educational needs.

ASD PARENT SUPPORT GROUP

http://asdparentsupportgroup.blogspot.com

ASD Parent Support Group is an ongoing, parent-run blog that posts other resources on the Web and hosts online discussions.

MEETING WITH YOUR EMPOWERMENT CIRCLE

In my own life, it seems to work best if I meet with most of the members of my empowerment circle on an individual basis. We rarely, if ever, meet as a group. You may find, however, that you prefer the dynamic support of a group. It is something I highly recommend and encourage at the Special Needs Network. An empowerment circle with regular meetings can take on a life of its own.

If you meet as a group, you will need to take responsibility for running the meeting. This is your opportunity to put **Advocacy Principle 1** to work, by taking on the role of a leader. You will set the agenda and make sure that it is generally followed. Your purpose is to empower everyone in your circle, and this can be done only through meaningful dialogue.

The time you spend at the beginning getting to know one another will be invaluable. Although it's time-consuming at first, it will eventually make the process more efficient. Eventually you might even become like the couples who can finish each other's sentences because they know each other so well and are so much in tune with each other's wants and needs. It all begins with the initial meetings, where you and your circle commit to the process, share your needs and talk openly about your experiences, feelings and expectations. These conversations will lay the foundation for all your subsequent meetings.

If you identify members who are fully committed, but who cannot attend physical meetings or help you with driving or other chores, this is perfectly acceptable. It's your circle; you get to decide what your priorities are and who is in the best position to assist you. Maybe your greatest priority is assistance with understanding the many treatment and educational options available to you, or having someone you can call when you need to vent or to bounce ideas off of another person. You know your needs and your schedule. If you are at a stage where phone calls and e-mails work better, then that is the circle you will create. Leave open the opportunity that at some later time, your needs may change and you may need greater support by having a circle of supporters you can actually meet in person on a regular basis. You can make this as formal or informal as you like, recognizing that your circle is an important part of your advocacy strategy.

At your first meeting, set the ground rules—without being too technical. For example, discuss your future meeting dates and times and elicit a commitment from each member to take on a specific task. One member may be asked to create a directory that has everyone's contact information so that information can be easily shared. Another member may be asked to be responsible for sending out e-mail alerts or bringing copies of articles related to autism treatment or care. Someone else may be responsible for establishing playdates or other activities, if the group decides this is a priority item.

Guidelines for Meetings
- Plan an agenda for every meeting to keep you on task and to make sure each member's concerns and issues are addressed
- Share the agenda with other members of the group when the meeting starts
- Discuss new research, experts, materials, theories or information relevant to autism, treatment, education or advocacy
- Consider choosing a primary theme for the meeting
- Set aside time for each member to comment on the theme
- Remind everyone of future meetings, events or activities

Collaboration is one of the most crucial principles of advocacy. Without it, many of your other efforts will have nowhere near the trajectory or impact that they could have had with a strong, supportive group. Whether or not you have ever attempted forming an empowerment circle before, make the effort now. Put **Advocacy Principle 6** into practice by becoming a team builder. It will change your life.

TRUST YOUR ADVISERS

In my law practice, it amazes me how many of my clients pay tens of thousands of dollars for legal advice that they don't follow. They come to my office, tell me that they have read about me in the press, seen me on television, talked about me to friends and colleagues, and they just know from everything they have been told and all of their research that I am the perfect person to help them. Yet the minute I tell them something contrary to what they have already decided to do, all of that goes right out the window!

A circle of "yes" people is not an empowerment circle; it's a waste of time. As I said, hopefully you will manage to find people who feel free to be candid with you. But of course, even when people feel free to give you their honest opinion, it's completely up to you whether to accept their advice.

If you find that you are rejecting more advice and assistance than you are accepting, however, it is time to reevaluate the situation. First, evaluate your own open-mindedness. If you are consistently turning down good advice because your mind is already made up, you are cheating yourself and your child of good options. Ask others in your circle if they have noticed this tendency in you. If not, it may be that the advice you're turning down is not well suited to you. In that case, you may want to consider bringing new members into your circle. If someone isn't working out, you should feel free to terminate the relationship. Be polite, but be firm. There are no plans or decisions that cannot be rethought or redefined.

Over time, some team members may also become less engaged because of personal circumstances or other commitments. As your child grows, your needs and your child's needs will naturally change as well, making new members more appropriate. Don't count this as a loss; see it as a natural process and evolution. It gives you an opportunity to connect with others, recalibrate your circle and strengthen its core.

I am well aware that the last thing you have is extra time. If an empowerment circle were going to end up being one more chore on the never-ending list of things you need to accomplish, I would not recommend it. But these circles have made amazing things happen in my own life and those of many, many others I have known. Believe me, your efforts will be rewarded far more than you can imagine.

PUTTING IT INTO ACTION

1. Write down every need in your advocacy for your child that could be met by an empowerment circle. Looking over the list, think of what kind of person would be best to meet that need. If you know such a person, jot down the name. If not, brainstorm about where you could find such a person. Ask friends to help you come up with contacts to meet these needs.

2. Turn to your empowerment circle for help in creating a script of ready answers for situations you face when you take your child out in public.

3. Identify the three Advocacy Principles that you can apply with the most confidence. Consider whether your strength in these areas can be of use to others in your empowerment circle, and find ways to offer your help.

4. Identify the three Advocacy Principles that you would most like to strengthen. Are there members of your circle who could help you develop these areas? Ask for suggestions and find ways to get help.

5. Commit to a date by which you want to have formed your empowerment circle; set a sample agenda and do it. Take the first step in creating a circle of trusted advisers who can assist you and your child.

CHAPTER 7

Balancing a Career and Autism: Making Your Life Work

When Marty was in second grade, I had at least one or two meetings every week with his teacher, his therapist and other members of his therapy team. Then he began having unusual symptoms, and I had to take him to various doctors and specialists, who were investigating whether or not he was having seizures, at hospitals and neurologists' offices miles from our home. Meanwhile my two young daughters were in school hoping their mom would be around to take them to their after-school activities and playdates, I was managing partner at the Los Angeles law firm I'd founded, and I was also president of Special Needs Network.

There were times when I felt I needed three versions of myself to keep up with my schedule—plus maybe a spare who had time to relax! More than once, I questioned whether I could continue to maintain my full-time law practice, my commitment to the nonprofit I had started, and the other professional obligations I had without neglecting my son and family. Over the years, through trial and error, I've created a better balance. It did not come naturally. I needed advocacy skills to explore my options and put my priorities in place. Even now, it takes constant effort to sustain that balance, but the quality of life that results makes it well worth the effort.

According to Barbara Schneider and Linda J. Waite, who coedited *Being Together, Working Apart: Dual-Career Families and the Work-Life Balance,* "More than forty percent of working parents arrive at work early or stay late for three or more hours." The expectations at work often demand precedence over their family needs. The pressures on the job are so great that nearly 60 percent take work home with them.[1] The expectations at the office often collide with and overpower their family needs. These demands can make it difficult to imagine that it is even possible to work full-time while raising a child with autism. Yet parents who have spent years pursuing a degree or building professional experience often do not want to limit themselves to working as full-time caregivers. They take pride in their career and business accomplishments and derive a great deal of satisfaction from the work they perform. Working is their way of making a contribution and fulfilling lifelong dreams and aspirations.

Even women whose kids don't have autism can feel guilty about working and may abandon the careers they love to become stay-at-home moms. But it's more complicated when a child has autism. Women may feel pressured by family, friends or employers to quit their jobs and make caring for their disabled child their full-time commitment. That pressure can also come from inside ourselves. Those of us who have the luxury of not working but who choose to do so anyway often feel a conflict between our personal career goals and our commitment to our autistic child.

WHAT TO SAY. . .

When People Say Mothers Shouldn't Work

In today's economy, most women don't have a choice—they have to *work, either because the family needs two incomes or because she's a single parent (and remember the high divorce rate among parents with autistic children). At the Special Needs Network, I see how difficult it can be for parents to make time for the urgent needs of their child while maintaining a career that is both rewarding and sufficient to cover the extraordinary cost of rearing that child. On top of that, whether there are two parents in the home or one, the everyday needs of the child are most likely to fall on the mother.[2] Knowing the kind of sacrifices the parents of autistic children are making on a daily basis, I'm constantly astounded that anyone can criticize a mother for working. If you are faced with this kind of judgment, don't hesitate to speak up and with authority (**Advocacy Principle 4**).*

CRITIC: How can you work when you have a child who needs so much help from you?

PARENT: Working gives me the skills and confidence I need to help my child even more.

CRITIC: I quit my job when my son was diagnosed. He takes 110 percent of my time.

PARENT: That's a valid choice. But I made a different one and I feel good about it. Additionally, at work, I have the chance to educate so many people about autism. Now, since they know someone with an autistic child, some of my coworkers have gotten involved with organizations that support autism.

CRITIC: Juggling your job and your family, something must suffer. You can't do it all.

PARENT: It's true. I can't do everything—whether I stay home or work. There are sacrifices. But I have to work to support my family, and I have learned to be smart with my time and enlist the help of others—my empowerment circle is the key.

HOW ADVOCACY CREATES BALANCE

Plain and simple—advocacy is not for the faint at heart. You can either let the challenges of an autistic child drag you along, or you can step up. Doing so may take a new level of determination on your part, but the principles of advocacy will show you how. Using advocacy to create a balance between the demands of your child and the demands of your career will take tenacity and vigor. But this is one area in which the results will be noticeable immediately.

Once you find the right balance and learn to keep it in place, it will open the door to moments of real joy with your child—unimpeded by a schedule reeling out of control. It will allow you to take the well-deserved moments of relaxation and quiet time that keep you sane, or the night out with your friends—when you never mention your child—that remind you who you are and keep your spirit alive.

It's worth it to make a firm and unwavering commitment to achieving a balance between work and autism, because it's going to pay off in very tangible ways. If nothing else, it will help you avoid burning out and giving in to the inevitable pressures that can derail your advocacy. Running ahead of a never-ending series of obligations that feel like a fast-moving train is not a plan. You can do it for a while, but eventually it will exhaust and destroy you. You need to be driving the train, controlling every stop. Taking control of your schedule is the most sustainable course—not only today but in the years ahead, when your child moves into the heightened drama of the teen years and on to be an independent adult.

Know Your Priorities

Parents who decide to work full-time, even when they bear the primary responsibility for caring for a disabled child, will be faced with sacrifices and hard choices. As an advocate, you will take responsibility for those changes from the start. Do not wait passively for life to force you into making decisions. Anticipate them. Decide beforehand what your priorities are—in practical terms—so you can be ready to make your choices accordingly.

It's one thing to say your family comes first. It's another to put that into practice. Most of us think we know our priorities, but we are not usually asked to choose between competing ones. As the parent of an autistic child, you may have to decide whether the needs of one child you love outweigh the needs of another. At what point do you sacrifice the music lessons for your talented guitar-playing son in order to pay for one more round of social-skills therapy for your autistic daughter? Which do you value more: spending money to fly across the country to explore an experimental treatment or keeping the college fund for your other children intact? If your connection with your spouse is starting to fray, do you find time to spend together, or would you place your child's needs first and expect your spouse to understand? No one can decide your priorities for you, and no one but you can put your priorities into practice.

As an advocate, you have to be alert to what kind of choices you consistently make. It's very possible to place a high priority on things we never make time for. When that happens, discontentment is inevitable. Think critically (**Advocacy Principle** 3) about each of your priorities, then notice what you actually do in practice.

Don't assume that your priorities are the ones you think you're supposed to have. Write down what you think your priorities are; then test them for yourself. Record your activities for one week and look at how you spend your time. Do you, in fact, spend the most time on your highest priorities?

If your weekly schedule shows that you are spending more time on the things you thought you valued less, you need to make an adjustment. First ask yourself why it happened. Do you need better boundaries to keep your priorities intact? Or are your priorities different from what you thought they were?

When it comes to career, a child with autism can bring you surprising insights about your true priorities. I have seen ambitious women in rewarding positions they have worked hard to achieve decide that spending time with their special-needs child is a much higher priority for them. But I have also seen women come to the realization that, with a child who requires so much of them, they need their career more than ever—not only for the income, but to maintain a vital sense of identity and purpose.

None of these decisions is sacrosanct. Just as your child's needs will evolve over the years, so will your own. But it is important to know what your priorities are as you proceed through life. Spend time thinking about what kind of balance you want in your life. Are you willing to give up your career entirely? Has the arrival of autism changed your dreams for your own life completely? Or is there a way to make it all work?

If you could make it work, what would you want your life to look like now? Sometimes one little shift can give you the breathing room you need, like hiring someone to clean the house periodically, sending out the laundry, installing bookkeeping software to help manage your cash flow, giving each of your children helpful chores around the house or finding ways to make meals easier. Anything you can do to reduce or eliminate the time-consuming things that mean very little will leave more time for your priorities.

If you are in the financial position to hire a full-time support, such as a nanny or health aide, you will have more options, of course. Put your time into finding a trusted person or team of people to attend important meetings and accompany your child to medical appointments, therapy treatments and playdates while you maintain your daily activities and obligations as before. For busy entrepreneurs, ambitious professionals and anyone else with significant financial resources, this may be a more valid option than you think.

Many two-family households dedicate a large portion of their income to the support staff at home that allows them to travel and work the long hours required to make their careers a success. If you have the resources and are willing to accept the emotional sacrifices involved, for you and your child, then hiring or extending your staff may be the best option. This may seem extravagant to you, especially if you have worked your way up from a background where support staff would have been impossible, but take another look at your priorities. While you might want to personally take your child to each appointment, for instance, delegating that task to someone else may actually give you more quality time with your child. Every autistic child will require a wide range of caregivers in his life.

Your own support staff—whether it is a full-time team or a flexible mix of part-time help—can become an invaluable extension of that caregiver support. The important thing is to screen each person you bring into your family very carefully. They must not only have your complete confidence, but they have to be able to make your child feel happy and secure. However, if you cannot afford this level of support or if you feel it is important for you to be more closely involved with your child's daily life, then you will need to take responsibility for coming up with creative alternatives.

If you are uncomfortable with a schedule that leaves you only a couple of hours each day with your child, then you have to assess your circumstances and decide what is workable. For example, if you cannot afford a nanny to pick up your child from school, you may have to leave work to do it yourself. Evaluate carefully how that decision will impact your career. If leaving the office at that hour will endanger your chances of promotion or advancement in your job, you must either be willing to accept this consequence or have an alternate plan.

Hold Your Boundaries

Lack of clear boundaries is often the culprit when we feel out of control in our own lives. The feeling of being overwhelmed inherently implies that the boundaries have been breached and we are burdened with more than we can handle.

Advocacy Principle 1 can help you. The secret to creating strong boundaries in your life is to take responsibility for setting them—and holding them in place. No one else can do this but you. According to Sandi Stewart Epstein, a Washington, D.C.–based work/life coach, "Setting boundaries is a step-by-step process. The first step is to identify what your boundaries are." Take the time to evaluate the areas in your life that would benefit from firm boundaries.[3]

Once you have set your boundaries, stand up for them. They will allow you to stop ignoring things that interfere with your ability to be productive. If you know you have the right to do them, you will start feeling less guilty about putting your own needs first. It's a part of the process of defining yourself and what is acceptable to you. When you don't have boundaries set, other people will step over the line without even realizing where it is. It is up to you to make your boundaries clear.

In some cases, you will recognize immediately when a natural boundary is being breached because it is accompanied by an unpleasant feeling of dread, anxiety or fatigue. Instinctively, you know that by allowing that boundary to be crossed, you are giving more than you have to give. It can be caused by an individual asking too much of you or by a schedule that requires more hours than you have in a day. Either way, the experience is draining.

Zoe Hamilton, an attorney and mother of two, told me that she and her sons go to bed at eight p.m. every night, so she can be energized for work and the multiple activities her boys engage in every day. It's a healthy pattern that keeps her family life running smoothly. But the pattern did not establish itself. Zoe is a parent advocate. She excels at **Advocacy Principle 1**. When she realized how much better it would be if they all went to bed early, she took responsibility for making it happen. Getting her growing sons to go to bed so early was a challenge initially, and Zoe lay in bed awake herself for the first few nights, but she knew they would all adjust, and they did.

In order to hold the boundary in place, Zoe had to get her family and friends to respect their early bedtime. She asked each of them to not call the house after seven p.m. unless it was an emergency. She let her friends know she would not be available for events after eight p.m. unless it was a special occasion. Many people in her inner circle were incredulous at first, but when they saw that she consistently held the line, they came to accept it. Now they always comment on how well rested she appears!

Setting limits will require you to be proactive, firm and honest. Simply put, setting boundaries is about deciding how far you will let others come into your life. Although it may be difficult at first, you can form the habit with repetition and practice. Researchers say that every time you repeat a behavior—such as going jogging in the morning or going to bed at eight o'clock—associations develop in your memory between the behavior and the context in which it occurs.[4] As your new habit begins to form, the context itself will start to trigger the habit automatically. When that happens, waking up in the morning makes you think of jogging right away. At eight p.m., you feel sleepy and want to go to bed. At that point, the new habit feels like the natural thing to do, and not doing it feels a little strange.

As a parent and advocate, you have to decide what your highest priorities are and develop the courage to—pleasantly, but unapologetically—say "no" to things. For many parents, this is the hardest part about setting limits. Whether it's a fear of being disliked, a worry that you will never be invited again, or some upsetting association from childhood . . . get over it! And don't worry: "getting over it" is a habit that gets easier with practice, too.

To be a strong parent advocate and keep up with your obligations at work, you must accept that there are some things you will not be able to do. When you draw the line and eliminate things, some people will protest, but it's the best thing for both of you. Avoid, at all cost, the temptation to say "yes" when you know (or suspect) that you will not be able to meet your obligation. This will only alienate people and cause you unnecessary stress. The best approach is to be honest about your boundaries and hold your ground.

You must learn to set limits at work, at home and in every personal relationship—including those with your boss, coworkers, children, partner, friends and relatives. Identifying your boundaries will make it a lot easier to rule out requests that do not match your priorities. With practice, setting limits will move from an occasional event to a deeply rooted habit that allows you to feel in control of your life, to accomplish your goals and to protect yourself from the burnout that is, otherwise, inevitable.

Michael W. Rabow, MD, an associate professor of clinical medicine at the University of California–San Francisco School of Medicine, says, "Recognize that for the caregiver to be of most use, he can't burn out. Create a system that gives you breaks and that is sustainable. If you try to go two months . . . providing constant care, you won't be all there. Families need to have hard discussions about sharing the load. Even short amounts of respite can help immensely, and that might mean time at work."[5]

Once you determine what your boundaries are, don't be afraid to share them with your family and the other people they will affect. In my own life, one of my most crucial boundaries is my time in the morning to meditate and pray. It took my family a while to understand how important this time is for me, but I knew I had to develop a morning routine that supported my need for time alone. This meant going to bed a little earlier, so I could get up earlier and savor that quiet time before getting the kids ready for school. After a couple of months, my family began to accommodate my practice. Rather than ask me a barrage of questions about breakfast and backpacks, they learned to walk quietly by and wait till I was ready, respecting my boundaries.

It is important to articulate your limitations in the workplace as well. I don't mean unilaterally rewriting your job description, refusing assignments, failing to be a team player, or, for that matter, doing anything that undermines your responsibilities at work! For example, an attorney in a litigation practice can't exactly refuse to go to court or take a deposition. However, it would be perfectly appropriate to let coworkers know that you don't have time to discuss non-work-related matters during work hours. I'm not suggesting that you alienate your coworkers by giving them the cold shoulder—strong relationships are certainly important in business—but many discussions (not to mention time spent chatting online, answering e-mails or surfing) could be eliminated to increase productivity. If you are not convinced of this, keep a diary for the next two weeks and track all of your office conversations, phone calls, meetings, and other activities. You will be surprised at the amount of time that you can shave from your day and reallocate to your child.

When I was a young lawyer working at a Wall Street firm, it was not uncommon for attorneys to work from nine a.m. until ten or eleven p.m. This pattern was considered the hallmark of a hardworking, ambitious attorney who clearly was on the fast track to partnership. A decade later, when I became a manager and started to track billable hours, I quickly learned that there was absolutely no correlation between time spent in the office, quality work product and billable hours. In fact, I managed many attorneys whose work days spanned fourteen hours but whose productivity level was *less than half* that of others who worked only nine hours. Plus, those who spent fewer but more productive hours in the office also complained less about lack of quality time with family and friends and overall had a better sense of work/life balance.

Increasing your productivity will often require you to be assertive.

Don't be afraid to tell colleagues how their conduct is affecting your job (and your ability to stay focused on your top priority—the care of your child). For example, if you rely on a coworker to complete her task in order to do your job, and that coworker is chronically late, explain to her how her tardiness prevents you from efficiently finishing your task: that it impacts not only you, but the company's bottom line.

If you are a hardworking team player, your bosses and coworkers will welcome your approach. Remain flexible and remember that you are part of a team. You are working toward a collective goal. By doing so, you can respect your own boundaries and continue to contribute to the bottom line.

According to Epstein, when it comes to boundaries, "Only you are the expert on yours. Nobody's going to come to you with solutions, so it's incumbent upon you to make your life the way you want it."[6]

Control Your Time

Time management and boundary setting go hand in hand. Creating a schedule for each day is essential. Good boundaries will help you formulate that schedule.

Effective time management isn't just about making a series of endless to-do lists and checking things off as you go. Think of time management as a way to organize your life around the priorities and boundaries that you have set. You'll choose what to do, and therefore what not to do, in a way that gibes with your goals. When I prioritized my morning ritual, I had to weigh all the possible things I could be doing in the morning—such as sleeping a little later, checking my e-mails, writing in my journal, exercising or making business calls to the East Coast. I had to recognize that opting *for* meditation essentially meant deciding *against* any other possible use of that time, however useful or appealing.

Most of us are not being asked to choose between something that's patently a waste of time and something we value. It's trickier than that. To fit everything into a day, it seems we constantly have to hold our boundaries against things we'd really love to do.

When you choose to have a glass of wine after work with your coworkers, go shopping with a friend, or attend a social event, you are simultaneously deciding not to spend that time with your child, your spouse or your family. They're all good ideas. These decisions are neither right nor wrong; they are simply a matter of choice. The important thing

is to make your decisions *consciously*. If you always make them sponta-
neously, I guarantee you that you will not make the best choices.

After a tiring day at work, a glass of wine with a coworker may be
just what you need in the moment, and if you were planning to spend the
evening with your child, you might be able to squeeze in the drink today
and that family time tomorrow. Maybe you can afford to spend two
hours with your coworker, or maybe you can't afford to spend even
one. Without checking your schedule, how will you know? If you keep a
schedule, you'll know whether or not this healthy moment of relaxation
will allow you to keep your priorities intact.

Whether you keep that schedule on your BlackBerry, your laptop, or
on your photo calendar hanging on the kitchen wall, keeping it is part
of your role as a parent advocate. It is yet another application of **Advocacy Principle 5**: Document, so you can be prepared. Without that documentation you cannot have the overview you need to be sure your
priorities are getting enough time throughout the week.

Within a family, decisions about time management have to be discussed collectively. It simply doesn't work for one parent to be away
from home, even for a brief period of time, if the other parent doesn't
know the plan. This is a formula for havoc.

In our family, we have family meetings on a regular basis, where my
husband, my children and I bring our respective schedules together. We
talk about any major events, sports, school- or work-related projects and
other activities coming up over the next thirty days. This gives everyone
an opportunity to voice their needs and expectations for transportation,
time and resources. I make sure to bring my office calendar, so I can
integrate my work assignments with my family's needs. This allows each
of us to have an overview of what's happening for months in advance.

For example, if I have an important client event after work on the
same night as a therapy session for Marty, I have to evaluate whether I
should attend the event or the therapy session. If I really need to attend
both, I make a note to reschedule one of them. If it's possible for someone else to go in my place, I consider whether I should ask one of my
coworkers to attend the event or ask my husband to attend the therapy
session. Other members of my family or my empowerment circle
may also be able to help. By being proactive, I give myself a realistic
chance of securing help; I respect the time commitments of others; and
I simultaneously involve my family in the process.

With the major items for the month scheduled, I next fill in recurring events that are important to me, my career, my children and my family, such as exercising, working on articles or other projects for my Web site, attending my daughters' tennis practices, and attending Marty's monthly therapy and school team meetings.

Before we started coordinating our schedules, I felt like I could never get ahead. I was constantly putting out fires. I might discover at four p.m. that my daughter had signed me up to bake cookies for her class's field-trip fund-raiser the next day. Without detailed documentation, I might not realize till two thirty p.m. that Marty's three p.m. team meeting was being held at a therapy clinic twenty miles away. The last-minute cookie sale and extra driving time might cut into the time I needed to write a complex brief for federal court. Although it seemed like a chore in the beginning, taking the time to thoroughly schedule months in advance—with all its details—allowed me to get in front of my obligations. I was amazed how much it inspired and empowered me.

Of course, despite our carefully crafted schedules, the unexpected is going to happen! As new things pop up in the month, I know that if I make time for them, I'm going to have to do so at the expense of something that I've already determined is a priority. Again, it's all about making conscious choices.

In the early days following Marty's diagnosis, I had to dramatically change how I spent my time. The learning curve for autism is steep. I had a lot to catch up on and I wanted to do it fast. So although I might have enjoyed doing other things, I spent weeknights and weekends reading or taking classes on speech delays and behavior issues for children with autism. For that intense period of time I decided it was worthwhile to forgo many of my routines. As I learned more and became more immersed in the autism community, my time commitments shifted again and I began to spend more time working with individual therapists on applying the theories I had learned in my reading and classes.

At first, I didn't realize that being a parent advocate was going to require a new level of time-management skill. Taking a holistic approach to my time and the management of my various responsibilities has reduced the stress of feeling like I'm constantly on the defensive—responding to external events without any real control over my time. My integrating my family and my office helped everyone learn to respect my commitments and one another's. Most of all, I've learned that it's important to me as an advocate to control my time, so that I can devote the most time possible to the things I truly value. I encourage you to do the same.

Initiate Change

An advocate takes the lead. Whether you are an employee in a corporation, a part-time worker at a small business or an entrepreneur running your own company, you can initiate changes in your work life that will allow you to balance your work with the needs of your autistic child.

Learning to hold your boundaries and control your time will certainly help you accomplish more of your top priorities. But if you find that that is still not enough, you may need to look seriously at changing how you work. Autism is not going to change. Of course, your child's *specific* needs will evolve and shift over time. But having an autistic child in your family—whether she is a child, a teen or an adult—is always going to demand a lot of your energy and time. Changing your work situation to accommodate that may be a good solution to finding the right balance.

Adjusting your work to accommodate autism may be more feasible than you think. Creativity and initiative can really pay off. In my law practice and at the Special Needs Network, I have watched parent advocates make remarkable changes in their work schedules to find the time they need for their children. Some of them are included here. If these do not meet your current needs, keep striving for a solution that works for you. Turn to your empowerment circle for more ideas. Read everything you can about alternative jobs online. Get a mentor. Learn new career skills. You *can* find a way.

Take Time Off

After exploring your options, you may determine that it is better to take time off, as some parents do with maternity leave.

You may, for example, decide it would be invaluable to take time off for a limited period while you organize your life, setting up adequate child-care services, interviewing prospective caregivers and researching your options in every area. Giving yourself this early grace period may help you gain your bearings. It will also allow you to support your child as he makes the transition to a host of unfamiliar people and new routines. In a few months, once things are better established, you may be able to return to work as before, or with a modified schedule. On the other hand, you may decide you need to take several years off to help your child and your family adjust. Your child may need more extensive medical care or interventions than you could handle while working.

In that case, your time-off plan should take both long- and short-term objectives into account—not only for your child's future, but your own. Ask yourself what impact this time off will have on your career. If you decide to take a few years off, will you be able to reenter the workforce, and at what expense?

After you have considered these questions, come up with a realistic plan. Identify exactly how much time you would like to take off and whether you will be able to continue doing any aspect of your job during that time.

Before setting a meeting with your employer to make this proposal, you will need to do some research. First, read your employee manual to find out your company's internal policy regarding any changes in schedules or time off. There may be provisions in the policy that directly apply to your situation. As an advocate, it is up to you to learn what you can, so you will be able to come to the meeting in a strong position. Remember **Advocacy Principle 2** and become an expert on your company regulations.

Second, research the applicable law. Whether your company has a leave policy or not, under certain circumstances, federal law allows you to take time off work to care for an ill child. If the Family and Medical Leave Act (FMLA) applies to your company, for example, you have the right to twelve unpaid weeks off to care for a new child or an ill family member. "To care for" may include giving psychological comfort, arranging third-party care and providing physical assistance—all things that you are likely to be doing with your child.

Employees also have the right to intermittent leave, when "medically necessary," to care for a child with a serious health condition. Courts have even upheld parents' rights to take time off to work on language and communication skills for their disabled children. Under certain circumstances, some states (like California, New Jersey and Washington) provide a limited amount of *paid* leave.[7] Find out if your state offers similar support. If it does, research the specifics before your meeting, so you will know what your options are.

President Barack Obama has said he wants to get more bills passed that support families in the workplace. He has already approved measures that give parents time off to attend their children's school functions and go to parent meetings without fear of losing their jobs. It is his

intention to create a federal fund to help states create paid-leave programs for parents.

In the past, rights given in the FMLA have applied only to limited
employees in companies with fifty employees or more. President Obama
plans to expand the FMLA to cover smaller businesses with only twenty-
five employees, as well. The proposed version will also allow parents to
take up to twenty-four hours' leave every year to attend their children's
school activities. Provisions will also be made for taking leave to care for
individuals who have resided in your home for at least six months.[8]

Armed with the knowledge of your legal rights in your own state and
well versed in the regulations of your own company, take your proposal
to your employer. Then, using **Advocacy Principle 4**, speak with authority. A proactive approach will allow you to control the message and to
collaborate with your employer to find the best ways to accommodate
both your needs.

If you believe the FMLA does apply to your situation but your employer does not agree, consult with the director of your human resources
department or legal counsel. Try to be conciliatory with your employer,
but also be well represented. Do not neglect **Advocacy Principle 5**:
Document everything that happens. Make note of the dates and details
of the meeting at which you alerted your employer to your rights under
the FMLA.

If you work for a small company, be prepared for the possibility that
it is not governed by the parameters of the FMLA or that your state does
not offer much support for family-related leave. If you are faced with
taking unpaid time off work and no guarantee of keeping your job at the
end of that period, you may want to consider other options.

Adapt Your Work Schedule

If you do not have the option of taking a considerable amount of
time off from work, or if you are fully engaged with your career and
would rather not interrupt it, consider requesting an alternative work
schedule. With an unconventional schedule, you could continue to do
your work, but in a way that is conducive to your child's needs. Progres-
sive employers recognize the value of good employees, and many are
willing to find creative ways to help them deal with short-term or even
permanent changes in their family situations.

As before, your first step requires **Advocacy Principle 2**. Learn your employer's policies and methods of handling previous requests. Use your empowerment circle to help you identify supporting data. If you are proposing an alternative schedule, try to find similar companies that have had success with such schedules. Any statistics, data or other objective information you have to support your request will enhance your credibility.

When you have put the information together, ask your empowerment circle to critique your proposal. Then go to your boss armed with that information. Ideally, your plan will show that you will be an even more valuable and productive employee if you can modify your current work situation. But be honest. If leaving three hours early will cause you to be less productive, make the offer fair to your employer by proposing a reduction in pay or the elimination of some other benefit.

One of the alternative schedules below may be appropriate for you. Assess each of these options in light of the priorities that you have identified for your career, your child's needs and your long-term goals. If several of them would be improvements over your current situation, present one as your main proposal, and be prepared to offer one of the others as a backup plan, if necessary.

KEEP IT IN THE FAMILY

Regardless of what your employer says, be sure to ask your partner or spouse for input. The decision to alter your work schedule or career track should not be made in a vacuum. If your children are old enough to participate, discuss your choices with your whole family. Your goal is to find the best outcome, use the best strategy to achieve it and get everyone on board with the schedule.

Flextime is a common example of adapting a work schedule. Children with autism often have appointments with doctors, therapists and tutors immediately after school. If you need to attend appointments with them, a regular nine-to-five schedule presents a conflict.

Consider asking your employer to allow you to start your workday one to two hours earlier, so that you can leave sooner and be available for your child. Or maybe you have team meetings at school before the day begins, or you'd like to drop your child off and help out in class; for you it may be better to come to work later in the morning and stay later in the evening. Either way, changing your work hours will allow you to respond to the many demands of your child's schedule.

If you explain the situation, your employer may understand and be willing to accommodate this kind of flexibility. In most businesses, there are peak hours when you are most needed at work. Start and end times, though, may be flexible.

Because most people need a steady income, employers resign themselves to the fact that they must pay their employees for a consistent number of hours throughout the year. If you are in such a business, you are in a position to offer a win/win solution to your employer. Reducing your hours during the slow periods may be as ideal for your employer as it is for you. It could help you be available for the school meetings that are clustered at the beginning and end of the school year and the individual education plan meetings that are held in the early spring to plan for the coming school year.

That said, your employer may not immediately recognize the advantages to her. She may have never questioned the fact that the employees work the same number of hours all year, regardless of the work flow. Be prepared to explain exactly how your plan will benefit her. Educate her (**Advocacy Principle 7**) so she can take you up on your offer.

Consider Job Sharing

For parents who can afford it, working part-time is another option. But part-time jobs tend to be less secure, and not all businesses can use part-time workers. Why not consider job sharing, which is dividing one full-time job between two people? A job can be shared on the basis of a split day, a split week or a split month. (Sometimes tasks can be split between two people, with each one taking responsibility for their half rather than for the whole job. This arrangement is more like two part-time jobs.)

For true job sharing to work effectively, you need exceptional management, organization and communication. Both people must know what's going on with the job at all times and work closely together as a team. This option works particularly well in service-industry jobs, such as insurance, real estate and hospitality.

At a recent women's conference I facilitated, a woman raised her hand to share her experiences in juggling her career and her autistic son. She said that she met her business partner at their sons' preschool and discovered they were working as real estate agents for the same company, in separate offices. Both expressed their frustration about how difficult it was to manage their clients while attending to their sons' special needs.

One day, it occurred to her that they could each work half-time and share the responsibility of servicing their combined client roster. As parent advocates, they were determined to make the plan work. They took responsibility for initiating the change (**Advocacy Principle 1**). They did the research into why the plan would work and how similar arrangements had succeeded in the past (**Advocacy Principle 2**). With a strong proposal in hand, they spoke with authority (**Advocacy Principle 4**) when they met with their senior management. But the idea was not warmly embraced.

The managers had never seen it done before, so they were skeptical. But the two women were persistent. They convinced the managers to allow them to implement the plan on a trial basis. According to the arrangement, one would work three days a week and the other would work two days a week. They both spent more time than that in the beginning to get to know each other's clients, listings and pending deals. It was each woman's responsibility to know the client's issues and to provide a timely response. The success of their pilot program depended on both of them making a serious commitment to being 100 percent available and efficient on their respective days. Together they learned to collaborate (**Advocacy Principle 6**) and made their plan a success.

Switch to a Virtual Office

Using technology to work at a remote or mobile location has been called telecommuting, e-commuting, e-working, teleworking, or simply working at a virtual office. Sometimes it includes a combination of e-work and office-based work. It is especially well suited to jobs with a high degree of mobility and autonomy, such as architecture, journalism and law.

With BlackBerries, iPhones and laptops, I virtually run my law practice remotely. Of course, I have to appear in court and meet with clients and other attorneys, but a great deal of my work is accomplished outside of a traditional office. This gives me the flexibility I need to attend school meetings and therapy appointments and meet the various demands of Marty's schedule.

A decade ago, the idea sounded preposterous. Early adopters of technology had a hard time getting people to see that it was very possible to do many different jobs with a few pieces of portable technology. In recent years, people have become more comfortable with the idea. With lighter laptops, faster broadband, smarter phones and Wi-Fi zones in coffee shops, libraries and entire neighborhoods, the virtual office is more viable than ever.

Between answering e-mails and talking to clients, I can literally go for days without setting foot in my office. Yet I am more productive than I have ever been! Of course, there's a trade-off. In order to be available to attend early morning school meetings and midday medical appointments with Marty, I have to be willing to talk with clients in the early morning and late evening. But the adjustments may be easier than you expect. I've discovered that the long hours you spend waiting in doctors' offices can be turned into productive time if you can work from a laptop or smartphone!

Times are changing. Everyone's lives are becoming more nomadic. How can you make this trend work in your own life? Are some aspects of your job more mobile than others? How many things do you do in the office that you can't do outside it? Even if you interact with a team, do you do it every day or could you come into the office a few hours a week? Could the meetings be held with Web conferencing?

The technology is available, but cultural acclimatization takes time. When Alexander Graham Bell invented the telephone, many people thought it was silly to call their friends when they could just walk over and see them. Today, the ability to make a call has literally accelerated our lives. It has given us a way to fit more into the day.

Many people who use e-mail avidly today could not appreciate at first how much it would add to their lives. Instant messaging, SMS, and VoIP are no different. As an advocate, why not lead the charge? If spending most of your workweek in a virtual office makes your life easier, find a way to do it, even if it means educating others about the advantages of technology.

WHAT TO SAY. . .

When Requesting an Alternative Schedule at Work

Approach the meeting with an open mind. Although not all workplaces are receptive to alternative schedules, do not assume the worst. Focus on the positive benefits the changes will bring to the company. Be reasonable in your request, but also be prepared to fight for what you want. If your employer reacts negatively to your first attempt, don't consider it a permanent "no" but a chance to create a "yes" at a later point in time.

Although you don't need to memorize these comments verbatim, this is one way that your meeting might go, when you make your request.

PARENT: I really value my job, my coworkers and the work that I do here. I don't want to jeopardize my status in any way. However, my child was diagnosed with autism. He has a series of medical and school appointments that can be scheduled only during the hours that I typically work. Rather than request time off for every appointment, I would like to explore possible modified hours.

EMPLOYER: What exactly do you mean by modified hours, and how will this impact your current job duties?

PARENT: Modified work hours can take many forms. In my situation, I am asking for [state the specifics]. My research shows that many of the Fortune 500 companies use flextime, job sharing and job splitting as a means of creating a work environment that is conducive to parents while boosting their revenues. Studies have found that such arrangements allow employers to retain their best employees and get the high-quality work performance they desire. For example, [cite a company name] is very similar to our organization, and they have been using flextime for years now with great success.

EMPLOYER: If I give you a modified schedule, doesn't that mean I must do it for everyone in the office?

PARENT: It's my understanding that the law does not require you to change everyone's work schedule simply because my schedule changes. It's a matter of looking at each individual job or class of jobs and setting a schedule that allows maximum productivity—

one that is consistent with the culture you want in the office. It's like salaries. Different employees always have different pay scales.

EMPLOYER: How can I guarantee that your work will not suffer with this new schedule?

PARENT: I value my position and take seriously my obligation to contribute to the growth and success of this company. I plan to continue to work to advance the mission of the company and to give my personal best. I guarantee you that with my new schedule, not only will my productivity not decline, but in some ways, I expect it to be better. If I know that I can comfortably attend my child's meetings and provide him the care he needs, I will be more productive.

Launch Your Own Business

Some careers are simply more stressful and time-consuming than others. If you need more time for yourself or your family, now may be the time to explore a career change, or perhaps simply take a less stressful job within your existing field. This change may involve working with your current employer to identify a new position, it may involve a full job search or it may mean temping or becoming a consultant or starting a freelancing or other home-based business.

Home-based businesses, often run by moms, include concierge services, catering, virtual-assistant services, academic tutoring, graphic design, day-care centers, Web-based businesses, day traders, investment brokers, real estate agents, artists and consultants of all kinds. By working at home, parents can set their own hours and run their businesses as they see fit. Because a home business can provide far more flexibility than any other kind of work, it is especially conducive to creating the time needed to care for a special-needs child.

Many parents of children with developmental disabilities start home-based businesses as a way of managing their child's schedule, but some have actually made autism a business! Ziba Nassab was working as a social-skills therapist when her son was diagnosed with autism. Ziba saw the need for more programs to provide early intervention and social-skills therapies. She also wanted to provide her own son with high-quality therapies to address his sensory and communication needs, so Ziba and her husband, Mark, opened Holding Hands, a therapeutic center that provides a full range of therapies for children on the spectrum. The need was so great that the center grew quickly. Today, Ziba and Mark operate two centers and provide care for over five hundred children annually.

After their child is diagnosed with autism, many doctors, lawyers, therapists and educators refocus their practices. By doing so, they gain the added benefit of being able to assist other children while caring for their own child's needs.

It may seem like starting a new business would only compound your scheduling issues, but before you reject the idea, do the research. Learn which business models will best suit your needs. Talk to others who are making those businesses work. You may find that starting your own business is the solution to finding the balance you need between work and autism.

FINAL THOUGHTS

Caring for a child with autism doesn't automatically mean that you must abandon your career aspirations. With existing and emerging technological advances, it is possible for parents to work full-time and provide excellent care for a special-needs child. You have to be willing to evaluate your priorities and circumstances and have the courage to make a choice that works for you and your family. When you develop a clear understanding and realization of what you want for your career and your family, you can make unencumbered choices that will lead to the necessary balance between the demands of work and autism.

PUTTING IT INTO ACTION

1. Write a list of the major obligations you have at work and at home over the next thirty days. Rank each item by priority, giving a ten to those items that are the highest priority and a one to the least important. Indicate how long each one will take and whether there are any potential conflicts.

2. Keep track of your time for a week. At the end, review the week in light of your priorities. Note any instances when you spent time on a lower-priority item in a way that left no time for a higher-priority one. Why did that happen? Was that low-priority item more important to you than you'd realized? If so, adjust your expectations and recognize it as a higher priority from now on. If not, think of two ways you could avoid wasting time on low priorities like these in the future.

3. Identify five people who are hard for you to say "no" to, even when their requests are unreasonable. Read this list over and over again for a week. At the end of that time, assess your feelings. Do you still find it hard to say "no" to them? If so, would you like to schedule a meeting with them to discuss your feelings?

4. Make a list of five things you can do to improve your productivity at work and start implementing them immediately.

5. Schedule a meeting with your family to discuss upcoming events and activities over the next three months. Give everyone an opportunity to get their schedules in sync.

6. Write an essay of five hundred words or more describing in great detail how you envision your life in three years, five years and ten years. For each time period indicate what you will be doing in terms of your career and how your time will be spent. This exercise will help you focus your priorities and give you a road map for creating the life you want for yourself, which is the first step toward achieving it.

PART III

Public Advocacy:
Getting Results

CHAPTER 8

Navigating the Therapy Maze: Educating Yourself

I n the Akira Kurosawa film *Rashomon*, four characters give completely different accounts of the same crime. Each person's perspective is distorted by his or her own interests. The phenomenon is so common that sociologists now call it "the *Rashomon* effect."

Very early on, as you begin to navigate the therapy maze, you will find yourself exposed to a similar effect. As therapists evaluate your child and recommend treatments, they will each bring a perspective strongly influenced by their own beliefs, assumptions and interests. Their opinions about the autism spectrum, the prospects of a cure and the different theories for handling your child may vary widely.

To make matters worse, these experts are likely to explain their points of view with abbreviations and initials you've never heard before. Just off the top of my head, I can remember hearing about RID, OT, TSA, APE, IEP, IDEA, LAS, DDT, ABA and PECS without knowing what they meant. When you scribble them down, they look like a flood of alphabet soup.

It's your responsibility to learn about these treatments and begin to evaluate which ones might be most appropriate for your child. You will have to educate yourself by reading, talking to experts, going to workshops and asking a *lot* of questions of other parents about results— always building on your knowledge, as your experience grows. Do you know what the hardest part is? While you're learning, you're going to have to build up a tolerance for your own uncertainty. At the turn of the twentieth century, Samuel Butler said, "Life is the art of drawing sufficient decisions from insufficient premises." No one knows this more

clearly than parents trying to choose among therapies for their autistic
child.

The first problem is that you will not have the luxury of waiting until
you're absolutely certain; it has been established by the National Institutes of Health that early intervention is vital. You must quickly get an
assessment by the therapists who seem to be a good match for your
child, then learn to evaluate them, finance them and coordinate them
with one another. As an advocate, you can rely on your advocacy principles to help you make the best choices.

APPLYING ADVOCACY PRINCIPLES
TO THERAPEUTIC CHOICES

1. **Take Responsibility.** Do not assume that someone else will
    make these decisions for you. When you feel unsure of
    yourself, it's tempting to make an emotional choice and go
    with the first therapist who appeals to you personally.
    Handing over your responsibility to an expert may feel like a
    relief, but it isn't advocacy. And it isn't the way to get the
    best treatment for your child.

2. **Learn.** Remind yourself that everyone who is spouting off
    terms like IDEA, LAS and DDT was as ignorant as you once
    upon a time. They had to learn the lingo at some point, and
    so will you. There is a steep learning curve with autism. But
    you can handle it. Be patient with yourself.

3. **Think Critically.** The *Rashomon* effect is so prevalent
    because we are all prone to see what we want to see. Hold
    yourself to a higher standard than that. Recognize that, to
    some degree, the preferences of therapists for a certain
    treatment are based on their own personal taste—which is
    fine, but it has nothing to do with your child. Teach yourself
    to look at the facts, regardless of their biases or your own.
    See what really works and keep doing that.

4. **Speak with Authority.** You are the number one expert on
    your child. Always treat others with respect for their
    expertise, but do not yield your own authority. When

evaluating therapies and treatments, keep an open mind. Then make *your* choice of therapies for *your* child.

5. **Document.** If you are sloppy about this, the information you gather will be lost. Contacts will be lost. Appointments will be missed. Don't let that happen. Cultivate better organizational skills. Become an avid note taker. Document every meeting and every phone call with a therapist. Otherwise, with so many terms and treatments being thrown around, how will you remember what was said?

6. **Collaborate.** A united group is far stronger than its individual parts. Maintain free and open communication among the therapists and others treating your child. Provide them with updates. Make them feel a part of a team that is making a real difference in your child's life.

7. **Educate.** As you learn vital information about these treatments and see the results—or lack of results—for yourself, share it! Let the professionals on your team know what works and doesn't work. Tell other parents what you've learned. Let the knowledge and experience you take in flow back out organically. Because of the natural flux of life, educating others is sure to keep more and better information flowing back to you as well.

EARLY INTERVENTION

In October of 2008, the American Academy of Pediatrics began recommending that all children be screened for signs of autism at eighteen to twenty-four months during routine "well baby" checks. "Early detection leads to earlier intervention. If we intervene by age three, children do far better than if we wait until age five," says Professor Amy Wetherby at Florida State University School of Communication Science and Disorders.[1]

Children who receive therapy for delayed development before they reach twelve months of age may not even develop autism at all. According to Dr. Lonnie Zwaigenbaum, it is because the human brain is still so flexible at that age. New behavioral therapies may be able to "override" the underlying genetic causes of autism and push the brain in a different direction. "The hope is that there's enough plasticity in the social system that intervention can help get children back on track in terms of their social and communication development," says Dr. Zwaigenbaum, of the University of Alberta in Edmonton, Canada.[2]

Even small children can benefit from intervention. Therapists can show you how to use your child's own interests to teach her new skills. For instance, an autistic infant may like being bounced up and down, but may not automatically smile and meet your eyes or make any sounds of enjoyment. By waiting and bouncing your child only after she has made eye contact and smiled or has asked to be bounced with a gesture or a sound, you can encourage a response that might be natural in another child. Since children with autism also often dislike loud sounds or touching, a therapist can show you interventions that will teach your child to simply ask for a break, rather than screaming or acting out when he feels uncomfortable.

Broadly speaking, early intervention services are specialized health, educational and therapeutic services designed to meet the needs of infants and toddlers, from birth through age two, who have a developmental delay or a disability. At the discretion of each state, services can also be provided to children who are at risk of *developing* delays if services are not provided. Once a child turns three, she is no longer eligible for early intervention services in most states.

For most children with autism, early intervention consists of speech and behavior therapy and social skills training. Many parents erroneously believe that they must choose one of the two most popular forms of behavior therapy: the Lovaas Method, developed by Dr. O. Ivar Lovaas, or Floortime, developed by Dr. Stanley Greenspan. Although these forms of behavior intervention may be appropriate for some children and they continue to be used by a large number of families, there are other options to consider.

Each state has one agency, known as the "lead agency," that is in charge of the early intervention system for infants and toddlers with special needs. It may be the state education agency or another agency, such as the health department. The National Dissemination Center for Children with Disabilities (NICHCY[3]) provides a comprehensive list of the agencies responsible for providing these services in your community.

If your child is eligible, you can meet with a team to develop a plan for early intervention services—for your child and, if necessary, your family. The plan outlining these services is called the Individualized Family Service Plan, or IFSP. As a general rule, if a service is not explicitly stated in the IFSP, the agency is not required to provide it. The IFSP should be developed as a whole-family plan, with the parents as major contributors in its development. Involvement of other team members will depend on what the child needs. These other team members could come from several agencies and may include medical professionals, therapists, child development specialists, social workers and others.

If you live in the United States, your child is entitled to early intervention and educational services under a federal law known as the Individuals with Disability Education Act. Enacted in 1975, following the passage of major civil rights legislation, this was the first comprehensive legislation mandating that public schools throughout the nation recognize the needs of children with special needs and work with their parents and other experts to provide a variety of services that would enable a disabled child to access the classroom curriculum, develop the skills necessary to matriculate in colleges and universities and ultimately provide a foundation for them to live independently as adults. States have followed the spirit of IDEA and have enacted education codes to provide children with disabilities a plethora of rights in both public and private school settings.

You don't have to be a lawyer to make use of these federal laws and educational statutes. Just knowing what your child is entitled to under IDEA and other federal and state laws can be invaluable to you. It will help you know what to ask for and what to do when you have concerns, enabling you to be a more effective advocate for your child.

Many times parents become preoccupied with learning the terminology and the science of a particular therapy or intervention service available under IDEA. Although important, the central issue in early intervention, continued therapeutic services and educational resources is advocacy. Being knowledgeable, prepared and persistent in your quest for services can make the difference between your child receiving two hours a day of behavior intervention versus the six hours that may be recommended by his assessment team.

TYPES OF EARLY INTERVENTION SERVICES

According to the National Dissemination Center for Children with Disabilities, some of the most common early intervention services may include:

- family training, counseling and home visits
- special instruction
- speech-language pathology services (aka speech therapy)
- occupational therapy
- physical therapy
- psychological services
- medical services (only for diagnostic or evaluation purposes)
- health services needed to enable your child to benefit from the other services
- social-work services
- assistive technology devices and services
- transportation services
- nutrition services
- service coordination services[4]

After early intervention, many families see dramatic improvements in their children's expressive and receptive language and social relatedness. Bryan made remarkable improvements in the first several months.

From the time he was eighteen months, Bryan's behavior was unusual. He smiled, but not in response to other people. Nor did he look at people's faces or babble like other children. "He was a very quiet baby," his father, Bill, said. "We dismissed it at first. We thought, 'He's a boy. It will probably just happen a little slower.'" After six months, when Bryan hadn't improved, his pediatrician persuaded the family to screen him for communication problems.

After he was diagnosed with autism, Bryan began an intensive course of early intervention, including behavioral, speech and occupational therapy. Therapists arrived daily at his home and worked one-on-one with him in the dining room for four to six hours each day. Bill and his wife had turned the area into a nursery school, with bright posters of letters, numbers, shapes and animals.

At first, it was extremely difficult for the team of therapists to get Bryan's attention, but eventually they managed to interest him in matching toys and identifying numbers. Soon Bryan was responding to his name and using a few simple words to express his desires for food or toys. Now and then, Bill even saw him look at his mother. "He was coming out of his world and joining the rest of the family," he said proudly.

Bryan now attends a local private school. He is in a special classroom for children with autism, but spends part of each day in a class with children without autism. He can communicate his wants, and his language has improved dramatically. Bill attributes Bryan's tremendous progress to early intervention services.

Researchers confirm that autistic children who receive early, intensive intervention services between the ages of two and five years old have a dramatically increased chance of being mainstreamed in school once they enter kindergarten. They are also far more likely to require fewer services as they matriculate to higher education, according to Geraldine Dawson, PhD, professor of psychology and director of the University of Washington Autism Center.[5]

ADDITIONAL THERAPIES AFTER EARLY INTERVENTION

At the age of three, your local public school becomes responsible for the therapies your child needs for school. However, some lead agencies in certain states will supplement the services provided by your school district beyond the age of three. It is important that you become familiar with the lead agency's scope of services and any related service providers that may be mandated by state law to provide intervention for children with autism. For example, California passed the Lanterman Developmental Disabilities Services Act in 1977, which establishes twenty-one regional centers throughout the state. These centers are responsible for providing intervention and support services for individuals with developmental disabilities from birth to death. Families in California can receive services from their local school districts and from regional centers simultaneously.

Below are the most commonly recommended interventions for children ages two to twenty-two diagnosed with autism and other developmental disabilities.

- **Applied behavior analysis (ABA).** ABA is an umbrella term used to describe a type of therapy used to increase positive behaviors and decrease negative behaviors in children with autism and related disabilities. ABA therapy is typically administered by a trained therapist or educator and relies on identifying antecedents to certain types of disruptive or noncompliant behaviors. Once identified, therapists use positive reinforcers, such as preferred toys, foods or activities, to teach replacement behaviors or to redirect the child from engaging in the negative behaviors. These reinforcers or rewards are used to promote positive and functional behaviors.

- **Discrete trial training (DTT).** This is a form of ABA therapy that focuses on breaking skills into small and discrete parts and teaching each skill in sequence. For example, to teach a child to brush his teeth, a series of steps will be developed, starting with picking up the toothbrush, wetting it, taking the top off of the paste, spreading the paste, brushing, rinsing, etc. This form of therapy is often criticized as teaching root skills that are not easily generalized in natural settings.

- **Early intensive behavioral intervention (EIBI).** This is another form of ABA therapy that is typically used as a form of one-on-one therapy for toddlers and young children. Most early intervention programs occur in the home or natural setting.

- **Pivotal response training (PRT).** This therapy model is based on increasing a child's motivation to engage in certain positive behaviors by giving the child more choices and opportunities to engage in preferred behaviors.

- **Floortime.** This therapy is based on engaging the child in play and other recreational activities initiated by the child. The theory is that you can increase language, social interaction and overall learning by creating opportunities for interaction outside of a structured setting. The hallmark of Floortime therapy is that it is child-directed.

- **Occupational therapy (OT).** A form of therapy designed to address both sensory needs and motor planning. Therapists use a wide variety of tools including balls, manipulatives and even Play-Doh to help children learn to tolerate noises, textures and certain environments. OT is also used to address both fine and gross motor skills.

- **Speech therapy.** This form of therapy can be provided individually or in a group setting. The goal is to increase receptive and expressive language and to help children learn to use language in a functional manner.
- **The Picture Exchange Communication System (PECS).** PECS is an alternative communication system. Children use picture cards to communicate everything from their wants and needs to their feelings.

KNOWLEDGE IS POWER

Despite your child's eligibility for services, at some point you are very likely to encounter service providers who refuse services, believing the requested service:

- is a want, not a need
- will not be effective for this child
- exceeds their minimum legal obligations
- is inappropriate
- is unavailable

Only strong advocacy can overcome or work around these obstacles. Clients often ask me, If the law mandates the services, how come states and school districts don't simply provide them? I explain that, despite the mandate, the reality is that there is a scarcity of resources available to school districts and other institutions. This is why advocacy is so important. In many cases, the person with the most tenacity gets access to resources, simply by being persistent.

Like many of the clients I see in my practice, Tammy came to me frustrated about her attempts to access services for her two-year-old son, Kyle. "I have called my local service provider multiple times and they don't return my calls," she said. "Whenever we do talk and I ask for a service, they say it's not available or that I have to be placed on a waiting list."

After your child's been diagnosed with autism, after you've looked into the various intervention services available, spent hours researching the latest "gold star" therapy methods and finally chosen the ones you believe will be the most beneficial, you'd think the worst is over, right? The clients I see in my office tell me otherwise.

Sylvia Landon, a parent of two children with autism, said that she never dreamed that she would have to spend days calling agencies, being placed on hold for hours and trying to sort out the conflicting information she was told about which services were available and which were not. "How can I trust anyone?" she said. "I was told that my child didn't need speech therapy, because she wasn't verbal. Someone else told me that *all* children with autism need speech therapy and my daughter should get *at least* three hours a week. Then my case coordinator said they only allot one hour a week. And, after all, my child was quickly approaching three years old. At that point, the school district would be responsible for her services, not the agency."

I hear the same thing from the hundreds of parents I meet every year in my practice and at conferences around the world. After every appearance on the *Dr. Phil* show, I am deluged with e-mails that make the same complaints: Parents' first experiences trying to access services almost always leave them utterly frustrated and confused.

My client, Joseph Luftman, MD, a sports-medicine physician, understands this frustration. Even the massive HMO where he practices has a systematic approach that ensures that his patients get what they need when they need it. "If we can reduce red tape and streamline the delivery of complex medical services for tens of thousands of patients across the country," he says, "then surely agencies and school districts can simplify autism care!"

When we were trying to obtain early intervention services for Marty, I once asked a provider if she could send me a list of all the early intervention services her agency offered, so I could discuss them with Marty's doctor and choose which one was appropriate. This struck me as a perfectly logical, systematic approach.

"This is not a restaurant with a menu of services for you to pick from," she said coolly. "Our assessment team will decide what your son needs and that's what we will offer." So much for the concept they promoted, that families were "a vital part" of their team! It was an important lesson for me and one that I use to help other parents: In the world of services for children with autism, it is survival of the fittest in the purest sense. Those with knowledge, fortitude and keen advocacy skills prevail. Those without perish. Plain and simple.

In a perfect world, the specialized services that your child is entitled to receive would always be available and easy to obtain. In the real world, however, the full range of necessary services may not be available unless you request them, demonstrate their importance, then actively work to get them—in other words, unless you "advocate" for them.

Some lead agencies, state departments of education and local school districts may not have the money and staff to do everything you and your team determine is best for your child. The shortage of certified teachers for children with autism and licensed speech therapists is notorious. The Center on Personnel Services in Special Education estimates that at least twice as many of these specialists are needed to meet today's demand for services.[6] As a result, many communities don't have a teacher or therapist trained to provide special services to every autistic child. And since the number of children with diagnosed autism is on the rise, agencies are finding it difficult to meet the ever-growing demands. In California alone, the number of children referred to its regional centers for early intervention with autism diagnosis increased 1,200 percent from 1987 to 2007.[7] The situation is even worse in rural areas and small cities.

Whether the services offered in your area are sufficient or woefully inadequate, your first task is to find out exactly what they are, so you know what to request. Don't be deterred by sarcastic remarks from caregivers, like those made by Marty's first service provider. Of course selecting services for a child with autism is not like deciding whether you will have turkey or ham for lunch. But if you don't know that music therapy is offered and you have not yet learned that it has been proven to assist nonverbal children with autism to develop functional speech, how would you know to ask?

No matter what opposition you face, don't let anyone deter you from learning as much as you can (**Advocacy Principle 2**). Once you know what services you want to investigate further, getting them is about persistent, but polite, pressure.

If your service provider refuses to share with you all of the services that the lead agency in your state funds for autistic children, ask other parents, your child's pediatrician or preschool teachers. Consider consulting a professional advocate or attorney who specializes in education law.

In my practice, I frequently meet with parents shortly after they receive a diagnosis and are simply trying to understand what the law is and what it entitles their child to receive. It takes me the first half of our hour-long meeting to simply go over the list of possible services. I also recommend that they read *A Work in Progress* by Dr. John McEachin and Dr. Ron Leaf, which provides a comprehensive strategy for developing an effective intervention program for toddlers, school-age children and teens with autism. The last part of the hour is spent on strategizing about how to access the services and how to advocate and win.

CONSULTATION EXCERPTS

Even when parents do obtain services, they often have challenges in obtaining the frequency and level of services recommended by professionals and participating in the process to determine what services will be provided. These are the types of exchanges I have with parents in our hour consultation.

PARENT: My son's speech therapist told me he is making great progress, but he needs three hours a week of therapy, instead of the one hour he's been receiving. I would love for him to get the extra time, but my lead agency says that they provide only one hour per week to all children.

MY REPLY: You must convey that the request is not a matter of your preference, but that it is based on the observations, assessment and expertise of the licensed professional working with your child. Politely inform your service provider that services for children with autism must be based on the individual needs of the child and made in the context of what the multidisciplinary team recommends, not the inflexible internal policies of any one agency. Offer to send a report from the therapist to the service coordinator and ask her to reconsider her decision based on that report. Ask that after her review, she send you a response in writing with a detailed explanation.

PARENT: At my last team meeting to discuss my son's services with the agency providing his speech and behavior-intervention services, I felt like no one listened to any of my concerns. I kept trying to tell them things about my son and it appeared they had their own agenda.

MY REPLY: You are a vital part of any team that is making decisions about your child's care. One way to get the attention of the others at team meetings is to prepare your own agenda and disseminate it in advance of the meeting. This will help to set the tone of the meeting and make it difficult for your concerns to be overlooked. At the top of the agenda, quote the language from that agency's handbook, Web site or literature that talks about how important it is for parents to participate in the development of a service plan. When you enter the meeting, tell them that, before you get started, you would like to schedule time during this meeting to address your agenda. This shows that you are prepared and in command of the issues. It makes it a lot harder to be marginalized.

PARENT: My child is currently receiving twenty hours a week of behavior-intervention services, but the agency told me that they don't provide behavior hours during the summer and I'm afraid she's going to regress.

MY REPLY: Remember the issue is your child's needs. Politely inform the service provider that, although you understand some agencies restrict their services to weekdays and months when school is in, IDEA places no cyclical limits on when services can be provided and that your child's multidisciplinary team has determined that your child needs continuous services to prevent regression and loss of acquired skills. If the information they give you is based on a law or statute, politely ask to see a copy.

Every autistic child is likely to receive a combination of treatments in their overall program. For example, your child's program may include speech therapy, social skill development and medication. Your friend's child may be receiving music therapy, sensory integration and dietary interventions, along with communication and behavior therapies. No single program or service will fill the needs of everyone.

One of the most popular forms of behavior intervention was developed in 1987 by the psychology department of UCLA under the direction of psychologist Dr. O. Ivar Lovaas. Considered a pioneer in autism intervention, Dr. Lovaas required all autistic children to receive forty hours a week of one-to-one ABA instruction.[8]

ABA interventions shape behavior with positive reinforcement that is specifically tailored to the likes and dislikes of the autistic child. A careful progression is set in place to break skills into manageable steps and reward success. In childhood, the reinforcers may be eating a snack, playing with a favorite toy or looking at a picture book. Social encouragement, like praise, hugs, tickling and "rides through the air," are also reinforcing. As the child grows older, the reinforcement is expanded to include reinforcers from peers in a natural environment.[9]

Good behavior is maximized with prompting and positive reinforcement, while inappropriate behavior is offset by teaching more socially acceptable ways to communicate the same needs. The ability to make requests—rather than acting out—is developed as soon as possible. Learning to talk, interpret vocal language, imitate other children and engage in social interactions, as well as cooperative play, are integral to ABA treatment.[10] Some of the technologies that have proven effective are:

- **Task analysis.** Breaking down a task into smaller parts for easy learning.
- **Chaining.** Each chain link is a skill associated with one small part of a task.
- **Modeling.** A demonstration of the desired response.
- **Prompts.** Cues that encourage the desired response.
- **Reinforcement.** Positive and/or negative reinforcers to increase target behavior.
- **Generalization.** The application of the skills in other settings.[11]

A number of scientific studies indicate that the UCLA treatment provides significant gains in development and reductions in the need for special services. It may enable some (though not all) children with autism to achieve levels of functioning that are typical of other children their age. Studies at UCLA show that 47 percent of children who had received forty hours of intensive therapy were mainstreamed into regular classrooms. Not only were they able to participate in regular classrooms; they were considered to be "indistinguishable" from their peers.[12]

"There is clear evidence, from many studies, that applied behavior analysis improves behavior and allows kids to lead more normal lives," says Andrew Zimmerman, MD, pediatric neurologist and director of medical autism research at the Kennedy Krieger Institute in Baltimore. "The benefit is greatest when ABA is started as young as possible. There has been a paper that showed that 60 percent of higher-functioning children can lose their diagnosis by age eight. The recovery rate is increasing; we're seeing it here all the time."[13]

Dr. Max Wiznitzer, associate professor of pediatric neurology at Case Western Reserve University in Cleveland, Ohio, cautions that the treatment should fit the child. In his view, ABA may not work as well as other therapies.[14] Lovaas's technique and ABA therapy in general have received an increasing amount of criticism over the years. Critics claim that the astonishing progress Lovaas achieved was based on only a small number of selected high-functioning autistic children, not on a random sample.[15] Others claim ABA is a very limited program, that what is taught does not translate into practical skills in other environments. They complain that ABA teaches a child specific responses that do not translate to other applications. A child may be able to count to one hundred during therapy, for instance, yet remain unable to say his home address. Another criticism of ABA is that children become mechanical, because they learn to have only one specific response for a given prompt.[16] For example, a child may be taught to respond to the simple question, "How are you doing?" by parroting back, "I am fine." But beyond that rehearsed statement, the child may lack the ability to tell you how he actually feels.

Staying informed about the latest research is important. For years, therapists concluded that any program less than forty hours a week was useless for autistic children. Current research shows that children who receive targeted, intensive therapy—no matter what the intervention—can be helped with as little at twenty-five hours a week.[17]

BIOMEDICAL INTERVENTIONS

Both conventional and alternative medicines offer approaches to autism. Many parents hope that alternative biomedical treatments will allow their child to fully recover from autism. As you investigate these options, be sure to consult with the trusted team you are building for your child. Ask the members of your empowerment circle if they have anecdotal information about these interventions. Do your research. And remember that none of these options work 100 percent of the time for every child. If they did, they would be widely embraced. Adjust your expectations accordingly.

In her article "Biomedical Therapies for Autism: Gluten-free Diets, Vitamins, Antifungals and Enzymes," Melissa Hincha-Ownby describes some of the most commonly used biomedical approaches, such as a gluten- and casein-free diet, methyl B12 injections, omega-6 fatty acids, enzymes, antifungals, chelation therapy and even hyperbaric oxygen chambers.[18]

Parents who are interested in finding out more about biomedical therapy may also benefit from contacting a doctor at Defeat Autism Now! (DAN), a project of the Autism Research Institute, which promotes wider acceptance of biomedical approaches.[19]

KNOW YOUR CHILD

Whatever therapies you choose, knowing your child and her limits is imperative. It may require constant adjustment, but be careful not to push beyond her limits. There is a difference between challenging a child and overengagement—at which point the child begins to react poorly and the therapy becomes counterproductive.

Because of the nature of autism, your child's communication, cognitive and social skills are extremely relevant to how much or little therapy she can tolerate. Take responsibility (**Advocacy Principle 1**) for knowing your own child and making whatever adjustments are necessary on any given day.

The optimal hours recommended by the experts are simply guideposts, not rigid directives to be followed by every family. Deviating from the norm may be what is most appropriate for your child. Taking a break from a therapy for weeks, maybe even months, can also be a way to rejuvenate your child and an opportunity for you to reevaluate the effectiveness of the therapy.

You must also consider the function of the intervention and the impact it will have on your child, as well as your entire family. A child going to school and receiving hours of therapy every day is keeping as active a schedule as a busy professional.

Certain types of therapies mean sitting in a confined area with an adult or small group of other children for hours at a time. Think about the impact of the therapy on your child and remember that a forty-hour program means a child will be in therapy eight hours a day, five days a week.

Once a child begins a full-day school program, many schools count the school day, or six hours a day, as part of the allotment of service hours. For some children, this means being in a structured school environment six hours a day followed by hours more after school. This can be a grueling schedule for an adult, much less a five- or six-year-old child. Many parents find that their autistic child is overscheduled and burned out from so many sessions of therapy.

In some instances, you will have no choice but to take your child to a therapy center. But often, particularly with early intervention programs, individual therapists will be willing to come to your home or your child's school. As an advocate, you will become a coordinator of the various therapists coming in and out of your home. With a typical twenty-five- to forty-hour program, it's not uncommon to have three or four basic therapists traipsing through your house every week—not counting the speech, occupational, music, movement and social-skills therapists who may also be a part of your child's program. Managing the schedules, ensuring the timely arrival, and coordinating the actual services will require you to be actively involved and, most of all, organized.

ASSESSING YOUR CHILD'S PLAN

After Diane Murphy started ABA therapy with Shiane, she called me, frustrated and ready to give up on the intervention. She said she felt the therapist lacked sufficient skills to make the most of the therapy. I suggested that, before she abandoned the intervention, she contact the agency and request that a supervisor attend several sessions to observe and provide on-the-job training for the therapist, and that, ultimately, if she didn't see improvements, she should make a decision to change one of the variables: either the therapist or the intervention.

The first measure of an intervention is: Does it work? If you don't see progress in a reasonable period of time (four to six weeks), don't be afraid to change the therapy, the therapist or both. Your child's plan should also have these components:

1. Systematic, planned, data-based instruction of twenty-five to forty hours a week that focuses on engaging your child, not just getting her to perform tasks.

2. Functional, meaningful and natural behavior development in your child, such as greeting people when she enters a room, covering her mouth when she sneezes and responding to questions that are posed to her.

3. Fluid goals designed to develop skills that match your family's goals, activities and lifestyle.

4. Regular meetings (every three to four weeks) with all members of your child's therapeutic team to discuss progress and challenges.

5. Training components for parents and, if appropriate, siblings. Teaching family members the strategies used in therapy allows opportunities for continuous learning and practice of newly acquired skills.

6. Data collection on the progress being made for each new skill.

7. Opportunities for generalization in a natural environment. (For example, if a child is learning to sort objects and identify food items in therapy, she should be able to go to a grocery store and find the vegetables, not just recognize vegetables on flash cards.)

8. Positive, rather than negative, reinforcers. Discover what motivates your child to use language, play with toys and engage others; then focus on encouragement rather than negative feedback.

FINANCING THERAPY

In 2006, Harvard psychologist Michael Ganz estimated that the lifetime cost of caring for a person with autism was a shocking amount— about $3.2 million.[20]

While federal and state laws mandate that certain interventions be free to autistic children, the reality is that, with the shortage of providers, parents often choose to hire private therapists rather than lose years of intervention while their names sit on a waiting list.

TYPICAL ANNUAL COSTS OF AUTISM INTERVENTIONS

Speech therapy: .... $18,000 $125 per fifty-minute session
Three times a week for forty-eight weeks

Occupational therapy: .... $12,960 $90 per fifty-minute session
Three times a week for forty-eight weeks

ABA therapy: .... $72,000 $60 per fifty-minute session
Twenty-five hours a week for forty-eight weeks

Other: .... $16,500 $150 per hour for ABA supervisor
Ten hours a month for one month

TOTAL: .... $119,460   per year, per child

(These costs were typical in 2009 in urban areas, such as New York and Los Angeles.)

When they are denied school services from local school districts and lead agencies, many parents look to their private insurance plans and HMOs for help, only to find that, in most cases, coverage is not available.

As of the publication of this book, there is a raging debate over whether insurance coverage should be extended to cover all or some part of autistic evaluations and related therapies. Only a few states have comprehensive mandatory laws requiring insurance companies to cover autism treatment, although many states have legislation working its way through the legislative process.[21] According to Michelle Matlock, in her article "How to Convince Health Insurance Plans to Pay for Autism Treatment," "Missouri and Indiana recently passed legislation requiring group insurers to provide coverage for the treatment of autistic children younger than age 18, starting in 2010. The laws say insurers must cover ABA, which would cost insurers up to $55,000 annually, but only for children younger than 15."[22]

Getting insurance companies to pay for most autism treatments is difficult, if not impossible, in many states. Understanding what different carriers cover and how much they will pay for what types of services is often confusing and conflicting. Many parents are automatically rejected for all types of services. Carriers claim that ABA and other forms of behavior interventions are experimental in nature and thus excluded, despite the fact that the American Academy of Pediatrics, among others, recommends this form of therapy for the treatment of autism. Others will deny coverage of treatment such as ABA therapy on the basis that the providers are not licensed providers under state law. Some states require ABA therapists to take a state-administered exam and qualify for a license similar to medical doctors, attorneys and a handful of other individuals who provide professional services. There are no national standards governing ABA providers and such licensing requirements are not universal.

Many doctors are forced to use different diagnoses and more acceptable codes in order to be paid for services. Doctors unwilling to bill under these alternative codes turn parents away, leaving hundreds of parents without recourse. Families with limited resources and those who are ineligible for government-sponsored insurance plans often go without services. The inability to secure insurance coverage is not only an issue of great concern to parents of children with autism, but it's an issue that impacts all citizens.

FIVE CREATIVE WAYS
TO FINANCE AUTISM THERAPIES

1. **Nonprofit and health foundations.** There are some organizations, like the UnitedHealthcare Children's Foundation, that provide grants for autism services to

middle- and low-income families for treatments such as speech and occupational therapy not provided by school districts or covered by insurance.

2. **Gifts.** Ask family members and friends to fund a therapy in lieu of a Christmas or birthday gift they would otherwise give to you.

3. **Scholarships and stipends.** Some groups like Special Needs Network, Inc., give special-needs students scholarships and stipends to assist them in transitioning from high school to college or the workplace.

4. **Professional bartering.** If you have an expertise in a particular area, such as law, accounting or dentistry, you can provide your services in exchange for therapy services for your child. You may also volunteer at a therapy clinic and, in lieu of being paid, arrange to have your child receive therapy hours.

5. **Supplemental services.** If you have a college student or other interested and available family member, have them take some training on a particular intervention strategy to supplement the professional services that your child is receiving. Although not a substitute for a professional, this is a way to extend the learning process at low or no cost to you.

Because of the growing number of lawsuits challenging insurance companies, some insurers are beginning to offer policyholders special riders for intensive early intervention programs for children between the ages of two and five.

After the $1 million settlement of a class-action lawsuit involving one hundred Michigan families whose claims for coverage of ABA therapy were rejected, Blue Cross Blue Shield of Michigan began to offer its insureds the opportunity to purchase additional coverage for autism programs in June 2009.[23]

This is a good example of what parent advocates can accomplish when they band together. By filing a class-action suit, these parents made a difference for thousands of others. If you live in a state without mandatory coverage laws or if your insurance company rejects your claim for coverage, be prepared to advocate. Take action and enlist others to join you. Be a team builder (**Advocacy Principle 6**).

Given the endorsements by major medical associations and the trend toward providing coverage, you may well be successful in getting your insurance company to cover your child's therapy. If you have a private health insurance plan and your doctor has tried unsuccessfully to bill your carrier, you need a strategy for seeking reimbursement. First, contact your insurance company directly and ask to speak with someone who can fully explain your benefits and what coverage is provided. You may also consider talking with someone in your company's human resources department. Depending on this person's expertise, they may or may not have specific information about your plan. Find out whether your group plan is fully funded by your company. Any plan that is fully funded is required to abide by state mandates. Expect to have to do a little investigative work to make this determination, as this is a complex area and you may find that there are more questions than definitive answers. But don't get frustrated. Once you obtain this information, it will be invaluable.

Next, contact your child's pediatrician and ask her to make a specific referral for the treatment you are seeking for your child. For example, if you are seeking ABA home-based therapy and have identified a specific provider, ask the doctor to include that specialist in the referral letter. Be sure the doctor makes specific references to any relevant state law mandates and states clearly that the recommended treatment is endorsed by a medical association, such as the American Association of Pediatrics.

After the referral letter has been sent, call to confirm that your insurance company has received the letter. Ask them to assign a case manager for you. Large insurance companies use case managers on a variety of claims, particularly complex ones and those involving long-term health issues. Explain that your child has a complex neurological disorder. Establish a good rapport with the case manager and remember to keep a phone log of every attempted contact and conversation, along with the date and time it took place. Make copies of all the documents that you submit and receive from the company. These will be critical later, in the event you have to challenge a denial of claim.

If, after you have submitted the referral and complied with any other requirements of your carrier, your claim is rejected, ask your case manager to send you a letter stating:

- the basis for the rejection
- the date of the rejection
- the process used to reach the decision, along with any documents, research and/or scientific evidence relied on by the decision maker.

Make sure you have the most current copy of the appeals process, which is usually contained in your benefits handbook. Review that process carefully, as there may be deadlines you must meet in terms of when an appeal can be initiated.

If you have an HMO plan, the process is essentially the same. Your HMO may require you to utilize an "in-network" provider. So make sure you know all of the providers available through your plan. If the plan does not have a preapproved provider, you can request a single case contract for a provider who is qualified to provide the services.

As an advocate, you will need to be both persistent and able to respond to questions or concerns the carrier may have. If, after exhausting the appeals process, you have not been successful in securing coverage that your doctor recommends for your child, you should consult with an attorney or law firm that specializes in insurance claims. Many states have enacted insurance statutes that prohibit insurance companies from bad-faith denials of legitimate claims of its insureds.

Sometimes a simple letter from an attorney may encourage your company to reevaluate your claim to avoid potential litigation that could result in their being assessed damages for not only the cost of the care that was sought, but also punitive damages for their "bad-faith" denial.

MAKING SUSTAINABLE CHOICES

Although, like most parents, you would eagerly do anything to help the child you love, all of us have to face the reality of our limitations.

After doing your due diligence to find out which therapies are covered by your insurance, local agencies or school district, and which are not, you may have to make some hard decisions. Your family's financial security is important. In order to protect it, you may simply not be able to afford every conceivable treatment you would like. Keep your eyes on the future and make choices that will be truly sustainable. This process can cause a great deal of stress. Some families have to choose between expensive therapies and basic household expenses, such as the mortgage, car payment and retirement fund.

Too many parents are beguiled by the promises of cures and quick, dramatic results, even when the support for these claims rests on the latest news story, not scientific evidence. When it comes to financial matters, a lack of discernment (**Advocacy Principle 3**) can be extremely expensive.

In my practice, I am constantly amazed at the number of families who attempt to fund their children's treatments by mortgaging their homes and borrowing money from friends or high-interest loan companies. Others relocate their entire family to a different part of the country in pursuit of services for an autistic child. A growing number of parents across the country are taking drastic measures to fund autism therapies.

Be very careful about this approach. Autism is a lifelong condition. Going into debt when an autistic child is young may deplete resources you'll need as that child grows up. As a child with autism matures, important decisions about college, housing and extraordinary health-care needs have to be made. In most cases, it is the family who will have to pay for these expenses. After a child with disabilities reaches the age of twenty-two, he is no longer entitled to the educational or intervention services mandated by IDEA. In some states, the family begins to pay 100 percent of the ongoing treatments. Some costs may be covered by Medicaid and Social Security benefits, but for the most part, the expense is paid by the parents of an adult with autism.

When it comes to financing your child's care, take a holistic approach, never losing sight of the big picture. Determine what your family's priorities are. Be prepared to set limits, just as you would in any other aspect of your life. Many parents dream of their children attending an expensive, private university but when the time comes they have to live within their budget. Let your budget—not guilt, your neighbor's accomplishments or the norms set in the media—be your guide to what you choose. It does not serve your child for you to exhaust your resources too soon. As an advocate, it is up to you to do the best that you can for your child, while balancing your life with autism.

PUTTING IT INTO ACTION

1. Make a list of all of the therapies your child is receiving, including the type of therapy, the date the therapy started and the frequency with which she receives each therapy. Next to the type of therapy, write the intended purpose. For example, if your child is receiving speech therapy, write a very specific goal, such as increasing the use of expressed language in order to use three- to five-word sentences.

2. For each item in number one, begin to track whether progress is being made toward the goal; if it's not, schedule a meeting with the therapist to discuss your concerns. If progress is being made, still meet with the therapist to discuss next steps and additional goals that can be added to your child's program.

3. Plan a meeting with all of your child's therapists and take fifteen to thirty minutes to learn about their backgrounds, experiences and skill sets. Ask each one about other programs or activities that they are aware of that might be of help to your child.

4. Identify at least one workshop or conference in your community on autism intervention and treatment. Commit to attending at least one workshop a quarter for the next year. You will be surprised how much you learn about the use of computer programs and the use of technology that can enhance your child's existing program.

5. If your area does not have the type of therapy that your child requires, contact the head of the psychology department at the university in your community. Tell that person you are willing to organize other parents to advocate for the development of the program needed.

6. Create a therapist notebook that includes the names, telephone numbers, e-mail and mailing addresses of all of your child's therapists. Also in this book, list the various types of therapies that your child has received, the dates he received it and the outcomes of the therapies. This will be a good resource guide that you can provide to doctors, teachers and other members of your team. It will also help you keep track of what your child has received and how effective it has been.

CHAPTER 9

Legal Consultation:
Making Decisions About
Your Child's Education

E very parent wants to make the best, most informed choices possible for her child. Unless they have already been involved in the special-needs community, however, very few parents are knowledgeable about the school choices available in their area. Most have even less idea about *how to decide* which one would be best for their child.

To make matters worse, the terminology used by educators is often confusing and inconsistent. While exploring various schools, you may hear a private school principal casually refer to the process of "mainstreaming" or "inclusion." When you speak to the principal at a charter school, she may use the same terms but mean something very different. Your child is entitled to attend a class in the "least restrictive environment," for example. But the least restrictive environment in a special day class, filled with disabled children, may be far more restrictive than the environment in a general education class.

The investigation can be time-consuming and complex. Busy parents, working full-time jobs, can expect to spend months of their free time looking for the best placement. Every moment you invest in becoming an expert (**Advocacy Principle 2**) on the nature of these choices will be well spent, but don't underestimate the enormity of this search and the dynamic nature of it.

In the course of your child's education, you are likely to attend at least sixteen federally mandated IEP meetings. You will meet with a team of school district and other advisers (such as your child's principal, teacher, teacher's aide and experts who provide assessments) to create a plan that defines the educational services your child will receive and builds the vital transition plan to prepare her for life after school. In other words, it's important to get it right.

As the school year progresses, you will also have to evaluate whether the classroom and school you and the IEP team selected are proving to be appropriate or not. It's not always possible to anticipate whether your child will be a good match with a particular therapist, for instance, or whether she will develop new behaviors that make the entire plan moot.

As a practical matter, at the end of each year's IEP, your school will make you an offer for placement, assigning your child a particular school location and type of classroom, along with other services. When you receive the offer, you can either accept or reject it. If you disagree with the school on the best placement, your child will stay in place until the issue is resolved by compromise, mediation or due-process hearing. You do not have to abide by the choices of the school. If you choose to reject the offer, the law is on your side. But in most cases, you will have to brace yourself for a fight.

Because the process of creating an IEP plan and deciding whether or not to accept the school's offers for placement is so complex, this is one area where you may need to consult an attorney or educational advocate (nonattorney professionals who assist families in IEPs).

Having grown up on the far side of the tracks in St. Louis myself, I know only too well that not everyone can afford a private consultation with a Harvard-educated attorney. In some states, it's difficult to even find an attorney or special-education advocate with experience in special-needs issues, much less one who can tell you how to get the most out of IEP meetings.

So, you're in luck. One of my main motivations for writing this book was to give you the benefit of my legal training and experience.

When clients come to me for advice about school placement and IEP meetings, we schedule several appointments, so I can thoroughly explain the school and classroom placement options. I describe the legal mandates, assessments and special service requests, as well as the elements they should consider when challenging IEP plans. In this chapter and the one that follows, I will provide you with the same information you would receive if you were to hire me to help you get up to speed and begin to lay the groundwork for your child's educational planning.

As you'll discover, the details can be somewhat intricate. Think of it as one of the advantages of reading this chapter instead of sitting on the other side of my desk, as my client, and taking voluminous notes.

You will have the luxury of reading these chapters once for a general overview, then coming back again at your leisure to read for the specifics. (Please note that this information is general and may not be applicable to your individual situation. It is not intended to be applicable to your child in particular and cannot be a substitute for specific legal advice.) You can also find information updates on my law firm's Web site (www.martin-martin.net), as regulations change and more current information becomes available.

Let's begin. If you were to consult me about your child's educational options and the years of IEP meetings that lie ahead of you, this is the most vital information you'd need to know.

UNDERSTANDING THE LAW

In our first meeting, I would begin by explaining the law that secures the rights for your autistic child. The first thing I would mention is the Individuals with Disabilities Education Act (IDEA), since it is the federal law that ensures services to children with disabilities. IDEA governs how states and public agencies provide early intervention, special education and related services to more than 6.5 million eligible infants, toddlers, children and youth with disabilities.

IDEA is designed to ensure that all children with disabilities receive a "free appropriate public education" (FAPE). The FAPE includes special education and related services designed to meet their unique needs and prepare them for further education, employment and independent living.

Because the IDEA is the governing law, it can be helpful for parents to remember a few key phrases. For example, you may need to remind school administrators and IEP team members that disabled children are guaranteed the opportunity to:

- meet the "challenging expectations that have been established for all children" and
- "improve academic achievement and functional performance . . . to the maximum extent possible."

When Congress reauthorized IDEA in 2004, they raised the bar. The newly revised law requires that individualized education programs (IEPs) must include "a statement of the special education and related services and supplementary aids and services, based *on peer-reviewed research*." It also requires that schools provide "high-quality, intensive pre-service preparation and professional development for all personnel who work with children with disabilities." All school staff are now required to have the "skills and knowledge to improve the academic achievement and functional performance of children with disabilities . . . including the use of scientifically based instructional practices."[1]

The reauthorized IDEA is intended to coordinate with the federal law No Child Left Behind Act (NCLB), the purpose of which is "to ensure that all children have a fair, equal, and significant opportunity to obtain a high-quality education and reach, at a minimum, proficiency on challenging State academic achievement standards and State academic assessments." IDEA 2004 requires states to establish performance goals for children with disabilities that are the same as the state's definition of adequate yearly progress under NCLB. Special educators who teach core academic subjects must meet the highly-qualified-teacher requirements in NCLB and must demonstrate competence in the academic subjects they teach. Congress found that "30 years of research and experience has demonstrated that the education of children with disabilities can be made more effective by having high expectations for such children," educating them in the regular classroom so they can "meet developmental goals and, to the maximum extent possible, the challenging expectations that have been established for all children."[2]

WHAT IS AN IEP?

IEP stands for *individualized education program*. At least once a year and at regular intervals, you will meet with your IEP team to discuss the best educational placement and additional services for your child. These IEP meetings will result in a written blueprint for the coming year. That written statement is the IEP.

It will be developed, reviewed and revised in accordance with these very specific mandates of IDEA:

"(I) a statement of the child's present levels of academic achievement and functional performance, including:

    (aa) how the child's disability affects the child's involvement and progress in the general education curriculum;

    (bb) for preschool children, as appropriate, how the disability affects the child's participation in appropriate activities; and

    (cc) for children with disabilities who take alternate assessments aligned to alternate achievement standards, a description of benchmarks or short-term objectives;

"(II) a statement of measurable annual goals, including academic and functional goals, designed to:

    (aa) meet the child's needs that result from the child's disability to enable the child to be involved in and make progress in the general education curriculum; and

    (bb) meet each of the child's other educational needs that result from the child's disability;

"(III) a description of how the child's progress toward meeting the annual goals described in subclause (II) will be measured and when periodic reports on the progress the child is making toward meeting the annual goals (such as through the use of quarterly or other periodic reports, concurrent with the issuance of report cards) will be provided;

"(IV) a statement of the special education and related services and supplementary aids and services, based on peer-reviewed research to the extent practicable, to be provided to the child, or on behalf of the child, and a statement of the program modifications or supports for school personnel that will be provided for the child."[3]

The IEP meeting will normally be held at the school where your child is enrolled. These meetings can last from one hour to the all-time record of twelve hours! They may include one or two other people or as many as fifteen to twenty.

Educational choices are based upon various assessments your child has undergone. These too can vary. A single assessment may be considered or a multitude of experts may be invited to present reports and offer their opinions about your child.

Some IEP meetings are pleasant and relatively painless for parents. Others are emotionally charged, adversarial and overwhelming.

Once signed, the IEP document becomes a legal document that governs your child's educational experience for an entire school year, unless it is formally amended. Any educational options you would like for your child must be *explicitly stated* in the IEP. Otherwise, your child has no legal entitlement to those options—whether it's as prominent as the choice of a school or as supplemental as a graphic organizer or squishy balls to help a child with significant sensory issues cope with stress.

Because the IEP determines those choices, there is a lot at stake. You must do everything in your power to appear at IEP meetings well-informed and prepared to serve as advocates on your child's behalf.

APPEARING AT THE IEP MEETING

If you were my client, I would advise you to prepare for an IEP as you would for any other business meeting. After all, you are developing and executing a legal contract with your child's school. If you were meeting to discuss an important business opportunity, you would dress for the occasion, review relevant documents and possibly even draft questions about the deal in advance.

Do the same for your next IEP. Put on your fanciest business suit and bring a nice briefcase. You will be surprised by how the dynamics of the meeting will shift when you walk into the room. You are, in fact, the single most important person in the meeting. Your professional attire will set the tone and establish you as someone to be taken seriously—not only a concerned parent, but an informed advocate.

Developing an appropriate IEP for your child's school year is one of the most significant actions you will take on your child's behalf. Securing an appropriate education can mean that he'll learn the skills he needs to live independently, matriculate to college, work and lead a productive life one day. So bring your A game to every meeting.

I recommend you also bring a professional-looking binder (**Advocacy Principle 5**) organizing all the documents that lay the foundation for a productive IEP meeting, including:

- any and all relevant reports or assessments you have access to
- a list of your child's strengths and challenges
- samples of your child's academic work
- copies of prior IEPs
- report cards and teacher evaluations
- a flattering photo of your child
- excerpts from IDEA that apply to IEPs
- a carefully drafted agenda for the meeting
- a list of well-developed questions

As a rule of thumb, never go to an IEP alone. One of my clients routinely takes five to eight relatives to her son's IEP. She says it not only gives her comfort and confidence, but she believes it also helps show the school that her son is surrounded by a cadre of supportive family and friends. She uses her team to stay focused. She has also advised them that, if she becomes emotional about an issue during the IEP meeting, one of them will step in and assist her. Even my clients who are veterans of IEPs say that they often invite a friend or family member to accompany them when they anticipate that requests for services may be challenged by the school.

Finding eight people who are free during the workday may be a challenge, but I recommend that you take one or two others with you, at least to your first few IEPs. Ask members of your empowerment circle, family members or friends. Whether or not they are trained in educational issues, the fact that they know you and your child can be a tremendous help. You may also want to educate them (**Advocacy Principle 7**) by requesting that they read Chapter 3 of this book before they go, so they can better understand your role as an advocate.

Your child is also an integral part of the IEP process. As he matures, his role in the IEP meetings will become more critical. Even students with significant challenges can participate in the IEP meeting. As much as possible, it is important that they know what is expected of them and what tools are being put in place to help them. Do not underestimate the fact that, no matter what the well-informed adults decide, without your child's participation, none of it will work.

IEP BASICS

Whether your child is in kindergarten or planning his transition out of high school, these are the basic elements involved.

- There are *no limits* on the number of IEPs a student can have in any given year.
- Parents or schools can request an IEP meeting. If the parent requests the meeting, the school has thirty days from the date of the request to convene the meeting.
- If assessments are to be conducted and presented in the meeting, schools have sixty days to complete the assessment and convene the meeting.
- Members of the IEP team include: parents; regular and special-education teachers; a representative of the school district who has supervisory responsibilities and is knowledgeable about the general education curriculum and agency resources; and someone who can interpret the instructional implications of evaluations.
- Parents have the right to record IEP meetings.
- Parents and school districts have the right to have attorneys, advocates and other interested parties present at IEP meetings.
- An IEP is a legal document. It cannot be implemented until it is signed by the parents.

YOUR CHILD'S SCHOOL AND CLASSROOM CHOICES

Two decades ago, the school choices for autistic children were fairly limited. As a parent, you would have had the option of placing your special-needs child in a public school or locating one of a small number of private schools that were able and willing to educate an autistic child. Things have changed dramatically. Today, many states offer a range of options for parents to choose from, including:

Public Schools

- regular public schools (local district school in your neighborhood)
- charter schools (operating with autonomy from the local school district)

Private Schools

- state board–certified therapeutic schools (private schools contracted by your local district to provide services for students referred by the school district)
- uncertified private schools for students with particular disabilities
- regular private schools and religious schools
- home schools

Because they are state funded, public schools are, in theory, in the best position to offer more varied types of classrooms for children with autism. However, many public school districts—particularly smaller districts and those in rural communities—have few choices for autistic students. The schools may have classrooms dedicated to students who have special needs staffed by credentialed special-education teachers, but these classes may not be suitable for a student with autism. A classroom of students with severe learning disabilities, mental retardation, emotional disturbance and other disabilities may be inappropriate for your child. You need to know all the options—and more about each option—before you can make an informed decision.

The education of your autistic child—more than almost any other area—requires you to become an expert (**Advocacy Principle 2**). Simply understanding all the options and terminology will put you ahead of most parents—and a surprising number of school administrators! It may be impossible to match the expertise of professionals who have been working in a field for years, but you should always do enough research to know the key issues and what some of the best options are likely to be.

Study these two chapters until you feel confident that you understand the basics—*before* you meet with experts at the IEP. Otherwise, you will have no real way of evaluating the options they suggest (**Advocacy Principle 3**).

This is a lesson I learned the hard way.

When it was time to enroll Marty in kindergarten, I had a general understanding that some special-needs children were included in the general education classes and others were placed in special-education classes. Since Marty was not yet speaking, he could not recite the alphabet or count to ten like other preschoolers. So I expected to be told his only option was to be placed in a kindergarten class with "slow" kids.

New to the whole world of autism, I didn't do much research, because I assumed that the IEP team from the school district was more knowledgeable and would explain the various options to me. I was fully prepared to accept their recommendations. They were the experts. I naively presumed they knew what was best for my child. What a mistake!

At our meeting, the team told me Marty had two options: he could be placed in an "intensive" class—for children with severe disorders and intense needs—or a "mixed" class—for children with mixed diagnoses and more moderate needs. Well, given these two choices, I agreed with their suggestion to place Marty in the mixed class.

No one told me that the law (IDEA) requires a) that students receive a free appropriate education (FAPE) and b) that their education take place in the "least restrictive environment," which is also known as *mainstreaming* or *inclusion.*

No one at my IEP meeting mentioned such concepts as *full-* or *partial-inclusion* classrooms or *mainstreaming.* I didn't realize that there were different philosophies about what kind of classroom environment suits autistic children best. I simply went along with what the experts on the school team recommended.

Because I was inexperienced, I didn't notice that they had already made their choice of a classroom without even asking about Marty's needs and my family's priorities for him. Today, I would see that as a red flag. It is a sign that the experts are applying preconceived notions about what is best to children across the board, without taking individual needs into account.

Whenever you meet with educators or other experts, never stop thinking critically (**Advocacy Principle 3**) about what you're being told. How much of what they say is based on opinion and how much is fact? Are they recommending a course of action that is well established or controversial? What are they leaving out? In some cases, what they *don't* tell you can be more relevant than what they *do* tell you! Try to find out what the experts' assumptions are; even when you are not as knowledgeable as an expert, you may know immediately if you disagree with his assumptions.

In our first IEP meeting, for instance, the school district assumed that it would be best for Marty to study and learn to fit in with other autistic children. Ultimately, we realized that *our* priorities were for Marty to be able to fit in with our family and friends, so he could be more fully involved in our life. Once we realized we had very different priorities from the IEP team, we knew we needed to choose different classroom options than the ones they offered.

SCHOOL AND CLASSROOM OPTIONS

We made the decision to have Marty included in a regular public school classroom, but that may not be the best choice for *your* child. Many of my clients jump at the chance to send their children to schools dedicated to children with autism. They like the notion of having their child grow up with others like her. While she may not have the advantage of children without autism as role models, it may be more possible for her to feel a sense of kinship and belonging in such an environment.

Students who are more severely challenged are likely to prefer the smaller classrooms and structured environment of therapeutic schools. Others may find the most natural fit in a home-school environment that can be tailored to the needs of each particular child. Whatever your decision, be prepared at each IEP to explore the full range of options and select the one that is most appropriate for your child based on his unique needs, taking into consideration assessments, teacher input, private evaluations, academic progress and classroom observations.

Public Schools

Regular Public Schools

Public schools are the most common form of education. They are funded by the federal, state and local governments. Their curricula, teaching, and school policies are generally established by locally elected school boards that have jurisdiction over the individual school districts. Most often, children attend the school in their residential district.

In general, the following types of classrooms are offered by most public schools:

- **autism classroom** (small class of ten to twelve autistic students taught by a teacher with specialized training in ABA or some type of behavior-intervention management)
- **special day classroom**, also known as a segregated classroom (small class of ten to twelve students with autism or other disabilities, such as cerebral palsy or Down syndrome)
- **resource classroom** (class for students with learning disabilities and/or speech delays but limited behavioral challenges)
- **collaborative classroom** (classes where half the students have a variety of disabilities and the other half are typically developing)
- **general education classroom** (class where the autistic student participates by way of full or partial inclusion, usually accompanied by a teacher's aide)

Charter Schools

In 2009, there were 4,364 charter schools with 1.25 million students in attendance.[4] All but ten states have charter legislation.[5] According to Special Education News, "Although charter schools are obligated to follow federal law and provide special education services, a study by the National Association of the State Departments of Special Education found that many charter schools lack the funding, staffing and knowledge to access special education services."[6] Because they rarely offer specialized classrooms for students with disabilities, they have been known to advise parents against enrolling. That's actually flouting the law. According to federal and state law, a charter school cannot discriminate against a student with disabilities. If there are more applicants than the school can accommodate, they must hold a lottery.

Although your child can't be denied admission because he has autism, as a practical matter, the school may not have the same number of classroom choices as your local public school. For example, the charter school may not have enough students with autism to justify having an entire classroom dedicated to autism, so instead places those kids in a general education class with an aide, which may or may not be appropriate for your child. On the other hand, charter schools may offer specialized instruction in math, science, music or other areas in which an autistic child may excel, and some parents may want to take advantage of that, knowing they'll have to hire tutors to address social and language skills.

The legal identity of the charter school under state law largely determines its responsibilities for students with disabilities. There are two main types: the charter school may be its own separate district, usually referred to as a local education agency (LEA); or the charter school may belong to a traditional district. (There are also charter schools that have ties with LEAs that fall between these two extremes.) If the charter school is its own LEA, it is responsible for all aspects of special education, including evaluations, programs and related services. In some states, however, responsibility for a child's special education lies with the LEA associated with his home address, even if he attends a charter school operated independently from the district.

Because charter schools are established by individual laws that vary from state to state, if you are considering a charter school placement, you should contact your state office of education and obtain information regarding the nature of the contract that the school has with its chartering district. This will tell you whether the school is solely responsible for special-education services or if those responsibilities are with the chartering agent. For example, the Los Angeles Unified School District operates as the charter agency for many of the charter schools in the city, so those charter schools are likely to have the same special-education services as all the other schools in the 750,000-student Los Angeles district. In contrast, a charter sponsored by a nonprofit or smaller agency may have limited resources and can offer students very little by way of services. Knowing the type of charter, its sponsoring agency and its financial resources will help you make a decision about whether a charter school can meet your child's unique needs.

UNILATERAL PLACEMENT

If you place your child in a private, religious or nonpublic school without the recommendation of your child's IEP team, it is considered a unilateral placement. While in that school, your child may receive some services from his local public school, but the services will be limited. IDEA does not require public schools to provide the same level of services to students who are enrolled in private school unilaterally.

Here's what they *do* have to do: Public schools are required to meet with the administrators of each private school to discuss what the service plan for their special-needs students will be. Public schools are required to fund the service plan up to the amount generated by the student in federal funds. That amount varies from district to district and from year to year depending on the number of eligible children in the district. The public school district's director of special education can tell you what the amount is and what the service plan includes.

It is important to know that the overall amount of money involved is typically not enough to pay for substantial services. For specific information on private school service plans in your district, contact the special-education administrator in your child's public school district of residence.

Since IDEA applies only to public schools, and additional legislation such as the Rehabilitation Act of 1973 applies only to entities that accept federal funding, most private schools are not covered. However, the passing of the ADA in 1990 changed that distinction. Parents have become more aware of ADA and its stipulations, and many have asked private schools to accept their children with special needs.

Some private schools, especially preschools, have begun making accommodations and changes to their curriculum to meet the needs of a diverse population. But you should always ask specific questions about what kind of preparation teachers and administrators in private schools have had in special education and what services are being provided to the students.

Private Schools

If your local public school cannot offer your child a classroom placement that meets his or her unique needs, the IEP team may refer him to a private school, for which they will pay the tuition and related costs. If the district does not make such a referral, you may still request a private school placement; if the IEP team agrees, the public school will sometimes pay the tuition and related cost.

If your request for a private school is denied by the IEP team, you can enroll your child in the private school, pay the tuition and then seek reimbursement from the district directly by filing a request for due process. In such situations, it is critical that you provide your school with written notice of your decision to unenroll your child from public school, to enroll him in private school and to seek reimbursement. This notice should be sent to the public school at least ten days in advance of the date that you enroll your child in private school; this gives the district an opportunity to reevaluate its decision and perhaps make you another placement offer. Since tuition can range from $5,000 to $50,000, and getting reimbursed may involve a legal battle with your district, this is an expensive proposition at best, and not viable for many parents.

If you want to secure a private or nonpublic school placement, there are steps you can take to obtain a referral from your district. First, identify and document the issues. For example, make notes if your child has consistently failed to meet the goals set by the IEP, despite adjustments; behavioral challenges that prevent him from participating in class activities; consistent failing grades; aggressive behaviors or any other forms of disruptive behavior. Indicate when and how often you have worked with the teacher and other team members to correct these problems.

Next, call for an IEP to discuss placement. At this meeting, present the information that you have gathered, including any medical or other reports that indicate that the current placement is inappropriate. Be prepared to provide the team with information detailing how the school you have in mind is more appropriate for your child.

If the team denies your request, ask for an evaluation of the current placement. This assessment can be conducted by a school psychologist or behavior specialist from the private sector. Be sure the evaluation includes standardized testing, classroom observations at your child's current school and the prospective new school, as well as interviews with teachers and other related staff.

After the assessment is completed, the school will reconvene another IEP to discuss its findings. At that time, you should restate your request for an alternative school placement.

Be prepared, be persistent and be persuasive in your presentation. If you have had private evaluations done, bring them to the meeting too. If you disagree with the school-based assessment, request that an independent evaluation be performed. Bring work samples, daily logs, journal entries and any other documentation that supports your request.

If you are still unsuccessful, you will have to decide whether to file a request for due process to challenge the issue of placement. As always, think critically (**Advocacy Principle 3**); weigh the strength of your claim and the cost of filing against the potential benefits. In some situations it will be patently obvious what course of action you should choose. It is important to know that federal case law supports reimbursement for private schools when parents can establish by documentary evidence and expert opinions that the public school cannot meet their child's needs, but a private school can. You must establish that the public school was given an opportunity to evaluate the child's poor progress and that, even with revisions to the IEP plan, the school could not provide an environment in which your child succeeds. (In one recent federal case, the courts even held that parents were entitled to reimbursement for private school tuition though the child had not been previously enrolled in public school.)

Therapeutic Private Schools

There are both elementary and high schools, whether nonprofit or for profit, that integrate academics and various therapies in the classroom setting.

Some of these schools are certified by a state's department of education to provide services to children with various disabilities. These schools must meet certain requirements established by the state to receive certification. They are often referred to as "nonpublic schools" rather than private schools, but they are private in the sense that they do not receive funding from the federal or state government. Instead, they rely on tuition from students and private donations. Many of these schools have contracts with local public school districts. If a local public school cannot meet the needs of a child, it will make a direct referral to the nonpublic school and will pay the tuition for the student.

Other schools use the same model of integrated services, but are not certified by the state's department of education. They rely exclusively on private tuition and private donations, without any tuition from public school districts.

Whether they are certified or not, therapeutic schools offer many advantages for children with autism. First, the classrooms tend to be limited to ten to twelve students. Teachers are more likely to have direct experience in educating children with autism. Speech and occupational therapies, and many others, are a part of the classroom routine. In some cases, speech and other professionals may even coteach the class with a special-education teacher.

Many parents also consider it a benefit to have the child enrolled in a school where all of the children have a similar disability, since it creates a deeper sense of community, familiarity and acceptance. Others worry about the lack of diversity. There is a risk that a child's behavior can worsen if his only models are other children with disruptive behavior. It has also been said that such schools can create a false sense of security and make involvement with the mainstream community and family outings more difficult. Therapeutic schools often have very limited extra-curricular and sports activities to offer, as well. Private therapeutic schools can be a viable option, especially when there is a bad fit between your child and his local public school.

Fourteen-year-old Gabriel Victorin had attended public school from the time he was in preschool. He made significant progress in each grade and was able to participate in classroom projects and field trips. His parents were excited about Gabriel's transition to high school and felt comfortable about their choice. After all, they had met with the school's administrator and Gabriel's teacher prior to the school year to develop a program that would allow him to make an easy transition to ninth grade.

The school year started with great promise, but by late September, there were unavoidable signs that the school could not meet Gabriel's needs. Gabriel had a difficult time adjusting to riding the school bus and was often upset when he arrived. His aide didn't have the experience to help him process his frustration, which often led to tantrums and even pushing and shoving. Rather than helping, the aide, the teacher and other adults in the classroom would just make things worse, and these episodes often ended with Gabriel being sent to the principal's office or sent home by midmorning.

His parents requested a meeting with his school team. Months passed and in meeting after meeting, the school staff committed to using different strategies to address Gabriel's frustration and his noncompliant behaviors. But despite their best intentions, Gabriel continued to struggle and spent more days outside of the classroom than inside.

By March, his parents had to accept the fact that Gabriel needed a smaller school with a team of professionals who were experienced and capable of addressing his needs. This was a difficult decision; they had hoped to see him continue his education in a public school, where he would have an opportunity to engage with children without autism, attend football games and pep rallies, maybe even go to a prom. But they also recognized that Gabriel the teenager had different behaviors and needs than did Gabriel the boy.

The search for a new school was not easy. Some of the schools were very intimate and had small classrooms, and Gabriel's parents were concerned that with his large build and increasingly aggressive behaviors he would feel confined and act out. Other schools lacked appropriate academics or necessary therapeutic programs. Some schools dedicated to students with autism even rejected Gabriel because of his behavior issues.

After several months of searching and interviewing, Gabriel's parents found the right fit for him, a private therapeutic school for children with learning and developmental disabilities. It offered an accredited academic program, vocational training, therapeutic services including speech and language, behavioral-skills training, and a variety of extracurricular activities similar to his old public high school.

Private and Religious Schools

Approximately six million children receive special education, according to the Department of Education.[7] Yet there are still thousands of families with disabled children who avoid public schools altogether. Instead, they enroll their children in private or religious schools. Such schools are not governed by IDEA, so they are not required to hold IEP meetings and are not mandated to provide special education or related services to students with special needs, though they may decide to do so. Many private and religious schools welcome children with disabilities and work closely with families to support their success.

If you are considering a private school placement for your child, discuss your child's needs with the teacher and administrator in advance. Find out, too, whether the teachers at the private school have special-education credentials. Ask whether the school will provide speech, occupational or physical therapy. Public schools and therapeutic schools routinely offer alternative physical education and psychological counseling that are helpful to autistic children. If you are considering a private or religious school that does not offer these special services, weigh their importance carefully before you make your choice.

When you talk to administrators, speak with authority (**Advocacy Principle 4**). Be completely candid. One of my clients enrolled her autistic daughter in a religious school without mentioning that she had autism. Her siblings were doing well in the school and, because her condition was mild, her parents believed she would fit in. But it was a disaster.

Although the classes were small, the staff had no experience in special education and had never worked with a child with autism. They had no experience with behavior-modification techniques, picture schedules or other teaching methods that are usually a part of a child with autism's school day.

After two years of meetings to discuss the girl's lack of progress, the school asked the family to leave. The mother was angry because she believed the school could have done more to work with her daughter, but it seemed clear to me that her failure to share her daughter's diagnosis had made success impossible.

As much as you may want a particular school choice to work, do not underestimate the fact that children with autism need support in order to be successful. If a school lacks expertise in autism, it is unrealistic to expect anything other than a frustrating experience.

Home Schools

Many parents opt for homeschooling because it allows them to offer structured instruction suited precisely to the needs of their own child. In order for the education itself to be valid, parents must consult with their state department of education and find out what requirements they must fulfill. Some states require all homeschooled students to take standardized exams and maintain transcripts, while others do not.

Many private and public charter schools offer homeschooling as an option. The public home-school option is likely to offer you more services, as they are required to comply with IDEA. Be well aware of your rights and the resources available to you for homeschooling.

In a home school, your child will have limited interactions with age-appropriate peers. Unless you are going to schedule playdates and other activities throughout the day to replicate the social engagement that takes place on a campus, your child may miss valuable opportunities to enhance her social and communication skills. Since this is the area that often presents the biggest challenge for autistic children, it is an important consideration.

SCHOOL CONSIDERATIONS FOR TEENS

In general, there are the same school and classroom options for autistic teens as for young children, but you have an additional consideration: whether the student uses a standards-based or alternative curriculum. The former is based on academic standards set by each state department of education, while the latter is a modified version of the state's standards with a greater emphasis on vocational training and life skills. The choice of curriculum is key, as it determines whether a student will graduate from high school with a diploma or a certificate of completion. You may receive a recommendation at an IEP meeting as early as elementary school, but certainly by the time a student is ready to enter middle and high school a decision needs to be made and identified in the IEP document, as it will dictate the types of classes your child will take and the level of support he will need. Many therapeutic schools have different classrooms or "tracks" for students who are on course to receive a diploma as opposed to those who will receive a certificate of completion.

There is no right or wrong in selecting a curriculum; it has mainly to do with your child's ability to perform at or near grade level. Many children with autism struggle with abstract concepts, making it difficult to handle the kind of upper-level English classes that are required by most states in order to earn a high school diploma. An alternative curriculum—one that is more focused on functional skills as opposed to core academic subjects—may be more appropriate. It teaches students a wide range of life, communication, leisure, academic, social and vocational skills.

A successful transition to high school for a child with autism requires early planning. Even in states where children remain in elementary school until the eighth grade, parents need to start thinking about high school by at least the fifth or sixth grade. If you believe your child is capable of meeting all of the academic requirements, including passing a state exit exam, make sure that his IEP plan enrolls him in the curriculum he needs to graduate—such as credits in math, English, science and the appropriate electives. If you select a specialized private school for children with autism, check carefully to see that they offer a diploma-track curriculum and that your child is indeed eligible to be a part of that program, as opposed to a certificate program.

If you are unsure about which curriculum is best for your child, you can obtain a school-based or private assessment to determine his academic level. If your child is behind his peers who don't have autism, it does not automatically mean that he cannot graduate. You can request educational therapy and intensive academic instruction as a part of your child's IEP. Often a child will fall behind in school in the early years due to noncompliant behaviors; but, after behavior therapy and with the proper support, that same child may be able to make significant progress on grade-level course work.

Throughout this process, remember **Advocacy Principle 2**: Learn to be an Expert. Improve your expertise at applying this principle by taking your research further. As a parent, you might learn only enough to answer your immediate question. As an advocate and an expert, what else would you want to know? The more you learn, the stronger foundation of knowledge you create. As your child grows, this base will give you a solid place to stand in the years to come.

PUTTING IT INTO ACTION

1. Start investigating the schools available in your area. Call the school district to find out the options. Are there charter schools that accept special-needs children? What therapeutic schools are available? Get the contact information for each school.

2. Now it's time to build the professional-looking binder that will hold the documents you need for productive IEP meetings. Begin by finding a high-quality legal or executive binder. (Children's school notebooks will not convey the impression you are trying

to achieve.) Then collect each item below and insert them into the binder.

- any and all relevant reports or assessments you have access to
- a list of your child's strengths and challenges
- samples of your child's academic work
- copies of prior IEPs
- report cards and teacher evaluations
- a flattering photo of your child
- excerpts from IDEA that apply to IEPs
- a carefully drafted agenda for the meeting
- a list of well-developed questions

3. Identify someone who will provide you with reliable support at your IEP meeting. It is a good idea to take a good friend or relative along. If you can find two or three people, you will be in a better position. Explain the situation to them ahead of time and let them know when the next meeting will occur. Educate them by letting them read this chapter to be better prepared; then call on them when the time comes.

CHAPTER 10

Legal Consultation:
Our Family's Choice for Inclusion

After explaining the types of schools and classrooms available to their child, I sometimes tell parents what the process was like for our family. Before we go into more legal information in our consultation, I will do the same for you. It can help to ground the laws, regulations and technicalities in personal real-life experience, as you are deciding which schools and classrooms to choose for your own child.

In the summer before Marty entered kindergarten, we had the good fortune of spending one day a week for two months in a behavior management program at Koegel Autism Clinic at the University of California–Santa Barbara. Under the direction of Dr. Lynn Koegel, Marty participated in six hours of pivotal response training to increase his language skills and his ability to communicate with his peers.

After she had had a chance to spend such intensive time evaluating Marty, Dr. Koegel and I had many long discussions about his planned placement in a special day class with other students with disabilities. Our conversations led me to do extensive research. I read her publications in scholarly journals, as well as those by Dr. Susan Marks and other prominent experts in the field.

Based on her research at UCSB, Dr. Koegel has found that even children who are considered moderate to severe on the autism spectrum can benefit from being in classrooms with children without autism.[1] By observing those peers, autistic children learn to model speech, practice appropriate social skills and adopt other social behavior that will help them in natural environments, such as restaurants and movie theaters. The downside is that the teacher in a general education classroom may have no experience of special-needs children. The pace will be faster. For an autistic child to keep up, he will need to have a special education aide with him all day.

Ultimately, my husband and I decided that full inclusion was a better solution for our family, since it was very important to us that Marty be included in all our family outings, travel and other activities.

With only two weeks left before school began, I phoned the assistant principal and requested an emergency IEP meeting to change Marty's placement. I was shocked by the resistance and stonewalling that followed that phone call.

The school administrators were dead set against it. Marty's school district had a practice of automatically enrolling students with autism in either autism classrooms or segregated classrooms for children with multiple disabilities. There were clear advantages to this placement. The classes would have only twelve children. The teacher had years of special-education training and had specifically chosen to work with special-needs children. Marty would be in a class with other children who had autism, and he would receive a great deal of personal instruction. The administrators were frankly amazed that I would reject what they saw as an ideal placement.

Naturally, they were also concerned about Marty's potential for interfering with the education of the other children in the class, and they assumed no one would want a special-needs child in a general classroom—not the teacher, not the students and certainly not their parents!

Weeks of calls to the superintendent—or just about anybody in a position of authority at the school who might be able to intervene—followed. When I reminded the principal that special-needs children had a legal right to be educated in the least restrictive environment, she agreed, but insisted that we move slowly. Marty would be one of the first students with autism to ever be fully included in the school and she was cautious.

"Let's start with thirty minutes a day and take it from there," she said. "We'll put Marty in the general education class on a trial basis and see how it goes."

When I asked if he would be fully included by the end of the first few months, she said, "No. In fact, I can't guarantee that Marty will be fully included by the end of the year. Sometimes it takes years for students to be ready."

Although our goals were different, I could see that the principal was doing her best to protect all the students in her school. She had offered a compromise. It would have been polite to accept her good intentions and go along. But that would have meant sacrificing our goals for Marty.

As parent advocates, once we determine our priorities for our children, we must be prepared to stand by them. I cannot emphasize enough that this is going to require a level of tenacity that most of us have never needed before. Every parent advocate must be prepared to hear the word "no" and remain undeterred. Despite the fact that we have every right to make choices for our children and we often have the law on our side, the level of opposition—and our capacity for discouragement—is astonishing.

Those of us who have been raised to be courteous and ready to compromise find it especially daunting to stand our ground against a definite "no" from an authority figure. I have a little trick I recommend to participants in my workshops: stand in front of a mirror and repeat the word "no" over and over to desensitize yourself to it. It may sound funny, but it really helps! Even so, at times I still have to remind myself that it doesn't matter if this principal or clerk or doctor or administrator thinks I'm overly aggressive or even a "bitch." I'm here on behalf of my child.

After many meetings, calls and letters to the school's district office, including a day when I put the superintendent's number on speed dial and called more than twenty-five times, the principal eventually agreed to fully include Marty in the general education classroom—in keeping with his legal rights—and I agreed that we would all meet again to revisit the decision after sixty and ninety days.

Each victory is encouraging, but you have to be ready to stand firm. And keep standing firm. Pace yourself for the long haul, so you can sustain your efforts. After our first victory, we still had those sixty- and ninety-day assessments hanging over us. Then, after we cleared those hurdles and Marty was allowed to stay, we learned that his teacher barely spoke to him. Although Marty was no more disruptive than the other kindergarten students, the teacher resented having a special-needs child in his class (and unfortunately, the school didn't provide him with supplemental training or support), so he either ignored Marty or sent him out into the hall whenever he made any noise. He never developed a respectful, mutually beneficial relationship with Marty's behavioral aide, despite our regular meetings. As a result, Marty had a very difficult year, half of which was spent sitting outside in the hallway!

It was disappointing, but I decided that it was not a reflection on the process; any child can have a bad teacher. And in the same year, Marty formed some incredible friendships with girls and boys that continue to this day. He learned to obey and respond to the instructions of the adults in the class, follow a daily schedule and communicate better.

With consistent advocacy and hard work, we have found new ways every school year to foster synergy between his teachers and his aide. All of us are on a growth curve, learning how to redirect his behavior, provide structure and ensure that he is fully engaged in all the classroom activities.

We've come to accept the fact that the victories will be mixed with disappointments. Sometimes, the secret to contentment is learning to notice and appreciate what's working. We are extremely lucky, for instance, to have added to Marty's team a wonderful professional who is an inclusion specialist. He modifies the curriculum, serves as a coteacher and provides Marty with support to make his experience better. To this day, Marty remains fully included in the school system and has even been the subject of a front-page story in the *Los Angeles Times* as a model for inclusion among special-needs children. The school, despite its initial objections, has been heralded for being bold enough to allow full inclusion.

And yet, amazingly enough, we face the same challenges every year, trying to get each new teacher on board. But as a parent advocate, I am prepared for that. I expect to have to stand my ground again and again. You are likely to face the same challenges with your autistic child. It's par for the course. Even when it feels like an uphill battle, always remember that you can do this. And more than that, you have to do it. There is no one else.

Rest assured that, along the way, you will meet some wonderful, kindhearted people who will open doors for you and give you advice that will help ease your way, at least for a while. Once you get your bearings and build up valuable experience, you can become one of those people who reaches out a hand to parents struggling like you did.

In the years since I sought full inclusion for Marty, I have assisted hundreds of families in securing full or partial inclusion in public and private schools for their children with autism. Like me, some parents never dreamed their child could be included in a mainstream school environment. It's heartwarming to see the progress these children experience. Sharing your knowledge with others (**Advocacy Principle 7**) can be every bit as rewarding for you as it is for anyone you help.

Whatever type of classroom environment you choose for your child, the key to getting it is collaboration (**Advocacy Principle 6**) between you, your child's teacher and the school administrators. If you believe your child will thrive if she is included in a mainstream environment, specifically request it in your IEP. Even if your child is not working at grade level and has some challenging behavioral problems, that's not sufficient for the school to refuse to consider your request.

Unusual behavior is a part of autism. The reality is that, even with the best modification and intensive interventions, some children still continue to exhibit behaviors different from neurotypical children. Sometimes schools try to use this as an excuse to segregate students with autism. Legally, these excuses are not valid.

Know your child's legal rights to inclusion and be prepared to advocate for success. You will need to apply each of the Advocacy Principles strongly as you work to secure the best learning environment for your child.

The legal requirement for a child to be educated in the "least restrictive environment" has spawned a movement across the nation for children with any disability, including autism, to be educated in general education classrooms. The fight against segregation of those who are disabled and have special needs has a long history. For decades, people with disabilities did not have access to public schools, facilities such as restaurants and office buildings, housing and health care. Segregation typically promotes ignorance, misunderstanding and lack of empathy. This is why educating others (**Advocacy Principle 7**) is such a vital part of advocacy. It strikes at the root of many of the cultural presumptions that make it so hard to meet your child's needs for education, medical care and, sometimes, even basic human rights.

WHAT DOES INCLUSION MEAN?

Since different educators use the terms in different ways, it can be difficult to know exactly what they mean when they talk about inclusion. Applying **Advocacy Principle 4**, *be proactive. If you discuss this option with your* *school administrator or IEP team, begin by confirming that these elements are a part of their definition of inclusion:*

- a language-based curriculum
- a curriculum that progresses in an orderly manner throughout the day and addresses multiple skill development
- frequent opportunities for the child to respond to instruction
- little time when the child is not engaged in instruction
- effective instructional techniques drawn from evidence-based research, including a strong focus on positive reinforcement, shaping, prompting, and fading of prompts
- training for both the teacher and aide (if any) in behavior modification or other intervention strategies
- a comprehensive behavior support plan
- daily recording of academic work and any behavioral problems
- frequent meetings of all staff to review progress and make timely changes in procedures, if progress is not being made
- a preplanned strategy to address any disruptive behaviors

While a growing number of parents and educational experts believe that full inclusion will give children the most opportunities, many schools are slow to agree. Often, they simply think it's too much trouble. Making allowances for children who have special needs requires extra work and attention. They assume that an autistic child will disrupt the classroom and divert resources from the rest of the class. Do they really forget that most parents of children with autism have typically developing children who are also enrolled in school? We also care about the well-being of the other children!

Although they may not want to admit it, even to themselves, sometimes people have deeply rooted prejudices against those with disabilities. Despite the tremendous progress that has been made over the last thirty years, bigotry still exists. That kind of stigma has reared its ugly head in Marty's case and in that of many of my clients.

Proponents of inclusion say that it gives children with special needs the opportunity to learn in a natural, stimulating environment. Inclusion makes it possible for friendships to occur with nonhandicapped peers who become role models for positive behavior, and may accelerate the learning of social skills that will lead to greater acceptance in the community. But make no mistake: The advantages work both ways. Children without disabilities can benefit by learning about differences between people and by having the opportunity to help their differently abled peers. Teachers can learn new techniques and broaden their range as educators.

Nonetheless, inclusion is not always the best choice for every autistic student. The twirling mobiles, fluorescent lights and constant chatter of typical classrooms can all add up to the kind of sensory overload that leads to meltdowns in autistic children. The added stress of making transitions to different classes, eating lunch in rooms echoing with shouts, incessant teasing from other children and baffling social expectations at recess can make school intolerable for some children.

If you are wondering whether inclusion would be realistic for your child, think carefully about his ability to adapt and fit into other environments in your family life. Imagine him in a regular classroom and ask yourself questions such as these:

- How much routine and structure does my child need?
- Can he tolerate new classmates and teachers?
- Will he be able to adapt to the constant stresses in a regular classroom?
- Which social and academic areas does he need most help with?
- Will the entire school day be a struggle or will only a few subjects be challenging?

Even if your honest assessment tells you that your child is not quite ready for full inclusion in a general education classroom, the right interventions may make it possible. When Irene Green was first diagnosed at two years old, she was engaged in extremely difficult behaviors and had very limited verbal skills. Instinctively, her mother, Cheryl, believed that Irene could improve with the right interventions. She envisioned her daughter in a full-inclusion classroom with children without autism, even though it seemed impossible at first.

At the time of Irene's diagnosis, Cheryl was going through a divorce. She was working full-time and caring for her daughter on her own. Her family lived in another state. She wasn't sure how she would get Irene the intervention she needed when she had so little time and so few resources.

I met Cheryl when she came to a parenting workshop I sponsored at a local church. I encouraged her to get involved with the Special Needs Network. She began to take steps to become a true advocate for her daughter, learning to become an expert (**Advocacy Principle 2**) and using the resources of the Special Needs Network to build a team (**Advocacy Principle 6**) to get extra support for her daughter and herself. When she learned more about her child's rights and the services provided by federal and state laws, she was able to get intensive early intervention.

By the time Irene was in third grade, she was able to successfully transition to a general education classroom. Though she was painfully shy and introverted before treatment, Irene has blossomed. She loves computer games and fashion. She has even made friends among her peers without autism. Having seen Irene make progress that once seemed unimaginable, Cheryl is hopeful for the future.

WHAT TO SAY. . .

When Your Child's Inclusion Is Questioned . . .

For those parents of children without autism and school staff who ask questions about why you want your child included or suggest that his or her enrollment will negatively impact other children.

TEACHER: I have never taught children with special needs. Frankly, I didn't go into teaching to work with this population. We have a great special day program with a credentialed special-education teacher. I think your son would do much better in that class.

PARENT: Thank you for your concern and your candor. I know that this is new to you, but I am committed to working with the school to provide you with the training and resources you need to be successful. And although some children may do better in the special class, the IEP team agrees that the most appropriate placement for my child is in an inclusion setting.

SCHOOL ADMINISTRATOR: Your child is not able to do grade-level work, so I don't think full inclusion is appropriate.

PARENT: Doing grade-level work should only be one of many considerations that the IEP team reviews in making a recommendation of placement. There are many other benefits from inclusion, such as learning to model children without autism and learning to work in a group. There are ways to modify the curriculum to ensure that my child makes academic progress. At our last IEP meeting, we identified supports and services that allow my child to receive his education with children without autism, as the federal law mandates. If we work together as a team, I am sure we can ensure that he has a successful year.

PARENT OF A CHILD WITHOUT AUTISM: Your son was crying loudly today and appeared to really be upset. I'm afraid his outbursts will make it difficult for the other students in the class to learn.

PARENT: Thank you for your concern. When I was in the class the other day, several children had outbursts. The teacher and her staff are very skilled in handling such situations and not allowing them to prevent the students from learning. Reliable research shows that classmates of students with special needs have equivalent or higher tests scores; develop more positive attitudes toward individuals with disabilities; and have improved social and problem-solving skills! So your child will benefit as much as mine.

Without a doubt, inclusion requires a great deal of coordination, effort and commitment on the part of the school, the teacher and the parent. But there is no evidence that inclusion is more expensive for the schools. IDEA and other state laws provide separate funding for special education, which would not otherwise be available to public schools. Although having a disabled child in a classroom may require a general education teacher to participate in additional training and the school to provide some extra level of support, administrative inconvenience is not grounds for a school to deny a child inclusion.

In the big picture, most educators have yet to take into account the exponential growth in the number of children with autism. If they continue to object to inclusion on the grounds of expense, they will soon find that building hundreds of segregated classrooms is far more expensive!

PREPARE YOURSELF

There is no question that your child's education is going to take an enormous amount of time and attention. Educating a child with autism or related disabilities is a dynamic process that spans nearly two decades— the most formative years of your child's life. Building a solid foundation of comprehensive information and understanding is the only thing that will make the process easier from year to year.

The choices will be complicated and the stakes will always be high, but as the parent of an autistic child, you have tremendous resources at your disposal. The IEP planning team discussed in the next chapter is comprised of specialists from the school district who make their living planning solid packages of classroom education, tutoring, teacher's aides and a wide range of therapeutic interventions.

Your own staunch empowerment circle, as well as the doctors, care-givers and other experts who treat and evaluate your child, will place a wealth of information and experience at your disposal. If you make good use of these resources, you can ensure an education that places your autistic child in the best position to lead a happy, productive life.

Tremendous opportunities can be created when you enter into a true partnership with your child's school. With the right match of education, talented teachers, and insightful caregivers, phenomenal outcomes can be achieved for children, even those with the severest disabilities.

I've now given covered all the information I give my clients in our first few meetings. Armed with this knowledge, you'll be able to go confidently into your first meeting with the teachers, caregivers and administrators who will make up your IEP team.

I encourage my clients to meet with me again after that first IEP meeting, so I can prepare them for the assessment, strategies and potential conflicts that may happen next. You will find all of that information in the next chapter.

PUTTING IT INTO ACTION

1. Begin to explore the direction your child's life may go in the future by starting the conversation early. If your child is verbal, ask

her what she wants to be when she grows up. Her answer may change over the years; it may be whimsical and inappropriate or not. Either way, opening the conversation—and returning to it now and then—will help you both keep the future in mind. Return to this topic on a regular basis. It is sure to evolve over time.

2. Make a list of ten things you can do to build a stronger working relationship with your child's teacher and classroom aides. The list might include things like scheduling regular team meetings, offering to volunteer in the classroom, requesting in your IEP that more training be provided for the teacher, etc. Start immediately implementing the items on your list.

CHAPTER 11

Legal Consultation:
Planning Your Child's Education

deally, everyone involved in planning your child's education at IEP meetings would put your child's needs first, as you do. In reality, the team members will be governed by their own agenda and restrictions. The principal has to consider the federal, state and budgetary restrictions in the school district. Regardless of how much she would like to provide support for your child's special needs, she has an equal obligation to consider the needs of all the other children competing for the same finite resources. Teachers and therapists often find themselves caught between pleasing the parents and the school, while finding good solutions for your child.[1] You are the only one in the room whose sole concern is your child.

No matter how seriously the members of your IEP team take your child's education planning, the bottom line is, *it's not their child.* One attorney in Connecticut says that whenever she hears IEP team members telling parents, "We care as much about your child as you do," she wants to say, "I'm sorry, but no, you do not!" She points out that, as much as she cares about the outcome of the meetings for her clients, it is very different from how she would feel if she were attending a meeting about one of her own children.[2]

As you plan your child's education, keep this awareness foremost in your mind. You are your child's primary advocate. No one else knows his needs or cares about him as deeply as you do. No one else will be following him as closely through this school year and the next year and all the years after that.

The Advocacy Principles grew out of my own realization that it was up to me to step up and become a staunch advocate for my child. When it comes to IEP planning, I cannot emphasize enough the importance of listening to the advice of the team, but making your own decisions.

You are the best person to make the final decisions for your child's education. Your advocacy will ensure he gets the appropriate assessments. Your role is vital in making sure your child has all the training and preparation he needs before he makes the transition to adult life.

ASSESSMENTS FOR IEP

The IEP team will request assessments of your child from any number of evaluators, including psychologists, speech pathologists, and occupational therapists, as well as other pertinent assessments. These evaluations will determine your child's level of academic performance and ability to function. They will then be used to select the most appropriate special-educational services. As a parent, you can also request or introduce assessments. There are generally three types of assessments: school based, private and independent.

School-based Assessments

A school-based assessment is conducted by an employee of the school district at the request of the parents or teacher. Those conducting the assessments must have appropriate state licenses and credentials in the subject area of assessment. For example, psychological assessments can be conducted only by the school psychologist. In some states, school psychologists need only a master's degree rather than the doctoral degree and thousands of supervised hours required to be a licensed psychologist in other states.

Private Assessments

If you believe the school evaluation is inaccurate or insufficient, you may obtain a private assessment at your own expense. Such evaluations can play a critical role in that they allow parents an opportunity to have their child assessed by someone whom they select and have confidence in. The assessments also provide the school team with a fresh perspective.

The school is required to "consider" any private evaluations you provide. However, "consider" does not mean "accept" or "embrace." If they reject the recommendations made in a privately obtained evaluation, they have to state the reason.

The timing of private assessments is crucial. If you have your child privately tested too close to the time of the school-based assessment in the same area (e.g., speech and language), the test results from your private assessment may be deemed invalid. As a general rule, students are evaluated once an academic school year at most.

Independent Evaluations

Parents may also request an independent educational evaluation (IEE), to be conducted at the school district's expense. Typically, such requests are made if parents disagree with a school-based assessment and want to seek a second opinion.

If you request an independent educational evaluation, the school district must agree to your request. In such cases, the school will normally give you the option of selecting a qualified examiner to conduct an evaluation, which they will pay for.

If the school denies your request, it must request a due-process hearing to defend the accuracy of the school-based assessment. (A full discussion of due-process complaints comes later in this chapter.)

Advice about Private Assessments

Parents often come to me for advice after spending thousands of dollars on private psychological or educational assessments, only to have them dismissed by their school district! If you plan to obtain a private assessment by a psychologist, neuropsychologist or educational psychologist, these questions can help you choose an evaluator with the right qualifications.

- Does the evaluator meet your state's requirements for conducting the evaluation? (For example, most states require a psychologist to be specifically licensed to conduct psychological evaluations.)
- Has the evaluator performed school-based evaluations in the past? If so, for which school districts?

- Is the evaluator versed in state requirements for school-based evaluations?
- Will your evaluator include an observation of your child in the classroom?
- Is the evaluator willing to attend the eligibility or IEP meeting to explain his findings, educate the IEP team about the reasons for the recommendations and, if necessary, be available to testify at any administrative hearings?

If the prospective evaluator answers "no" to any of the above questions, reconsider. Although the evaluation may be helpful to you and your family, it is not likely to be accepted by the IEP team. States have very specific requirements for educational assessments. Any expert's findings must be made in the context of the IDEA requirements.

Many parents make the mistake of having a qualified professional assess their child in a clinical setting. Again, the analysis may be valuable, but it will not be suited to the requirements of the IEP. For those evaluations, observation of a child in the school setting is imperative.

Most schools have routine procedures that outside evaluators must follow when performing observations. I cannot stress enough the significance of these classroom observations. If you do hire a private evaluator, ask him to make multiple trips to the school to observe your child, as well as to interview the teacher and other staff members working with your child. Without these components, a private assessment will carry very little weight with your IEP team.

OCCUPATIONAL THERAPY

Children with autism often need occupational therapy to help their nervous system process sensory input in a more typical way. Occupational therapists evaluate and provide assistance with motor planning, sequencing, gross and fine-motor skills. Young children often get OT in therapy clinics, where there are lots of ball pits, swings and other playground-type equipment. As children get older, the therapy tends to consist of tabletop activities that can be performed in a classroom. The purpose of such therapy is to address many of the sensory-integration and motor-planning issues that children with autism have that often prevent them from learning simple tasks such as buttoning their shirts or riding a bicycle.

Many parents obtain private evaluations for occupational therapy from a clinician who has treated their child in an occupational therapy clinic. It seems like a logical choice. However, if the goal is to obtain school-based therapy, the assessment may not be appropriate. The school's primary interest is in services that help the child in a classroom setting. The question is not whether she needs the therapy, but whether it will improve her ability to make academic progress at school.

All assessments related to the IEP must be based on how they affect a child's ability to function in the classroom. Whenever you hire a professional to make a private assessment, be sure that she has experience with school-based services, that she can observe your child repeatedly in the classroom and that she can make recommendations in a manner consistent with your state's guidelines.

REQUESTS FOR ADDITIONAL SERVICES

Whether your child has received school-based assessments, private assessments and/or independent evaluations, the results will help you and your IEP team determine what additional services he may need.

The law states that the IEP may also include "related services and supplementary aids and services to be provided to the child . . .

- to advance appropriately toward attaining the annual goals,
- to be involved and progress in the general curriculum (that is, the curriculum used by nondisabled students),
- to participate in extracurricular and other nonacademic activities, and
- to be educated and participate with other children with disabilities and nondisabled children."[3]

If a student is eligible for special education, the related services recommended by the IEP team will be provided free of cost to the parent and the child. "The services may include:

- speech-language pathology
- psychological services

- physical and occupational therapy
- recreation, including therapeutic recreation
- early identification and assessment of disabilities in children
- counseling services, including rehabilitation counseling
- medical services for diagnostic or evaluation purposes
- school health services
- social work services in schools
- parent counseling and training
- transportation
- inclusion counseling
- behavioral intervention and supervision
- one-on-one aides"[4]

This is by no means an exhaustive list. Related services may include other developmental, corrective or supportive services—such as artistic training; cultural programs; art, music or dance therapy—if the child needs them to make educational progress and receive FAPE. The services can be provided directly to a child or in the form of training for the teacher.

Be prepared to advocate for these services. Simply because your school acknowledges that your child is entitled to special services does not automatically mean that you will agree on what those services are or the frequency with which your child should receive them.

Many of my clients with children entering kindergarten are frustrated by their first IEP meeting, when they discover that their school districts will not continue to provide their child with the same level of speech, occupational and behavior-intervention therapies as in their early intervention programs.

For example, from the age of three, Jason received two hours of speech therapy, two hours of occupational therapy and twenty-five hours of behavior intervention every week. His mother, Cathy, was shocked when the IEP team recommended a completely different program.

First, the IEP team stated that Jason would benefit more from group speech therapy than the individual sessions he had been receiving. They also recommended that the frequency be reduced from two hours a week to one. The team recommended eliminating his occupational therapy altogether and replacing it with one hour a month in consultation with the classroom teacher.

In place of the twenty-five hours of home-based ABA therapy Jason had been receiving every week, the IEP team recommended that he be assigned a classroom aide and that he attend a school program. Cathy was told directly that if she wanted to continue with other therapies at home, she would have to look for other sources of funding. Shocking though it seems, this is not an uncommon situation.

Although parents can be quick to perceive a district's recommendation for reduced services as a personal attack or a greedy attempt to conserve school district resources, that is not usually the case. Most teachers and school personnel genuinely care about children and work very hard to provide them with a good education. Some have their own children with special needs and have both a professional and a personal interest in special-needs children. The disparity is often caused by the difference in what IDEA obligates a school to provide and what parents expect from their children's school.

In an important case, *Board of Education v. Rowley*,[5] the United States Supreme Court held that a school district is required to provide only a "basic floor of opportunity" for special-needs children. Schools must ensure that children have access to specialized instruction and related services that are individually designed to provide educational benefit to the child. But while parents want school districts to provide the best education possible—one that maximizes the potential of the special-needs child—the court specifically stated that school districts were not obligated to do so.

Because of this ruling, it is important that you replace the word "best" with "appropriate" when requesting services from your school. Also, avoid framing your requests in terms of what you "want" for your child. This will only be received as an emotional plea. Instead, focus on what your experts say is necessary to help your child access the curriculum and make meaningful educational progress.

When I first met Jason's mother, I asked her to bring assessments that supported the services she believed were appropriate for her child. Unless she had evaluations from a speech pathologist, occupational therapist and psychologist showing that Jason needed those services as frequently as before, the school wasn't likely to consider her request.

After we discussed her case, I advised Cathy to request another IEP meeting. This time, when she met with the IEP team, she provided them with a detailed statement of her son's challenges. She gave them documents showing how the requested services were designed to help him, academically and socially, within the school setting. She also pointed out specific instances where the previous, school-based IEP reports alluded to the same issues. She showed private assessments that recommended her son receive more frequent services. Although these findings did not always agree with those from the school's evaluating team, the IEP team made concessions and provided Jason with many of the services they had previously denied.

It is important to work with a team of experts including school evaluators and private assessors, if possible, to determine what related services your child needs in the school setting. Many of the doctors who assisted you in assessing your child can also help you in determining what services your child needs. Reach out to professionals in your empowerment circle, teachers, hospitals and other parents of autistic children. They can be a great resource.

Don't be afraid to be creative. At a parent workshop that my firm hosted, Dr. Delania Martinez told parents about a wonderful social-skills "lunch bunch" group she established while working at the Manhattan Beach Unified School District. Under her direction, a group of third- and fourth-grade students met a few days a week for lunch to learn to take turns initiating conversations and reading nonverbal cues. In this relaxed and natural environment, children were learning invaluable communication and social skills with peers. The program was so popular that there was a waiting list of children without autism who wanted to participate! Dr. Martinez encouraged parents to request this as a part of speech and language services in their IEPs if social interaction and engaging with peers were issues their children experienced.

The IDEA also recognizes that parents and staff need intensive training to assist a child in making substantial progress. Look for individuals within your school district as well as experts at nearby universities and colleges who can provide training to the entire staff at your child's school. A child may need an aide to help him on the playground, during recess and at certain school functions.

No matter how unusual and creative your request, you will improve your chances of securing services for your child with the strong support of a qualified evaluation. The assessment should clearly indicate the area of need, the present level of performance, the service specifics, the ways in which the service will address the need, as well as the frequency and duration required. To be effective, it must also state in no uncertain terms that the service is needed to help your child to make significant progress in an academic or functional area.

TEN STRATEGIES TO IMPROVE YOUR NEXT IEP MEETING

You can positively influence the outcome of your next IEP by changing the way you think of the meeting. Treat it like a board of directors meeting where you are the chairperson. You are there to guide, direct and build consensus. This may involve differences of opinion, sometimes even heated debates, but everyone present is working toward the same goal— improving the educational outcomes for your child.

1. **Know the players.** In advance of the meeting, find out who is planning to attend on behalf of the district, and their respective roles. You don't want any surprises and you want to know the dynamics of the personalities.

2. **Line up your team.** Since no one person has the ultimate decision-making powers, you want to stack the deck with supporters.

3. **Prepare an agenda.** This will tell you what areas you need to spend more time on in advance of the meeting.

4. **Research each agenda item.** For example, if one of your agenda items is behavioral therapy, look for articles and information on evidence-based practices, and research which ones best support autistic children. This will help to establish credibility.

5. **Organize documents.** This is your meeting. You want to make an impressive presentation. Have all prior IEPs, assessments, reports and other documents neatly organized in a tabbed binder, so that you can easily refer to them.

6. **Come prepared with assessments.** Have copies of all assessment reports for each team member. Remember, assessments drive services and placements. If you are

requesting a service, make sure you have obtained an assessment from a qualified expert or a school-based evaluator indicating the need for the service.

7. **Make a positive introductory statement.** Start the meeting by thanking the team for the hard work they are doing. Tell them what is working and how much you appreciate their efforts. Remember you are building consensus. By your setting a positive tone and acknowledging what is going well, team members will be more responsive when you move into more sensitive areas.

8. **Appeal to the heart.** After you make an introductory statement, show the team a picture of your child, a sample of some work that she has done, and tell them a brief, moving story about your child.

9. **Have a strong request.** Be clear about what is appropriate for your child and state it affirmatively. Be prepared to listen to differences of opinion, but stand firm.

10. **Document the meeting.** Even if you exercised your right to record the meeting, there may be a subsequent challenge to the school district if there have been differences of opinion. Take notes to memorialize what was said during the meeting. Put it in a letter that you ask to be added to the parent-comment section of the IEP.

PLANNING YOUR CHILD'S FUTURE

You should always be planning for the future—not only your goals for the next school year, but for the life of your child after school. The goals you set for your child in middle school and high school will lay the educational groundwork for the future.

Even when the time frame is a single school year, developing goals is one of the most difficult areas to navigate during an IEP meeting. Writing specific and measurable goals that address both academics and functional behavior can be difficult, even for seasoned educators on the

IEP team. It's even more challenging for parents without a background in special education. Still, this is what you will be required to do at each IEP meeting.

To be prepared for this portion of the IEP, you must do your research (**Advocacy Principle 2**). You don't have to become an expert on the current methods used at the university level to teach teachers, but you do need to have a general understanding of what all children are expected to learn in school at each grade level and how a child with autism learns some, or substantially all, of the same curriculum.

One way to approach goal setting is to correlate your child's academic goals with your state's existing standards for her grade level, available on the Web site of your state department of education. Functional goals can be based on vital life skills. Standards used by schools to develop curriculum are based on validated scientific methods as required by IDEA.

For example, if your child is going into fifth grade, look at what the expectations are for a typical fifth grader. Is she expected to develop and write five-sentence paragraphs using a topic and ending sentence? Is she expected to be doing long division, fractions or geometry? If your child is working at or near grade level, you can use the state standards almost verbatim when setting IEP goals for your child.

If your child is going into fifth grade but working at third-grade level, it is still important to be familiar with the standards for other fifth graders in your state. Although developing a five-sentence paragraph may not be a realistic goal, you might choose a modified goal of writing two to three sentences about the person or place of his choice. This will give him an opportunity to build the skills that approximate those of typical fifth graders. (An exercise like this can have a functional component as well: Not only will your child learn how to write, but he'll learn important facts about the people and places in his own life. For example, if the subject is Dad, he can write his father's full name, job, place of employment and hobbies.)

Make goals measurable by making them specific. Here are a few examples:

- Select a family member. Write a four-sentence paragraph about her occupation and hobbies with 75 percent accuracy, three out of four times.
- Add and subtract twenty three-digit math problems in thirty minutes with 80 percent accuracy three out of four times.

Each of these goals can be measured by the teacher, and your child's progress can be evaluated at incremental dates. If the school year ends in June, but he is completing only five problems in the allotted time by March, it is unlikely that he will meet the goal of twenty by June.

Progress reports and grades are also ways to measure whether your child is continuing to improve. If your child has failing grades or is not making adequate progress in academic areas identified in the IEP, it is a clear sign that the IEP plan needs at the very least to be reviewed and possibly revised. This may also be a signal that your child needs more intensive instruction or additional support in order to be successful.

If one of the goals in your child's IEP is that she learns to tell time, you can ask her the time on a regular basis, in her natural home environment. If she has been taught to tell time but cannot do it at home, you must communicate that to the team. Even if she is demonstrating mastery of a skill in the classroom setting, her inability to use it in her natural environment makes it nonfunctional and inconsistent with the dictates of IDEA. Both parents and educators can determine whether adjustments need to be made to the child's special-education program and IEP.

Remember to pace yourself. These adjustments and plans are likely to go on for many years. Not all children with disabilities finish school with their age group. As a result, you may be engaged in IEP meetings until your teen has become an adult.

The IDEA allows students with disabilities to remain in high school through the age of twenty-one. During that time, they can continue to receive special education and related services. Unfortunately, however, many schools begin to reduce services even as early as the preteen and teen years. There is a strange misconception that children with autism are more likely to benefit from intervention during their primary-school years. This presumption, along with school deficits and inadequate staffing, can cause schools to offer fewer services to older students.

As an advocate, you must continue to press for those services that your teenage student needs. There is no question that intervention continues to be essential in the life of an autistic child, whether at age four or fourteen. According to the *Journal of Applied Behavior Analysis*, behavioral analysis can measurably improve the quality of life for autistic teens and adults. I always emphasize to my clients that they must think beyond the elementary years and be prepared to expand their advocacy for those critical middle and high school years. It is important to know that the interventions that help a child learn how to play with others at recess need to remain in place to teach a teen how to behave at a school dance, surrounded by unpredictable movements and loud music. Speech therapy can help teens learn to initiate the more challenging social interactions of their high school years, to read social cues and to stay on the topic while talking to their friends.

WHAT TO SAY. . .

To Your IEP Team

Do not assume that your school's team is familiar with the newly revised provisions of the IDEA 2004 and its requirements. Before 2004, IEPs may have used short-term goals. These have been eliminated under the new law. Now IEPs must include "annual measurable goals, including academic and functional goals."

According to IDEA 2004, your IEP must contain "a description of how the child's progress toward meeting the annual goals . . . will be measured and when periodic reports on the progress the child is making toward meeting the annual goals (such as through the use of quarterly or other periodic reports, concurrent with the issuance of report cards) will be provided."[6] If you know the law yourself, you will be able to ensure that its provisions are included by the IEP team. These examples will show you the kind of thing you might say in response to your IEP team.

SCHOOL PERSONNEL: We send parents three progress reports throughout the year. This should give you the information you need regarding how your child is performing.

PARENT: Thank you for that information. However, I would also like to receive more frequent reports of my child's progress toward his goals in the event we need to make adjustments. I know that the U.S. Department of Education recommends that teachers use short tests every week or two to measure progress and that the results of those tests be placed on a graph that demonstrates progress toward the annual goals. Is it possible for you to use this method and to provide me with a copy of the graph at least twice a month?

SCHOOL PERSONNEL: We don't like to set too many goals because we find that it's too stressful for the child and we don't want to set him up for failure.

PARENT: I completely agree that we want my child to have a successful year. We also want to make sure that the goals are consistent with the high expectations I know you set for your other students. Even if he falls a little short of meeting all of the goals, it's important that he is challenged and that we stay focused on helping him make maximum progress this year.

SCHOOL PERSONNEL: The teacher next year is new to our school. Although she has some experience with children with autism, she has mostly worked with students with learning disabilities.

PARENT: I trust your judgment and know that you hire only the best teachers available to you. However, if she does not have specific training in working with children with autism, I am going to request that my son not be assigned to her class. No Child Left Behind requires special-education teachers to be highly qualified, and the unique needs of my child require someone with both the proper credentials and experience.

SCHOOL PERSONNEL: We have some thoughts about transition services, but our transition coordinator is not available for today's meeting, so we will defer this discussion to next year's annual IEP meeting.

PARENT: I appreciate your recommendation about deferring the discussion to the next meeting, but my son is already in the sixth grade and it's critical that we begin discussions about his transition to middle school as well as high school. I am requesting that we reconvene in thirty days and that the transition coordinator be present. Please ask her to bring to the meeting information regarding the district's various programs for middle school, high school and adult students.

TEEN TRANSITION PLANNING

No sooner than you've found the right combination of services, treatments and environments for your child's education, it will be time to start planning her transition out of school. At least, that's how it will seem. In reality, you won't have to start thinking about it in earnest until just before the teen years—when your child is twelve.

The law requires the IEP team to develop an official transition plan for your child's life after school by the time he is sixteen. Before you begin that long series of meetings, you will need to think critically (**Advocacy Principle 3**) about your child's interests, strengths, aptitudes, abilities and academic progress. Proactive planning is vital, because the process of thinking through, planning for and creating an ideal living situation for a person on the autism spectrum may take a long time.

The IDEA of 2004 recommends starting to think about the future immediately, so a child with disabilities can be prepared "for further education, employment and independent living."[7] It indicates that discussion of this important transition should begin no later than the very first IEP meeting, so that transition services can be in effect by the time the child is sixteen.[8]

QUESTIONS ABOUT THE TRANSITION

Questions to consider as you start the transition planning process:

- What skills does your child have?
- What issues (such as limited speech, rigid behaviors, tantrums, etc.) may make it difficult for your child to work with others?
- What interests does your child have?
- What has your child excelled in—even if not job-related?
- Would he benefit from remaining in high school past the age of eighteen?
- Does he have an interest in attending college? If so, what type of college is most appropriate?
- What financial and other resources are available?
- What job and skills training programs are available?

At your child's transition IEP, be a team builder (**Advocacy Principle 6**). Invite key representatives from the Department of Rehabilitation, Social Security, independent-living facilities and job programs, as well as the high school's college counselor, to discuss the options. Make your child a part of this process as well. It is important that you know the direction she wants to go in before you go to the meetings, even though you will hear more about her prospects at the meeting itself. Without her agreement, the program will not work. As soon as she becomes eighteen, you legally lose your right to make educational decisions for her, in the absence of conservatorship.

Transition plans can take several years to complete. Use the meetings to become as well informed as you possibly can (**Advocacy Principle 2**). Consider them part of your education on the way to becoming an expert in the many opportunities for you and your child to consider. Ask questions and document all the information you obtain, so that you can do follow-up research (**Advocacy Principle 5**). It is critical that all of the services recommended be well documented.

Early Occupational Training

Any transition plans that are set in place with the IEP team will require action. Suppose that by the time your child is fourteen, he has shown strong aptitude for computer skills and expresses an interest in working in data processing after graduation. As a part of his transition plan, your child may begin leaving school early a few days a week to work with an aide at a data-processing office. The vocational rehabilitation office can not only help set up such an arrangement, but they will provide the support. Before starting this job, your child will be taught appropriate social skills for the office, along with important office procedures.

A teen who prefers to be outdoors may be more suited to work with a forestry department or community landscaping project. Autistic students with musical talents or aptitude in sports can look for ways to pursue those interests, just like any other teen planning a life after high school. Those who have academic aptitude may prefer to go on to college. As long as the goals are adjusted appropriately and you begin planning the transition early, there is no reason not to base a plan on your child's skills and preferences.

A long transition period also allows autistic students to experiment to find the best fit. Many professionals believe that three or four different job experiences during the transition, while he is still in high school, can help assess the match between a teen's interests and his capabilities. Started early enough, a structured transition period, carefully planned with the help of an IEP team, can offer your child many advantages and help ensure a smooth start to the next important phase of his life.

When students turn twenty-one or graduate (whichever comes first), they lose the educational benefits afforded by most federal and state statutes. (Some states, like California and Illinois, allow developmentally disabled students to stay in high school until age twenty-two.) For that reason, many parents are well advised to keep their autistic children in school until they have the basic education and living skills they need for a successful adulthood.

Preparation for Adulthood

As you begin thinking about your options for your child's future life as an adult, heed the advice of Mary Anne Ehlert, founder and president of Protected Tomorrows, which specializes in helping people plan for the future of adults with special needs: "You have to be candid with yourself. What will this person really be able to do on his own?"[9]

I understand how challenging this is; it means separating what you had hoped your child would be capable of achieving from what he is actually able to do. Answering this question may require the assistance of the doctors, therapists and others who work with your teen.

Whatever options you choose (or assist your autistic child in choosing), they must be things he can realistically and safely accomplish. Some parents of children with Asperger's syndrome or high-functioning autism allow their young adults to make their own decisions about whether to attend college or not, and about what kind of living arrangements they prefer. This is perfectly appropriate for an autistic young adult who has the skills and ability to handle complex decision making, money management and daily life.

If independent living isn't an option, your child still may be able to live in his own place with a roommate and with assistance. Living with siblings and other relatives may be possibilities. Even autistic adults living independently may require help and support when facing adult issues such as transportation, interaction with law enforcement agencies, voting, military service, dating, marriage, financial management, health and safety.

You will need to determine whether it is appropriate for your young adult to make his own decisions or whether you should obtain power of attorney that allows you to make his decisions—or something in between.

The adult with more involved cognitive challenges and fewer life skills may not even have the ability to understand the implications of giving his parents power of attorney. If not, parents may file a legal document seeking full or limited conservatorship. They will then be able to extend their responsibilities for their autistic child into his adulthood, including arranging for long-term care.

Autism alone does not decrease a person's life span. The reality is that many autistic adults will outlive their parents, as children do. You must consider carefully who will step in to care for the autistic adult once you pass away or in the event you become incapacitated.

To make such decisions, you must fully research what resources are available from both federal and state sources, including Social Security, medical, housing and other benefits. In addition to the many laws governing education and public accommodations, there are laws prohibiting discrimination in housing and employment that apply to autistic adults.

FOR THE EIGHTEEN- TO TWENTY-ONE-YEAR-OLD AUTISTIC STUDENT

- **Life-skills Training.** Many states have residential independent life-skills centers where autistic adults can learn to live independently. Many of these centers offer one- to four-year programs, like colleges, but the focus is on life skills, not academics. There may be state funding available for some portion of such programs.
- **Power of Attorney.** When an autistic child turns eighteen, he is an adult. Parents no longer have the right to make decisions for him unless they have a power of attorney or a conservatorship ordered by a court.

- **Housing Options.** Autistic young adults have a variety of options: living at home with parents; living alone in an apartment, with or without agency assistance; living with a roommate, with or without agency assistance; a group home with six to eight other residents and around-the-clock supervision; or an institutional setting, which is normally for those with severe disabilities.
- **Social Security and Medicaid.** When your autistic child turns eighteen, he should apply for Medicaid and for Supplemental Security Income, a form of Social Security benefits. To qualify, he must have assets of no more than $2,000. If he has greater assets, such as money from an inheritance, a special-needs trust should be established to protect those resources.
- **Special-needs Trusts.** Parents should consider establishing a special-needs trust: a legal instrument that allows you to provide supplemental financial support for your autistic adult child. Consult with an estate-planning attorney or other professional to develop the trust.
- **Discrimination Issues.** Federal and state laws prohibit discrimination against autistic teens and adults in the workplace and in housing. Employers have a legal obligation to make reasonable accommodations if doing so does not constitute a substantial hardship. For example, an employer may be required to dim the lighting or lower the volume of noise in order to accommodate an autistic person's sensory issues.
- **Work and Day-care Centers.** Most states have work centers, adult day-care centers and other structured programs for autistic adults. Many provide free or low-cost transportation, skills training, job coaches, assistance with résumé writing and interviewing, and other services to help autistic adults find and keep jobs.
- **Recreational Programs.** Many states offer structured recreational programs for adults with autism, including Special Olympics, dances and other social gatherings. These programs can make the difference between an autistic adult having regular social contact or being isolated.
- **College Options.** Many junior colleges, colleges and universities have programs that are appropriate for autistic

adults. If your child attends college, he may be entitled to reasonable accommodations under Section 504 of the Rehabilitation Act to assist with note and test taking and other aspects of navigating the campus. (This act does not provide services such as occupational and speech therapy, one-on-one aides, behavior therapy and other services available under IDEA.)

All parents dream of and imagine their children's futures. When our children are neurotypical, we assume that they will gradually mature and take the reins, making a good life of their own. Not all autistic children can have that future. By thinking ahead, you can start planning for your child's life as a young adult, even when he is still an early teen. Advocacy involves long-term, even lifetime, engagement. In the event that your child does not finish high school until she is twenty-one, or is unable to work and live independently, you will have to continue to make plans and watch over her. Coordinating the life of an autistic adult will be a far more manageable task if you begin to lay the foundation for it in the first years of high school. Enlist your IEP team to ensure that your child's education leads directly to your well-informed expectations about what life may be like for him as an adult. The IEP team will help decide what related services and support will be required to realize that future.

Transition services can help prepare your child to live on her own, give her adaptive skills and expose her to a variety of job-related experiences, depending on her interests and education. Although generally these services can be provided up to the age of twenty-one, your own state may provide services for an even longer period of time. The cutoff varies. It may be governed by the date when the student meets her goals or when she graduates from high school. Check now to confirm the duration of the services available in your state.

ADVOCACY CHALLENGES

With every school year, many of the teachers, therapists, evaluators, aides and sometimes even school administrators on your IEP team may change. Since you will be working with this constantly shifting team from the time your child is three until she is nineteen or even twenty-one, it is inevitable that you will not always agree with every member of the team. When those differences are reflected in IEP offers that you cannot accept or strategies that are not working for your child, you will have to take a stand as an advocate.

It is not uncommon for IEP plans to require adjustments. Usually, these adjustments can be made by calling another IEP meeting and providing the evidence. You may be met with resistance over certain issues, but generally these issues can be resolved by further discussion. Unfortunately, that's not always the case. No matter how hard you work at it, there will not always be consensus.

Complaints don't result only from disagreements with your IEP team. In certain cases, the school administration may recommend that you file a claim or complaint, because the school does not have the authority to resolve the issue. Suppose, for example, you have paid $10,000 for private therapy called for by the IEP plan and would like to be reimbursed by the school district. The school administrator, therapists and teachers do not issue reimbursements; your only recourse is to file a complaint, and your IEP team may well encourage you to do it. The same is true if you and your team decide that your child would be best served by going to a private school with special facilities and you feel warranted in asking the district to pay the tuition. Your IEP team will not have the authority to approve those tuition payments, so, again, you will need to file a claim.

When you file a complaint that results in putting a good program in place for your child, the IEP team will respect you for being a strong advocate who took action on behalf of your child.

Sometimes my clients express concern about alienating their child's teachers or being labeled "troublemakers" by school administrators or their IEP team if they file a claim. As we've seen, that's not necessarily the case. But either way, advocating for your child is not about being popular. It's about protecting the rights of your child. If you have made reasonable efforts to address a dispute with your district and your efforts have failed, stand up for your child. As long as you are professional, avoid personal attacks on individual teachers and administrators and have a good-faith basis for your claim, move forward with confidence and conviction.

Filing a Due-process Complaint

At the conclusion of an IEP meeting, the district will make what is called an offer of FAPE. This will include its recommendations regarding placement and services. If you agree with the entire offer, you can sign the IEP and it will become effective immediately.

Before you sign, make sure it includes all the services you discussed, as well as their frequency and duration. If something is not in the IEP document, the school has no legal obligation to provide it even though it may have been discussed in the IEP.

If you disagree with the school's offer, *do not sign* the IEP. You have the right to file a due-process complaint with an administrative office established by your state's department of education. As a result of your filing, you and your school district will be given the option to participate in voluntary mediation or to proceed to a hearing before an administrative law judge. This is not a jury trial like you may see on legal television shows; it's a hearing where attorneys examine and cross-examine witnesses and introduce documentary evidence. But hearings, which can last from one to thirty days or more, can certainly involve some of the high emotions and drama portrayed in TV trials.

Due-process complaints can involve complex legal issues and hours of expert legal testimony. Although parents can represent themselves, in most cases, both parents and schools are represented by attorneys who specialize in education law. The decision of the judges can be appealed in federal court and taken all the way to the Supreme Court. It's not unusual for a single case to last three to five years, costing school districts and parents hundreds of thousands of dollars in legal and expert fees. Most parents are at a disadvantage at a due-process hearing. Not only do they have the legal burden of proving that the district's offer is not adequate, but they also usually lack the financial resources of the school district. The expense discourages most families from filing due-process claims.

If they win the case, parents are entitled to be reimbursed for their legal fees, but they will not be reimbursed for expert fees. Furthermore, they are likely to have been required to pay their attorneys ahead of time. This advance (also known as a "retainer") can run in the tens of thousands of dollars.

With few exceptions, IDEA does not provide for monetary damages. The "damages" include compensatory special-education services, reimbursement for educational costs and related expenses, and attorneys' fees, assuming you are the prevailing party. (If you are seeking monetary damages, you may speak to an attorney about civil rights and discrimination laws, which provide private citizens the right to money damages against school districts. These cases are filed in state and/or federal court.)

Pending the filing of a due-process complaint, a child's education program is in "stay-put" mode, which means that, until there is a resolution, the child remains in the same placement with the same services provided on the last signed and implemented IEP document.

You have every right to file due process; just go into it with your eyes open. It's a huge commitment of money and time, but many families have successfully won cases against their school districts and have even had their victories confirmed by the appeals court. I won one of my first educational cases many years ago on behalf of a child with learning disabilities, ADHD and severe behavioral issues. In this matter, the school had failed to initiate assessments or an IEP despite the mother's repeated requests for assistance and the child's demonstrated lack of academic progress over a couple of years.

However, an overwhelming number of cases are settled in mediation (the same is true of most civil cases filed in state and federal court). If your case is well prepared and supported by objective evidence, there is a high probability that you and your child's school will reach a prehearing settlement. As an advocate, you can assist your attorney by having maintained and organized all school documents, evaluations, assessments, invoices and correspondence between you and the school. As difficult as it is to compromise, in most cases, mediation makes sense. It gives the parties an opportunity to craft an agreement, have certainty in the outcome and bring closure to the matter. In most states, districts will voluntarily pay all or some of a parent's attorney fees in mediation. Mediation also mitigates the adversarial nature of a hearing, which requires testimony from the teachers and staff who work with a child. After listening to school staff testify, parents often feel betrayed and angry. Such feelings can undermine the teamwork that is necessary to support a child in the classroom.

If the offers to resolve your case by the district during a mediation fail to address your major concerns, consult with your attorney and be prepared to proceed to hearing. Policies are often made or changed when individual citizens use the litigation process. The rights of disabled people have been expanded by decades of disability-rights litigation.

Before filing a due-process complaint, do your homework. Check with the state office that administers special-education hearings and determine what percentage of parents in your area prevail. Research the administrative law officers, getting copies of decisions they have issued as judges. Many of them are attorneys who formerly worked in the government or in private practice. Try to determine, based on their prior history, whether they have a predisposition to support districts or parents.

Be warned that school districts can also file due-process complaints against parents. When this happens, it is called "reverse due process." Many districts do so to gain a strategic advantage and to prevent parents from getting reimbursed for attorneys' fees. If parents refuse to sign the IEP plan and the district senses they are going to file a complaint, the district may file first, placing the parents on the defensive. Even if parents successfully defeat the school district's claim, they lose any rights to attorneys' fees.

Think critically (**Advocacy Principle 3**) before filing for due process without representation by an attorney. This is not a plug for lawyers, but an acknowledgment of the complexity of special-education hearings. You can count on your district being represented by skilled counsel who will cross-examine your witnesses, and make opening and closing statements and evidentiary objections that can undermine your entire case. There are many nonprofit agencies that provide low-cost or sliding-scale rates for parents who don't have the money to pay an attorney's hourly rate. Your state and county bar associations can provide you with names of special-education attorneys or nonprofit legal-aid agencies in your area. It is important to know that once there is a determination that the district's offer is FAPE, you will have a difficult time making subsequent changes to your child's IEP.

SHOULD YOU FILE A DUE-PROCESS COMPLAINT?

If your answer to most of the following questions is "no," you are not yet ready to file a due-process complaint.

1. Are you prepared to have your child testify at a hearing? Even if you don't call her as a witness, the school district may.

2. Is the expert who has evaluated your child in classroom settings prepared to testify that the district's program is not adequate?

3. Do you have objective evidence to support your claim, such as test results, progress reports, journal notes, etc.?

4. Have you provided the school district with copies of the evaluation reports on which you plan to rely and given them an opportunity to provide FAPE?

5. Does the benefit of the requested service outweigh the legal expense, emotional investment, time commitment and potential stigma in the school district that are likely to accompany a due-process hearing?

Filing a Compliance Complaint

With a due-process complaint, a parent challenges the school district's IEP offer of placement and services. By contrast, a compliance complaint is filed if a parent believes the school is not following the law or required time lines. A complaint can be made about an individual, a school, an entire school district or a statewide practice.

A compliance complaint would be appropriate, for example, if your child's IEP plan provided for one hour of speech therapy a week and the therapy was not being provided. In that case, the district would be "out of compliance" with the legal mandates of the IEP agreement. If your efforts to have the therapy provided are unsuccessful, you could file a compliance complaint to force the district to "comply" with the terms of the IEP.

This kind of thing can happen because the school is short of trained staff. Budgets are being slashed in schools and, despite the fact that you've been promised a qualified therapist in your IEP, the school doesn't have the funding to provide it. Maybe your child's speech therapist quit. You've notified the school and asked for a replacement, but it's been months and nothing has happened. When you speak to the principal, he may even encourage you to file a compliance complaint, because without funding, his hands are tied.

Before filing a complaint, however, you must do a little homework. To find out which state agency is responsible for administering educational complaints, go to your state's department of education Web site or call its main office to request that information.

After the appropriate agency receives your compliance complaint, they will assign an investigator. Be prepared to explain the situation to the investigator, but also provide supporting documents for your claim. For example, if your compliance complaint states that speech therapy wasn't provided for two months during the first semester of the school year, you will need copies of the IEP itself showing that the service was approved. You will also need copies of any logs from therapists, notes from teachers, notes from your own journal (e.g., documenting the times your child failed to receive services) and letters to the school voicing your concerns. The investigator may also ask the names of potential witnesses who have information about the complaint, as she may want to interview them.

This is your opportunity to make your voice heard. Propose a clear resolution to the problem. For example, you may suggest that the school hire a full-time, on-site speech therapist within thirty days or contract with an outside private agency to provide ten hours of speech therapy to make up for the hours that have been lost.

Make your information precise and accurate, so the investigator can complete the investigation quickly. Based on the results of the investigation, the agency will issue a report that explains the issues, sets out the legal requirements, and makes findings. The report should indicate whether any violation has been found, and if so, what actions the agency must take to fix the problem, with appropriate time lines.

Resolving Expulsions and Suspensions

Some parents assume that, simply because their child is autistic, he cannot be disciplined or held accountable for his behavior. This is untrue. In fact, it's not uncommon for children with autism to get suspended or even expelled for aggressive behavior toward teachers, school personnel or other children. IDEA 2004 permits the school to suspend any disabled child—including children with autism—or place the child in an interim program for up to ten days, if he violates a "code of student conduct."

If the school wants to suspend your child for longer than ten days, it must convene an IEP meeting to determine whether or not his behavior is a manifestation of his disability. When this happens, you may request a functional-behavioral-analysis assessment, an assessment designed to determine the origins or antecedents that may have caused the behavior. It also helps professionals develop a program of positive support and reinforcement to actively prevent the behavior in the future.

If, after the assessment, the school concludes that your child's behavior was not related to autism, the school can discipline him like any other child. IDEA 2004 does not require the IEP team to reassess whether the child's IEP and placement are appropriate (and thereby contributing to the behavior). The law requires the IEP team only to determine whether the child's behavior "was caused by or had a direct and substantial relationship to the child's disability" or whether the behavior was the "direct result of the local education agency's failure to implement the IEP."[10]

Unfortunately, sometimes schools remove autistic children without formally expelling or suspending them. They simply send them to the library, the principal's office or the computer lab for hours. On an ongoing basis, these informal removals can easily add up and impede your child's education. They also violate federal law.

Recently, Gabe's parents came to me for advice when he was on the brink of suspension. Gabe, the fourteen-year-old boy discussed earlier, often fell asleep in class. When the staff tried to wake him, he became agitated and swung at them with his fists.

Gabe was being sent home from school once or twice a month as a result of lashing out at his teacher. I recommended that his parents meet with the teacher and teacher's aide to discuss whether a functional-behavior analysis was required or whether the existing team could develop a more effective IEP plan.

After several meetings, the IEP team decided that the class placement was inappropriate and inadvertently contributing to the problem. Rather than constantly sending Gabe home from school, the team agreed that they could not meet Gabe's needs and that it would be better to enroll him in a special school for children with disabilities. Gabe's parents are optimistic about the ability of the specially trained teachers at the new school to provide Gabe with the kind of activities that will keep him from falling asleep in class.

As an advocate, you will have to be diligent to ensure that your child is not inappropriately removed from school. If a student is repeatedly being removed from class, it is a clear sign that either the school placement or the services are inappropriate. Under these circumstances, parents should request an IEP meeting to develop a behavioral support plan. The IEP team should consider additional services to address the behavior and, if necessary, a new placement.

RELY ON YOUR OWN JUDGMENT

Always remember that you are the best person to plan your child's education. As your child becomes a teen and later an adult, she may be able to participate in some or all of the choices. But even before then, the stakes are too high and the process too demanding for you to shoulder it all alone.

My client who goes to IEP meetings surrounded by loving relatives has it right: You need support—not only at the IEP meetings, but also as you familiarize yourself with the laws, the standards, and the legal options available to you. If friends and relatives are unavailable, build an empowerment circle with this particular function in mind. Be sure to offer the same support to the other parents in the circle. Whatever one of you experiences will provide growth and information for you all. Sharing your experience will help reduce the stress and provide you with an outside perspective.

If necessary, set up a consultation with a qualified legal counsel.

Keep this chapter and the previous ones available for reference when you plan for those IEP meetings, and check my Web site for articles and updates. These will all help support you through the process and give you up-to-date information about changing regulations.

Despite their complexity, IEP meetings are fundamentally about helping ensure that your autistic child is ready for the future. You can do this. As a parent advocate, you bring all the skills and experience necessary to make these meetings a success.

PUTTING IT INTO ACTION

1. If your child is in high school, make an appointment with her school guidance counselor to discuss college programs that may be appropriate.

2. At least a year before your child reaches eighteen, call a family meeting to discuss whether it's in her best interest for you to obtain a power of attorney. If your child is high-functioning, include her in this discussion. If your child is less high-functioning, she may not be able to give you a power of attorney, so you may have to obtain a court-ordered conservatorship. This process can be lengthy, so you need to plan ahead.

3. Identify a workshop or seminar in your community on special-needs trusts to determine whether it would be appropriate to set one up for your child.

4. If your child is not going to attend college, start to think about what types of jobs he may be able to do. Find someplace where he can volunteer for the type of work he would hope to do later. Identify other any resources that may assist with his preparation, such as job coaching, skills training or part-time work.

CHAPTER 12

In the Community: Integrating Your Child

When Marty was in first grade, he was invited to a classmate's party at the gymnasium. It sounded like the perfect place for Marty to play. He could jump, tumble, run around and even shout if he wanted. To give him the comfort of a familiar face, his eight-year-old sister, Morgan, came along.

You probably know where this story is going. To my surprise, the gymnasium party was not ideal for Marty at all. The host had organized a series of games that required the children to wait in line and follow very specific instructions. It was fine for children without autism, but not at all compatible with an autistic child. Frustrated by the wait and unable to focus on the instructions, Marty soon refused to participate. As he stubbornly turned his head away, his eyes locked on the trampoline lessons going on at the other end of the gym. Every attempt I made to redirect him only made him more determined to jump on that trampoline. At one point he pulled away from me and actually started crawling up on it!

The teacher scowled and the parents of the class complained. When I brought Marty back to the party, the host asked sternly if I would "watch Marty, since he's not following the rest of the group." Embarrassed, Morgan asked me why Marty was "ruining the little boy's party." The tension was building. I had to keep telling myself, "Stay calm. You can do this. If you walk out of every challenging situation, you and Marty will be locked in the house for the rest of your days!"

I needed to employ **Advocacy Principle 4**. Instead of giving in to frustration and discomfort, I called on myself to be proactive and speak up.

I explained the situation to the host of our party, who was unaware that Marty was autistic. Then I took Morgan aside and talked to her. "Marty isn't intentionally trying to ruin the party," I told her. "He's just overstimulated by all the activities, and the rigid structure of the party is a bit too much for him. He assumed he could run and play freely, like he does on the playground. It's nobody's fault. It's just what it's like when you live with autism."

After multiple walks outside and experiments with different activities, we finally found a game Marty enjoyed. So we played that game for the remainder of the party. After a while, the other children came over and joined us. Although it didn't go as we'd planned, both Marty and Morgan had a good time. And I was proud of the fact that I had been able to stand my ground, to help Marty engage with the other children, to educate a few adults about autism, and to even laugh a little at the situation.

As an advocate, you need to prepare yourself for these moments. Develop affirmations to give yourself strength. Plan a brief explanation beforehand that you can use if you need to put your child's behavior in the right context for a stranger.

When your fight-or-flight urges kick in, it's always easier to head for the nearest exit. But committed advocates expect more of themselves than that. Rise to the occasion. Impress yourself. Every time you accept the challenge and step into the fray as an advocate for your child, it will make you stronger, more confident. And that strength will make it easier the next time.

STRATEGIES FOR SUCCESS IN THE COMMUNITY

Fortunately, it's getting a little bit easier for autistic children to take part in community activities. Because of the growing prevalence of autism, many public parks, restaurants and movie theaters are beginning to offer special programs that accommodate children with autism. Many AMC theaters, for instance, sometimes offer particular showtimes where the volume on the film is turned down and the loud, startling trailers are eliminated. Such accommodations are not just the right thing to do; they are a smart thing to do, since they allow these public places to tap into new markets and revenue streams, thereby creating a win-win situation for the parents, their children, and their communities.

Local Activities

Children with autism spectrum disorders can attend children's programs like those at the local YMCA, Girls and Boys Clubs or sports teams. They can even take part in organized classes, such as dance, music and art, and join special-interest clubs on any topic from bird-watching to the latest computer games. Even if your child does not participate to the same degree as other children, exposure to these activities will help him build confidence and social skills. While your child is engaged in these activities, you will have a chance to meet parents with similar-aged children.

If there are staff members leading a program, be sure to explain your child's situation. Sharing information about the strengths, preferences and interests of your child will allow them to focus on his abilities, rather than his inabilities. All too often, behavioral problems are highlighted and autistic children develop a "reputation" that doesn't convey the whole picture. I've found that staff in these settings are sometimes even willing to receive basic training in autism spectrum disorders when it's offered.

In most settings, you will need to advocate for the special accommodations that your child needs to be successful:

- Routines that are somewhat consistent.
- Visual schedules showing the routine.
- Drawings or photos explaining activities to come.
- Warnings ahead of time for any transitions or changes.
- Knowledge of the child's communication system.
- Limits, boundaries and rules to provide clear and consistent expectations.
- Modifications to the nature and duration of some activities.
- Additional adult support.

Tell the staff the strategies that help calm your child and explain what they can do if he is having a difficult time. The more people know, the less they fear. As parents, we have learned that, even though autistic behaviors can be alarming at first, there really is nothing to fear—just a lot to understand.

Parties and Invitations

As a parent advocate, you need to have a sort of PR strategy for your child's social life. For a child without autism, this approach would seem a bit extreme, but the truth is, if you don't intervene in your child's social life—at least at first—it may never get off the ground.

You cannot rely on your child to initiate relationships; nor can you assume that he will be invited to parties and other social events. If your child is in a general school setting, a lack of social skills can make other children assume she isn't interested in parties or other activities, such as playing on a sports team. These children's parents may make similar assumptions when they plan parties at holidays and birthdays. In your application of **Advocacy Principle 7**, you must go out of your way to educate them in this regard.

Start by hosting your own event. Invite both parents and age-appropriate peers. Select activities that you know your child enjoys and tolerates well, so that she's relaxed and in her element. With the right environment and positive reinforcement, the others will see your child in the best possible circumstances. Do what you can to give her an opportunity to shine.

These settings also allow you to let other parents see the behavioral interventions that work well for your child. It is a subtle way of demonstrating that even the most unusual behavior can be redirected. And it gives them a good model for what they might do in the future, if your child is visiting their house on her own.

On the heels of these experiences, take it upon yourself to develop a strategy for playdates, school field trips, sleepovers, movies, family outings and the wide array of other activities that young children are invited to attend.

If your goal is for your child to develop friendships and participate in activities with children without autism, you will have to be actively involved. Unlike other children who make friends in class, on the soccer team or on a routine trip to the park, the process is less organic for autistic children. It requires premeditation on your part!

Vacations

Recently, the Autism Society of America took two thousand people with autism to Orlando because Walt Disney World had developed special accommodations, such as front-of-the-line passes for autistic children who find it difficult to wait in long lines. Other theme parks, including Sea-World and Busch Gardens, also have similar programs. Resorts like Club Med and cruise lines like Norwegian, Carnival and Disney are also trying to be more inclusive of special needs for their organized activities.[1]

Families traveling with autistic children can now alert many airlines in advance to obtain special accommodations, as well. Delta Airlines has developed a special training program for its staff to help them understand more about autistic travelers.

TRAVEL TIPS

If you are traveling with a child with autism spectrum disorder, here are some tips from the experts to make the experience easier:

- **Call ahead.** Preparation is the best defense. Call the airline and the hotel, resort or cruise line of your destination. Inform them of your child's condition and ask what special accommodations are available. Ask for any special considerations you need, such as a refrigerator, a quiet inside room, etc.
- **Control the environment.** Be sure to select an environment your child can handle and come prepared to make adjustments as necessary. Bring your own sheets, pillows or anything that will make your child more comfortable.
- **Do an autism check.** Talk online with other parents who have taken their autistic children to this location. Simply Google the destination and "children with autism." Sometimes you can join a chat and connect with local parents.
- **Go off-season.** Not only are most vacation spots, cruises and resorts less expensive in the off-season, but they are less crowded too. The staff will also have more time to devote to your needs.
- **Create privacy.** Travel by car if you think flying will be too difficult. Opt to stay somewhere you can take some of your meals in your room.
- **Have an explanation ready.** Be forthright in explaining the situation to those you meet. Memorize a few lines that convey

what you want to say about your child to strangers. Jot down a few from the "What to Say" sections in previous chapters, in case people are rude. And then relax.

- **Prepare your child.** Develop "social stories," complete with pictures, that explain to your child exactly what you will be doing and where you are going.[2]

YOUR TEEN AND THE COMMUNITY

Your teen will need your help to adjust to the peer pressure, the need to fit in and be cool and the many social encounters they face. I'm sure I don't have to tell you how difficult the teenage years can be—whether or not a disability is involved!

When autistic children become teens, they are at a distinct disadvantage. Their lives suddenly revolve around the very nuances and subtle cues that are the most opaque to them. It can be a time of frustration and heartbreak. Like any teen, they may not know it when they make a social faux pas, but they can feel the pain of rejection quite clearly.

This predicament may motivate you more than ever to get involved in your teen's social life, but, ironically, adolescence itself sets new limits on parents' involvement. In her address to the Cambridge Center for Behavioral Studies, Catherine Maurice described the very typical reactions of her thirteen-year-old autistic daughter, Anne-Marie. "She has friends, she argues with me about clothes, and her chief embarrassment, of course, is me—especially when I open my mouth to say something in front of her peers, or, God forbid, actually sing in public."[3]

To help your teen integrate into the social community, you must first accept that you can't do it alone. Your role as a parent and authority figure is inherently suspect to your teenager. This is a healthy development, made more complicated by the fact that your child may not have the social skills he needs to find acceptance among his peers.

You need other adults and experts to assist you. Check your local university to find out if they offer social-skills programs. Many community colleges and universities sponsor mentoring programs for autistic teens. Washington University in St. Louis has a program that pairs college students with teens, as in Big Sister and Big Brother programs. It is especially designed to give teens mentors who can model for them and advise them about socially appropriate conduct.

With a greater level of autonomy, your teen may be ready to volunteer at a college or hospital. Volunteering is a good way to show your teen how her own particular fascinations can bring her rewarding connections in a larger community. An interest in dinosaurs, for example, can lead to part-time volunteer work in a museum, or even an internship on a dinosaur dig. An overwhelming interest in LEGOs can be the ticket to a LEGO Mindstorms competition and a whole world of opportunities in robotics. Community experiences can not only enrich your child's life, but be a wonderful way to build lasting relationships and a firm foundation of self-esteem.

Parents have to be keenly aware of the many new and varied challenges that teens face and use those six or seven years before their teens will be adults to help them develop strong social skills. Otherwise, autistic teens will become isolated adults.

Autistic teens are more likely to be socially awkward because they typically have an inability to read social cues. The nuances conveyed by facial expressions and body language are often missed by an autistic child. High school is rife with sarcasm, wry humor, constantly changing slang and even derogatory remarks that cannot be understood literally. The inability to gauge these nuances of social interaction may make an autistic teen seem out of touch or even rude, which makes it even harder to make friends and fit in with his peers.

Many common autistic behaviors, such as rocking or screaming, can create a powerful stigma. Let's face it, teens have been known to ostracize their peers for far less! Even wearing unpopular shoes or not knowing the latest songs can be a subject for ridicule in the unforgiving social milieu of high school.

The discernment you have been practicing through **Advocacy Principle 3** will come to your aid now. Your encounters with caregivers, school boards and strangers require you to put these principles to work on an almost daily basis. (We've talked about some examples in the course of this book, but trust me, you will have many more situations to apply them to in every area of your life!) Every time you improve your discernment by thinking critically about a health-care worker's proposal or a new possibility for treatment, you prepare for a moment like this, when you can use that discernment to help your child even more directly.

Use those critical-thinking skills now to identify the behaviors that present the greatest challenges for your teen. Think about what you know. What has been the most effective in modifying her behavior over the years? In which areas does she seem most able and willing to adapt? Apply **Advocacy Principle 3** to come up with an effective intervention strategy.

Once she has improved her social skills, seek out opportunities for her to participate in activities such as proms, dances, sports events, movies and other functions geared to teens. Organizations such as the Help Group[4] sponsor special training programs that teach teens specific social skills, such as prom etiquette and dance moves. If you can't find a class in your area, take responsibility (**Advocacy Principle 1**) for getting your teen that training anyway; start a group or ask your therapy team to create a program targeted for the particular activity. By taking the initiative, you can avert many of the issues that will make your teen vulnerable to difficult social situations and eventual isolation.

BULLYING

Bullying takes many forms on a school campus. Hitting, pinching, tripping, name-calling, derogatory remarks, stealing, sexual harassment, threats and physical violence may be involved. It can happen anytime your child is around others—on the playground, in the hallways, in the bathrooms, in the classroom and even on the Internet. The bullies may be older students, peers, teachers or other school staff members.

I am currently representing five autistic children from Las Vegas, Nevada, who were repeatedly bullied and abused by their special-education teacher. Four of them are nonverbal. One of the mothers discovered the abuse by noticing a bruise on her son's head. Other parents were concerned when their children would not ride the bus and would cower when adults approached them. An investigation revealed that the teacher had been physically and verbally abusing these children over a period of months. If the parents hadn't noticed something was wrong, these vicious acts might have gone undetected and the abusive behavior would have continued.

Autistic children are easy targets for bullies. A nonverbal child is defenseless against taunts. A verbal student who can't read social cues is equally vulnerable to wisecracks and even physical abuse.

Bullying is unacceptable. Period. If your autistic child is being bullied—or is bullying someone else—you must put an end to it immediately. There are no excuses and no exceptions.

Teachers, school administrators, staff, parents and students must accept responsibility for identifying, reporting and intervening to prevent such conduct. In recent years, numerous suicides—as well as homicides, such as at Columbine—have been attributed to bullying.

If you have been waiting to pick your battle, pick this one. This is a battle to win. If you even suspect your child is being subjected to bullying, speak up and take action.

- **Learn the warning signs.** Get in the habit of asking your teen about the details of her day. Listen carefully for any unusual changes in schedules or activities. With a nonverbal teen, you will have to rely entirely on other clues, such as bruising, excessive crying, irritability or uncharacteristic behaviors, including the sudden onset of aggressive conduct.
- **Talk openly with your child.** Make sure he understands what constitutes inappropriate conduct from teachers, staff and other students. Even if your child is nonverbal, you can use pictures, social stories and other visual tools to communicate appropriate and inappropriate behavior in the classroom. According to Kidscape.org.uk, children and teens are sometimes reluctant to talk openly because they are afraid: (1) the bully will retaliate, (2) they will be labeled a tattletale or snitch, (3) others won't believe them. You can defuse these concerns by teaching your child that he has the right to be safe and bullying is harmful. If your child isn't comfortable talking with you, let him know that he can also speak with a school counselor or another adult he trusts. The important thing is for him to talk and confide in someone.
- **File a written report** immediately with the school principal if you suspect your child is being bullied. Send a copy to the superintendent of schools. You should also call for an IEP

meeting. The team will need to address the situation. You may decide that your child needs more intensive services to help him protect himself and to learn to report bullying.

- **Increase supervision.** Depending on the nature of the bullying and where it occurred, you may also decide that more adult supervision is required. For example, the team may conclude that an adult aide needs to be in the hallway during transitions, or that your teen needs a one-on-one aide for safety reasons. This new level of support needs to be written into the IEP and implemented immediately.
- **Monitor the situation very closely.** Continue to check in with your teen every day. Ask specifically about the people who have been involved in bullying and how they behaved that day. Be aware that a child who has been bullied has a heightened sensitivity to pressure. Try not to make him feel he's being bullied into talking about whether or not he was bullied.
- **Take legal action.** Be prepared to take more aggressive action, if necessary—filing a police report, contacting the Department of Social Services, making a complaint to your local school board, contacting the media or even filing a civil rights action against the school and/or the parents of the perpetrator. If the school has been placed on notice of the conduct and they fail to take corrective action to prevent the bullying, a police complaint and civil action may be your only alternatives. These actions have to be filed in state and/or federal court, so you will need to consult an attorney.

The bottom line is that bullying is intolerable. Your forceful advocacy may not only shield your child from abuse, but it can directly result in a change of school policies that protect other children as well.

BEHAVIORAL INTERVENTION FOR YOUR TEEN

Although children and teens with autism are often the brunt of bad behavior, their own behavior can also be a substantial problem. As

MSNBC.com reported, "When a thirteen-year-old Minnesota boy was banned from church after parishioners complained about his behavior, it exposed a painful truth so politically incorrect that some people feel guilty just saying it out loud: Some autistic children can be annoying and disruptive in public."[5]

Some children and teens with autism may have violent tantrums, scream or make loud noises, or act aggressively. Even adults who understand that these acts can be a way to express pain may find that their patience is stretched past the limit. Uncontrolled, problems such as these can rip apart a family, making family routines and public outings stressful and traumatic for everyone involved. Ordinary activities, such as getting ready for school, having a family meal, making a trip to the store or spending a Saturday at the park, become burdensome.

Not only are these behaviors upsetting to the entire family, but they require elaborate accommodations. A family can feel trapped and under siege by a child who becomes violent or out of control in public. Sadly, it's quite common for families to stay home to avoid the social humiliation, not to mention the physical and emotional risks of going out!

This reaction is understandable but unfortunate, since it actually makes the problem worse by giving the teen fewer chances to learn how to behave in public. But the reality is that severe problem behaviors can create significant impairment to a family's functioning and quality of life.

Don't rule out behavior intervention for teens and young adults. Yes, it can be more difficult than when they were younger to get the kind of cooperation you would like. Intervention earlier in childhood is ideal, since it can help reduce this type of resistance and lay important groundwork for the teen years, when your child is bigger, stronger and more intimidating to others when he behaves in unconventional ways. But even teens who did not have behavioral intervention as children can learn to improve their behavior.

For example, some children with autism have a difficult time assessing the appropriate amount of space to allow between themselves and others when they are holding a conversation. An autistic person often gets so close—even to a perfect stranger—that it makes the other person uncomfortable. This can lead others to avoid the conversation, which only creates further isolation for the autistic child. However, this behavior can be addressed with very specific interventions that teach personal space and boundaries, such as having the child extend his arm to ensure that he is standing at least an arm's length away during all social interactions.

With an autistic child or teen, more time may be spent on each skill, and the behavior being modified is different, but to some degree this approach employs the same sound teaching skills that can be applied to any student. Catherine Maurice, author of *Let Me Hear Your Voice*, says she is an advocate of ABA because of the children it continues to help on a daily basis:

> As time goes on, I have seen many different rates of progress in children who are receiving behavioral intervention. I have spoken to parents whose children have been in therapy for five years and will probably continue to need some sort of support for most of their lives. I've seen children who, after two years of intervention, are now enrolled in first grade with normal peers. And yet I have seen very few if any of these parents abandon Behavioral Analysis. . . . [It] has given them a model of effective teaching. It has truly empowered them to make a positive difference in their children's lives, even while they may be searching for other biomedical solutions.[6]

The important thing is that the intervention chosen—such as a social-skills class or private therapy—or the strategy used to change the behavior respect the interests and desires of the teen. Children with or without autism often do not want to do things that parents force them to do for their ultimate benefit. However, teens and young adults with autism have long-developed preferences that should be respected. Always alert the professionals conducting treatment to your child's preferences, so collaborative treatment plans can be developed.

ASSERTING YOUR LEGAL RIGHTS

Your child has a right to be out in public, taking advantage of what the community has to offer. Even if he exhibits autistic behavior. Even if that behavior is strange or upsetting to others.

A restaurant manager, for instance, cannot ask you to sit in another area because he is concerned about other customers' reactions to your child's vocalizations. If your teen joins a fitness club, the club cannot require him to be accompanied by a companion at all times, unless there is a specific, demonstrable safety risk.

These are acts of unlawful discrimination and they infringe on your child's rights. As a parent advocate, it's your responsibility to learn those rights—in order to stand up for them.

WHAT TO SAY. . .

MANAGER: We are getting complaints from other customers that your child is making too much noise. If you can't control him, we are going to have to ask you to leave.

PARENT: My child has a disability and, as I am sure you are aware, there are federal laws that prohibit discrimination against individuals with disabilities in public places, such as restaurants.

MANAGER: I am not discriminating against you or your child. I am simply doing my job and responding to the other customers who are complaining about the noise.

PARENT: I appreciate that you are trying to do your job. However, singling my child out, when there are other children here making noise, is a form of discrimination. So although you may not be intentionally discriminating, when you request that my child be quiet while allowing the others to make noise, you are discriminating against him.

MANAGER: Maybe I can move your family to another table, where your noisy child won't bother the other customers.

PARENT: Thank you for the offer, but we are enjoying our table. Moving the complaining family may be the best option.

Most states have adopted laws similar to the ADA and the Rehabilitation Act of 1973 (Section 504).[7] These state and federal laws prohibit discrimination in public places against anyone with disabilities.

These federal laws specifically protect "qualified individuals with disabilities." To be a "qualified individual," your autistic child must be able to participate in the situation. So, for example, if your adolescent daughter with autism wants to swim in a public swimming pool and she is medically allowed to swim, the pool management cannot turn her away because of her disorder. (Religious entities and private membership clubs are exempt.)

"Discrimination" occurs when your child is treated differently from others because of her disability. If she is capable of participating in the same setting as others, without danger, she has every right to participate.

In addition, public accommodations are required to make reasonable modifications to enable anyone with a disability to participate. If one or both federal laws apply, then a public program must offer the same services, in the same setting, and at the same costs to a person with a disability as it would to a person without a disability.

"Public accommodations" are, generally speaking, places that provide public services. These places are required by law to make reasonable changes in their policies, if it makes it possible for your autistic child to participate. Just as a store may be required to waive its no-animal policy to allow for a Seeing Eye dog, so a day-care center may be required to allow a trained therapist to accompany your child on a field trip.

SUMMARY OF ADA

The Americans with Disabilities Act requires that public places must:

- Include children with disabilities, unless their presence would pose *a direct threat* to the health or safety of others, or require a fundamental alteration of the program.
- Make reasonable modifications to their policies and practices to integrate children, parents and guardians with disabilities into their programs, unless doing so would constitute a fundamental alteration.
- Provide appropriate auxiliary aids and services needed for effective communication with children or adults with disabilities, when doing so would not constitute an undue burden.
- Make their facilities generally accessible to persons with disabilities. Existing facilities are subject to the readily

> achievable standard for barrier removal, while newly
> constructed facilities and any altered portions of existing
> facilities must be fully accessible.[8]

Parents often struggle with how they should respond and whether they are in fact being unlawfully discriminated against. In the Minnesota case I mentioned, the judge barred the teenager from the local church services based on testimony of the priest that the severely autistic, "225-pound teenager was disruptive and dangerous, that he spit, wet his pants, made loud noises and nearly ran over people while bolting from the church after services." While the boy's mother insisted that was an exaggeration, other members of the congregation agreed with the statements made by the priest and the judge accepted their word.[9]

The public's response to this case reflected deep divisions in public opinion and a greater need for parent advocates to educate others (**Advocacy Principle 7**) about the nature of autism. Although public awareness and acceptance are growing along with the autism epidemic itself, there are still people like syndicated radio talk-show host Michael Savage who defined autism for his eight to ten million listeners in this blatantly uninformed way: "I'll tell you what autism is: In 99 percent of the cases, it's a brat who hasn't been told to cut the act out."[10]

Every time we stand up for those rights, we are standing against this kind of bigotry and ignorance—just as surely as if we were carrying banners around the White House with the women suffragists, demonstrating against apartheid with the Bantu, or marching with the students in Tiananmen Square.

The defense of human rights—for our own autistic children or anyone else—belongs to a long tradition. When the United Nations was formed to protect rights and freedom around the world, the first Article of its Declaration of Human Rights said:

"All human beings are born free and equal in dignity and rights. They are endowed with reason and conscience and should act toward one another in a spirit of brotherhood."

The Advocacy Principles that empower you to defend your child's rights to go to Sunday school or swim at the YMCA place you in proud company, alongside those who have fought to pass the laws that protect those rights.

ADVOCACY THAT GETS RESULTS

The law may not always be on your side, but most of the time, with a little ingenuity and compassion, you can get results anyway. Even if, like me, you can quote chapter and verse from the law, the legal route is not always the most effective approach. Sometimes, as the saying goes, you can catch more flies with honey!

Church is a big part of our family's rituals and traditions. The loud gospel music, two-hour sermons and thousands of members at First AME in Los Angeles were not easy for Marty. He would squirm, make loud noises and fidget throughout the service. We worked with his therapist to develop a specific behavior plan just for attending church. We brought along a few of his favorite toys to distract him. At first, one of us would take him outside for breaks throughout the service, but over time, he was able to tolerate the entire service. Now, he even participates in the singing and other rituals, such as kneeling and communion. Our biggest surprise was when he started hugging other church members during the designated time!

Religious celebrations are a big part of many families' traditions. Parents should be proactive in discussing their children's needs and be willing to contribute to help the church develop opportunities for their child to join them in worship. This could mean educating staff about how to respond to difficult behavior, offering to assist with other special-needs children during the service, or requesting special seating arrangements with access to exits. Luana Garrison worked with her church to create a Sunday-school program for special-needs children. Dr. Dwayne and Naomi Cox started a ministry at their church for parents of special-needs children.

At our own church, I made it a point to meet with the pastor and several of the ministers to tell them about Marty's condition. It was important to let them know what to expect. To bring the congregation into the loop, they agreed to have a local celebrity activist speak about disability issues at one of the services. The presentation not only educated those who knew little about special needs, but it helped other parents with special-needs children feel more comfortable telling their own stories.

After that day, we sat in a special section of church and invited other families with disabled children to sit near us. Yes, we were separating ourselves, but we were also banding together to support one another. And if it got a little noisy, there were no unwelcome stares. Attending church continues to be a community outing that we share as a family.

PRACTICING TOLERANCE AND ACCEPTANCE

In social settings with an unpredictable mix of strangers, it is not always easy to know how much noise is acceptable for an autistic child to make. All of us wonder when a child should be removed from the situation for her own good and the good of those around her. How do we recognize those moments? Is it possible to accommodate the needs of strangers without infringing on the rights and well-being of our own children? Can there be any rules at all, when every situation and every-one's opinion seems to vary?

In our society, we all share unspoken rules of appropriate behavior. Most of us consider it rude if someone cuts in front of us to grab a park-ing space or shouts into their cell phone in a crowded elevator. Our first assumption, whether or not it is correct, is that these people are indulg-ing themselves at our expense.

But even in the most common of everyday interactions, the social lines of consideration and politeness can be blurred. Personally, a baby crying at a school play wouldn't bother me. But what if it bothers my neighbor? Should the mother take the baby outside and miss her child's performance for the sake of that neighbor? What about the unhappy woman seated on a long flight next to a 350-pound man whose body overlaps the armrest between them? Should the airline require the man to buy two seats? Or should the woman learn to be more tolerant?

When you are trying to determine limits for your own autistic child, you have to ask these questions—even if there's no definitive answer—and then try to do the best you can. In my practice, I've developed a few questions to help my clients identify the line between respecting their children's rights and respecting the rights of others.

- Is the behavior your child is engaged in something that is harmful to him or to others—such as biting, kicking or hitting? If it is, not only is it in the child's best interest to be redirected, but it's not reasonable for anyone else to have to endure this type of behavior. If this is a problem, remove your child from the situation for now, but seek out behavior therapy to help him control these impulses.

- Is there a simple and nonintrusive way to moderate or control the behavior so as to minimize the imposition on others? For example, can you move to another seat in the movie theater, so that every time your child stands up, she doesn't block someone's view? It's both simple and considerate.

- Is there is a game, a piece of candy, or a toy you can always keep with you to help your child regulate her behavior? If so, don't leave home without it.

- How important is the activity to your child and your family? Once you identify those things that matter to your family, you will automatically know where to pick your battles. Why waste time on battles at the shopping mall if it's not a high priority? When important outings are causing conflicts with others, you can work harder to create a win-win situation.

In the early years, when Marty was first diagnosed, we were not quite sure what he could take or how quickly he might be able to adapt. How long would he sit quietly in a movie theater? If we introduced him gradually to crowded shopping centers or busy parks, would his tolerance improve? What was an acceptable level of noise and disruption? We had to find our own answers, as every parent with an autistic child must do.

While we were still looking for the right boundaries, we attended the funeral of a distant relative. My daughters and I sat in one row of the church; my husband and Marty in another. Before long, Marty started making noise and my daughter whispered to me that her father should take Marty outside.

At first, I anxiously thought she might be right, but when I glanced around to see who was being disturbed, I changed my mind. My eyes fell on one dear friend or relative after another. And almost every one of them had some "trait" the rest of us had had to put up with over the years. We loved them in spite of that "trait." Or maybe because of it. That's the way it is with families. If we can accept the aunt who gets drunk every Christmas or the teenager plugged into an iPod and unwilling to speak, why can't we accept an autistic little boy who makes funny noises and can't sit still in church?

It was a moment of insight for me that I've never forgotten. Although we can't expect everyone to make allowances for us and our unique idiosyncrasies, it's good to be reminded that we're such a diverse society. Every time people in a public setting interact with a child who has special needs, the noises and movements of that child become more tolerable and familiar. It's important to set limits and look out for other people's rights, while protecting our own. But at the same time, exposure to differences can help promote understanding and break down stereotypes. We have to live within a margin of tolerance for all kinds of behavior going on around us. And I believe that learning to accept diversity does us good.

PUTTING IT INTO ACTION

1. Identify five accommodations that would help your child participate in a public setting, such as a park or swimming pool. Is it important, for instance, that she have consistent routines? Will she need to be warned ahead of time about transitions? Are there things you could explain about her style of communication that would help the staff? Have these accommodations ready and meet with staff ahead of time to discuss them, whenever it's necessary.

2. Choose three replies from the "What to Say" sections of this book that appeal to you most. Ask a friend to play the opposition and practice saying them until you can remember the reply without reading it.

3. Adopt the habit of asking your autistic child or teen about the details of her day. It's far better to make this a regular practice now. If you start asking only once you sense that something's wrong, it may make your child defensive.

EPILOGUE
_____

It Begins with Hope

*[We] reject the cynicism that tells us that these kids can't
learn; that those kids who don't look like us are somebody
else's problem. The children of America are not "those kids"—
they are our kids—and we will not let them fall behind. . . .
Not this time.*[1]

—*Barack Obama*

When I graduated from Harvard Law, I was given the opportunity
to work with some of the country's foremost civil litigators at a
corporate law firm on Wall Street that had offices in twelve
countries. I represented Fortune 500 companies in commercial disputes
where millions of dollars—rather than the rights of individuals—were at
stake. With the generous compensation package, the skyline view of New
York from my office on the thirty-fifth floor, and dinners at the hottest
restaurants every week, it was such an exciting life that, for a fleeting moment, I thought: What more could a poor girl from the projects want?

The answer was: a lot.

No matter how much I appreciated the pleasures of that life, I knew
I needed to do something that would have an impact on *people's lives*,
not on corporations.

What I could not anticipate was that my decision to leave that glam-
orous Wall Street life would lead me to the same long road that advocates throughout history had trudged before me. With the birth of my
own autistic son, I soon found my true calling as an advocate—not only
as a special-rights attorney, but as a mother.

Our need to advocate for our special-needs children is as compelling today as it was forty years ago—before the passage of civil rights legislation or disability rights laws. Fortunately for us, the civil rights icons—like Martin Luther King, Jr., Julian Bond, Rosa Parks, Andrew Young, James Farmer, Robert Burgdorf, Tony Coelho, Tom Harkin and thousands of others—have made the way clear.

By standing up as advocates, we have an opportunity to walk in their great footsteps and take part in the vital and historic struggle for human rights—a struggle that today involves the more than fifty-four million Americans living with disabilities and the hundreds of millions who love and care for them.

When we cradle our autistic children in our arms and gaze into their eyes, the love that fills our hearts is reason enough for us to defend their rights. But we are doing more than that. By defending these rights, I believe that we are defending our humanity as well.

What does it say about us, as human beings, if we do nothing while the strong trample the weak? How can we stand silent while any innocent group of people is denied their rights over an accident of birth? We are better than that. As human beings, we may be fully capable of discrimination and intolerance, but we need not accept it.

As advocates, we have an opportunity to take a stand for the better parts of our nature. With patience and compassion, we can educate others to do the same. When we face obstacles that seem insurmountable—whether great or small—we can band together to encourage one another. And, when all else fails, we can stubbornly cling to an abiding sense of hope.

In the darkest hours, it was a stubborn sense of hope that pulled Pat Grayson Dejong through. Her son Christopher was diagnosed with autism at age three. For two years, Pat worked hard to help him develop language skills, but by the time he was five, he was only partially verbal and still showed aggressive behavior. Believing that a school environment might speed his progress, Pat tried to enroll Christopher in kindergarten.

This was in the early 1970s, before the passage of the IDEA, and the public school refused to enroll him. The administrator told her flatly, "We don't educate children with autism here. Christopher belongs in the local school for the disabled."

Pat knew that school was not appropriate for her son, but there were no public programs for students with autism and very limited private school choices. So Christopher was enrolled.

Three months later, the principal called a meeting to discuss Christopher's progress. His assessment was harsh and unforgiving. He told Pat that Christopher didn't belong in the school and said that she would save herself and her family a world of pain if she would place her son in an institution.

Pat wept, but she believed in her son. She knew he had the ability to speak and learn. She vowed to make a difference—not only for her own child, but for any others who might be subjected to a similar indictment. Joining forces with the Autism Society of America, she advocated for a local classroom specifically devoted to children with autism. In 1975, just months before the passage of the IDEA, the Los Angeles Unified School District opened its first and only classroom for autistic children. Christopher was one of the eleven students enrolled.

Becoming an advocate for her son changed Pat's life. She went back to college and became a special-education teacher, then a school administrator and, ultimately, the head of Los Angeles United School District's autism department, where she brings that same stubborn hope to the lives of more than five thousand children.

Today, Christopher is forty years old. He lives in his own apartment in Los Angeles, catches the bus to his girlfriend's house twice a week, plays on a basketball team at the Special Olympics, and recently traveled alone to Santa Barbara to participate in a tournament.

LIFE WITH AUTISM

Many parents wonder what the future will hold for their autistic child. They worry that their son or daughter will stay isolated, housebound and out of touch with the world. They ask if it's possible to live a full, rewarding life with autism.

As the following examples have proven, the answer to that question is yes! It is not only possible to lead a good life; it is possible for some to reach the heights of achievement in our culture. Only a small percentage of any group ever reaches those heights. The fact that there are examples among people with autism and Asperger's syndrome should be encouraging for parents everywhere.

- **Temple Grandin** may be one of the most famous autistics. She is a bestselling author and a consultant on livestock behavior with a PhD in animal science. Grandin is highly respected for her work in autism advocacy.
- **Tim Page** is a Pulitzer Prize–winning music critic for the *Washington Post*. His 2007 article in *The New Yorker* described how long it took to identify the source of his "lifelong unease." Page explains his experience further in his memoir, *Parallel Play: Growing Up with Undiagnosed Asperger's*.
- **Caiseal Mor** is a bestselling fantasy novelist and a musician. An Australian of Irish descent, Mor is known for the lavish book and album covers he designs himself. Although he was diagnosed with autism as a child, it was disclosed only in his 2007 autobiography, *A Blessing and a Curse: Autism and Me*.
- **Heather Kuzmich** is a fashion model with Elite Model Management in Chicago. Kuzmich is best-known as one of the final five contestants on the television show *America's Next Top Model*.
- **Dawn Prince-Hughes** is an anthropologist, primatologist and ethologist with a PhD in interdisciplinary anthropology from Universität Herisau in Switzerland. Formerly the executive director of the Institute for Cognitive Archaeological Research, she is associated with the Jane Goodall Institute. In her book *Songs of the Gorilla Nation: My Journey through Autism*, Prince-Hughes describes how her work with gorillas helped her learn how to manage her condition.
- **Michelle Dawson** is an autism researcher who has challenged the scientific foundations of applied behavior analysis (ABA) interventions. Dawson argues that too much emphasis is placed on compensating for autism, on the assumption that it is a flaw. Dawson believes more could be learned from determining how the autistic brain works.
- **Vernon Lomax Smith** is a professor of economics at Chapman University, who shared the 2002 Nobel Memorial Prize in Economic Sciences with Daniel Kahneman. After studying at

Caltech, the University of Kansas and MIT, Smith received a
PhD in economics from Harvard. He is currently an adjunct
scholar of the Cato Institute in Washington, D.C.

PUTTING IT INTO ACTION

1. Identify two ways that advocacy can make a difference within
your own family and initiate these actions today. Examples may
include advocating for:

- more involvement with the family from your autistic child
at mealtime
- playdates with new friends for your child
- quality time alone with your partner every week
- better communication with your child's teacher or
caregivers
- an hour a day of private relaxation for yourself.

2. If you would like to get more involved in advocacy outside your
home, look into these possibilities in your community:

- volunteering at a nonprofit special-needs organization
- joining an autism support group
- lobbying local school boards and commissions for needed
services
- getting a graduate degree with a specialty in autism
- speaking at your church, community groups and PTA
meetings
- participating in policy advocacy to promote legislative
changes
- creating fund-raising events for autism research
- joining autism fund-raising events, such as marathons
- starting a blog to promote greater tolerance and acceptance
for autism.

Frank Bowe, the professor who led the sit-ins in 1977 for Section 504,
said the popular assumption is that real change is brought about by
those who have reached the end of their rope, who feel downhearted and
fed up with the way things are. But actually, that's rare. As an aide to

Martin Luther King, Jr., once said, "People think revolutions begin with injustice. They don't. A revolution begins with hope."[2]

As a parent advocate, you are the keeper of that flame. Long after you have mastered the principles of everyday advocacy, it is your abiding hope that holds the promise of a better future—for your child and for the generations to come.

Glossary of Key Terms

Accommodations: Changes made to an environment to make it more conducive to a person with a disability. For example, an accommodation for a student with a hearing impairment might be a seat in the front row of a class.

Administrative hearing: A hearing conducted following the filing of a due-process complaint before a state hearing officer. Administrative hearings are minitrials, but there are no juries.

Alert Program: A program that teaches individuals to self-regulate their levels of stress.

Alternative Dispute Resolution: A process used to settle legal disputes that avoids a hearing or trial. For example, mediations are a form of alternative dispute resolution.

Americans with Disabilities Act (ADA) of 1990: Federal legislation enacted to prohibit discrimination against individuals with disabilities in the workplace and in public accommodations.

Antecedent: Events that occur immediately prior to a behavior.

Appeal: The process by which you challenge a final determination. For example, following a due-process hearing, each side has the right to appeal the decision to federal court.

Assessment: A process used by doctors and other professionals to determine an individual's strengths and weaknesses.

Audiology: Related to one's ability to hear.

Baseline: A determination of an individual's skills or abilities prior to interventions or medications being administered.

Basic skills: In a school context, a student's reading and writing skills.

Consent: The process by which someone affirms their agreement to something. In the school context, parents must give consent before their child can be evaluated by any school district personnel or agent.

Decoding: In the context of reading, the method of using phonics to sound out or read words.

Due process: The process by which parents challenge a school district's decision regarding placement, services, eligibility and other issues related to the district's obligation to provide special education services. A due-process hearing is a hearing that follows the filing of a due-process complaint with a state education office.

Early intervention: Therapy services provided to children usually between the ages of two and seven.

Executive function: The ability to organize and process information. Individuals with autism often have difficulties with executive functioning, and as a result, they often act impulsively.

Family Education Rights and Privacy Act (FERPA): Law giving families the right to inspect and correct their children's educational records.

Five-point scale: A visual aid that helps individuals with ASD identify their stress levels.

Fluency: The ability to read materials accurately and precisely. This term is often used in the context of assessing someone's ability to read.

Free and Appropriate Public Education (FAPE): A right provided to students with disabilities eligible for special education under the IDEA.

Frequency: How often a behavior occurs.

Generalize: To demonstrate a particular skill in multiple natural environments such as home, school, church, etc.

Hidden curriculum: Social rules or norms that most people learn through experience and observation, while those with ASD do not.

Hyperlexia: Ability to decode single words without the corresponding level of comprehension of words and texts.

Hypersensitivity: Overresponsiveness to sensory input.

Hyposensitivity: Underresponsiveness to sensory input.

Impulsivity: Behavior occurring suddenly, without warning.

Individuals with Disabilities Education Act (IDEA): Provides for the disabled to have a free and appropriate public education, protections and right to an education that is standards-based.

Joint attention: Ability to coordinate attention and share focus on an event or object; the awareness of the focus of another person's attention.

Mastery: Understanding and ability to utilize a particular skill.

Mediation: An information meeting between parents and a neutral third party designed to resolve disputes between parents and schools.

Modeling: Learning skills through observation.

Modifications: Substantial changes in curriculum in order to make it consistent with the ability level of a student with disabilities.

Paraprofessional: An individual employed in public school who must have at least a high school education and who works alongside a general curriculum teacher and special education coordinator.

Phonemic awareness: The ability to hear and identify individual sounds, or phonemes.

Phonics: The relationship between letters of written language and sounds of spoken language.

Primary reinforcers: Reinforcers that meet innate needs, such as food and water.

Priming: The process of reviewing material in advance in order to help a student master it. This is a form of preteaching that is often used with students with disabilities in general education classes.

Proficient: Solid academic performance; demonstrates competence.

Qualitative data: Informal, anecdotal information.

Quantitative data: Formal, numerical information.

Reasonable accommodation: A legal term indicating that a school, workplace or public place has altered its environment to make it more conducive to a person with a disability. For example, an employer who makes his lights softer to make it easier for the autistic worker to focus has made a "reasonable accommodation" as required by the Americans with Disabilities Act.

Remediation: The process by which an individual receives instruction and practice in skills that are weak or nonexistent in an effort to develop/ strengthen these skills.

Standardized test: A norm-referenced test that compares a child's performance with the performance of a larger group of similar children (usually peers).

Statutory rights: The rights protected by statutes enacted by a local, state or federal governing body.

Task analysis: Determining the difficulty level of a task and listing all the steps within it.

Theory of mind: The ability to think about and infer what someone else may be thinking or feeling.

Token reinforcement system: A system of rewards that is used to promote positive behaviors.

Transcript: An official record, such as school records and/or the transcribed recording of a hearing.

Acronyms[1]

ABA	Applied Behavior Analysis
ADA	Americans with Disabilities Act
ADD	Attention deficit disorder
ADHD	Attention deficit/hyperactivity disorder
ASD	Autism spectrum disorders
AT	Assistive technology
BD	Behavioral disorder
CARS	Childhood Autism Rating Scale
CDC	U.S. Centers for Disease Control and Prevention
CDD	Childhood disintegrative disorder
CFR	Code of Federal Regulations
CHADD	Children and Adults with Attention Deficit/Hyperactivity Disorder
CHAT	Checklist for autism in toddlers
CP	Cerebral palsy
DD ACT	Developmental Disabilities Assistance and Bill of Rights Act
DDT	Discrete trial training
EI	Early intervention
EIBI	Early intensive behavioral intervention
EMR	Educable mentally retarded
ESEA	Elementary and Secondary Education Act (aka No Child Left Behind)
ESY	Extended school year
FAPE	Free and appropriate public education
FERPA	Family Education Rights and Privacy Act
HHS	U.S. Department of Health and Human Services
IDEA	Individuals with Disabilities Education Act
IEP	Individualized education program

IFSP	Individual family service plan
ITP	Individual transition plan
LD	Learning disability, learning disabled
LEP	Limited English proficiency
LRE	Least restrictive environment
NCLB	No Child Left Behind
NIH	National Institutes of Health
NIMH	National Institute of Mental Health
OCD	Obsessive-compulsive disorder
OHI	Other health impairment
OSERS	Office of Special Education and Rehabilitative Services
OT	Occupational therapy
PASS	Plan for Achieving Self-Support
PBS	Positive behavioral support
PDD	Pervasive developmental disorder
PDD-NOS	Pervasive developmental disorder—not otherwise specified
PECS	Picture Exchange Communication System
PRT	Pivotal response training
PT	Physical therapy
RDI	Relationship development intervention
SCHIP	State Children's Health Insurance Program
SEA	State Education Agency
SID	Sensory integration dysfunction
SLD	Specific learning disorders
SLP	Speech and language pathologist
SSI	Supplemental Security Income
VBI	Verbal behavior intervention

Appendices

APPENDIX A
RECOMMENDED READING LIST

Books

Charman, T., and W. Stone. *Social and Communication Development in Autism Spectrum Disorders: Early Identification, Diagnosis, and Intervention* (New York: The Guilford Press, 2006).
- Teaches social and communication skills.

Firestone, Barbara, MD. *Autism Heroes* (London: Jessica Kingsley Publishers, 2008).
- Provides inspirational stories of families and their autistic children.

Gray, Carol. *Comic Strip Conversations* (Arlington, TX: Future Horizons, 1994).
- Teaches basic social skills to individuals with ASD.

Gray, Carol. *The New Social Story Book* (Arlington, TX: Future Horizons, 2000).
- Teaches play, emotion and communication skills to individuals with ASD.

Kearney, A. J. *Understanding Applied Behavior Anaylsis: An Introduction to ABA for Parents, Teachers, and Other Professionals* (London: Jessica Kingsley Publishers, 2007).
- Teaches parents how to develop and understand a behavioral treatment and management plan.

Koegel, Lynn Kern, and Claire Lazebnik. *Overcoming Autism: Finding the Answers, Strategies and Hope That Can Transform a Child's Life* (New York: Penguin Group, 2004).
- Provides information parents can use to implement a treatment plan for

their children and tells the inspirational story of a family and the doctor who worked with their son.

Leaf, Ron, MD, and John McEachin. *A Work in Progress: Behavior Management Strategies & A Curriculum for Intensive Behavioral Treatment of Autism* (New York: DRL Books, Inc., 1999).
- A guide to help parents develop and implement a behavior intervention program.

Richman, S. *Raising a Child with Autism: A Guide to Applied Behavior Analysis for Parents* (London: Jessica Kingsley Publishers, 2000).
- Teaches parents how to use ABA therapy at home and in the community.

Sundberg, M., and J. Partington. *Teaching Language to Children with Autism or Other Developmental Disabilities* (Walnut Creek, CA: Behavior Analysts, Inc., 1998).
- Teaches parents how to implement a verbal behavior plan.

Articles

"Psychosocial Treatment for Child and Adolescent Disorders: Empirically Based Strategies for Clinical Practice," Hibbs. E. D., and P. S. Jensen, eds. (New York: American Psychological Association Press, 1999), pp. 311–340.
- Describes empirically supported treatment for childhood mental disorders.

Paul, R., and D. Sutherland, "Enhancing Early Language in Children with Autism Spectrum Disorders," in *Handbook of Autism and Pervasive Developmental Disorders*, 3rd ed, vol. 2 (New York: John Wiley & Sons, 2005).
- Teaches language and communication skills.

APPENDIX B
SAMPLE ADVOCACY LETTERS[2]

These five advocacy letters provide examples for you to adapt to your own situation, rather than generic forms for you to fill in. Read them carefully and then create your own letters, suited to your child and circumstances.

Letter 1
Sample Letter to Special-education Coordinator
Requesting More Hours

Carol Beck, Special Education
Coordinator
Potter Street School
600 Haven Blvd.
San Ramon, New Mexico 80000

Dear Ms. Beck,

Thank you for talking with me on the phone last Tuesday about my request to secure twenty hours a week of discrete trial training for my son, Adam. I understand that he does receive some ABA in his LAUSD preschool setting, but I would like to get extended hours because Adam's team of professionals believes he will benefit from more discrete trial training. With twelve children in the Potter Street preschool class and only one aide, who has been absent a total of five days this month, the few hours he receives at school are not enough.

I would like to cite the National Institutes of Health report and a New Mexico State University report that both stated that ABA is the only proven and effective intervention for preschool children with autism. These reports also state that the more ABA the child is exposed to, the more beneficial his long-term outlook is for living a productive and independent life.

I have spoken with both Adam's developmental pediatrician and the Lanterman Regional Center psychologist, who also believe that he would benefit from an additional twenty hours of ABA work a week. As you may remember, I told you that we have a relationship with Itsy Bitsy Learners, a provider for the school district, which supplies these after-school discrete trial services. We were very happy with our previous behaviorist there, and if possible, would like to retain her again to work with Adam.

Please let me know at your earliest convenience when we can initiate the twenty hours a week of additional discrete trial hours for Adam. We can either have these done at the Itsy Bitsy Learners clinic on Melrose Avenue or in our home. I look forward to hearing from you. Please call me at 555-555-5555 upon receipt of this letter so we can discuss this in more detail.

Sincerely,

cc: Ben Reynolds, Early Childhood Special Education Office

Letter 2
Sample Letter Asking for Pre-IEP Meeting to Discuss Concerns

Ms. Susan Sample, Special Education
   Coordinator
Third Avenue Elementary School
123 Third Avenue
Oak Park, CA 90000

Re: Jerrold Smith, DOB 1-16-01
Fourth grade, Third Avenue
Elementary School

Dear Ms. Sample,

I am writing to request a meeting with you prior to my son's IEP this October. I have reviewed last year's IEP and I realize now that I didn't quite understand certain terms, especially about the scoring of assessments.

Also, I would like you and the other members of the IEP team to be aware that Jerrold still has some challenges that I will summarize in the following list. At age nine, Jerrold cannot:

- read labels or simple sentences
- tie his shoelaces
- hold a pencil or pen properly
- participate in group sports with his peers
- remember to flush the toilet
- stay seated for more than a few minutes
- play with peers or contribute to group discussions
- talk with peers (in fact, he has no friends in or out of school)
- stand in line without pushing other children.

I would like next month's IEP to address these concerns, which is why I am getting the list to you now, so that you may share it with those who work with Jerrold. They may have some ideas that we can incorporate into the IEP.

Thank you for your help with this matter. Please call me should you have any questions.

Best regards,

Letter 3
Sample Letter Documenting Failure to Implement IEP

Mr. Ralph Cousins, Principal
Third Avenue Elementary School
123 Third Avenue
Oak Park, CA 90000

Re: Breonna Haroldson, DOB 6-5-01
Fourth grade, Third Avenue
Elementary School

Dear Mr. Cousins,

In reviewing Breonna's IEP, I noted that she is to have speech therapy twice a week with Laurie Gwenn, Third Avenue Elementary School's speech pathologist. I have checked with both her classroom teacher, Carolyn Smythe, and her aide, Karla Baldwin, and found that after five weeks of school, Breonna has yet to have one session of speech therapy.

I would like to meet at your earliest convenience to discuss why my daughter has not yet received these valuable services and to discuss how the school might compensate her with additional services to make up for the missed sessions.

Please call me at 555-555-5555 as soon as possible so that we may get this situation corrected.

Best regards,

cc: Susan Sample, Special Education Coordinator
    Carolyn Smythe, Fourth Grade Teacher

Letter 4
Sample Letter to Request Additional Services

Mr. Ralph Cousins, Principal
Third Avenue Elementary School
123 Third Avenue
Oak Park, CA 90000

Re: Breonna Haroldson, DOB 6-5-01
Fourth grade, Third Avenue
Elementary School

Dear Mr. Cousins,

I am writing to set up a meeting with you regarding obtaining more adult supervision during recess and lunch so that my daughter Breonna is not left to fend for herself during these unsupervised times.

As you may know, Breonna has a one-on-one aide, Karla Baldwin, who takes her break when Breonna has recess or goes to lunch. This routine doesn't protect my daughter, as during these unsupervised times a number of challenging situations present themselves:

Today during lunch, no other students would let Breonna sit next to them, so she tried to eat her lunch standing up, her lunch box fell on the floor and the lunchroom supervisor yelled at her. Breonna became hysterical and I had to come to school to bring her home.

Two days ago, during recess, Breonna stood in line for handball, but never got a turn because the other children pushed past her.

Last week, again during recess, Breonna got lured into the boys' bathroom by two classmates and only the presence of Mr. Rand, the janitor, saved her from further embarrassment.

My goal is to give Breonna the opportunity to form relationships with her fellow students, and learn to stand up for herself. With the correct supports and modeling, this could happen. But this will never happen as long as she is left to fend for herself during these unsupervised times. We believe she needs more support. Please call me at your earliest convenience so that we can set up this meeting with you, her teacher, her aide and Susan Sample, the special-education coordinator.

Sincerely,

cc: Susan Sample, Special Education Coordinator
     Carolyn Smythe, Fourth Grade Teacher

Letter 5
Sample Letter to Legislator

Senator Don Perata, SD 09
State Capitol, Room 205
Sacramento, CA 95814

Dear Senator Perata,

I am a registered voter in your district. I am writing because my family and my community need your help. As you probably know, autism now affects one of every 150 children born in America. One child born every twelve hours in California will be labeled with ASD.

I urge you to introduce and support legislation that requires private insurers to pay for both diagnosis and treatment of ASD.

You may already know that a lifetime of support for an individual with autism costs $3.2 to $5 million, according to a 2008 study conducted by Harvard University. The cost to a family raising an ASD child from birth through high school is approximately $1 million. And that's just the cost in dollars; the emotional toll is much higher. Almost 80 percent of marriages involving children with ASD end in divorce, according to the Autism Society of America. Surely some of this marital stress is due to the financial burdens placed on the families raising children with autism.

I urge you to vote in favor of any Senate bill that relieves families of this incredible burden and places at least some of it squarely on the shoulders of the private insurance industry that in 2007 gave the CEOs of the top seven for-profit private insurance companies an average of $14.2 million each in total compensation—or enough money to buy almost eight thousand American families a year's worth of health insurance.

I believe it is unfair that individual families, public agencies and the public school systems carry this burden alone when private, for-profit insurance companies are raking in profits.

Thank you in advance for your support.

Sincerely,

APPENDIX C
STUDENT SELF-MONITORING IEP SHEET[3]

(The following chart can be modified to accommodate students in grades one through twelve. The example given is of a middle schooler's self-monitoring IEP sheet.)

SCORING:

0 = never   1 = not very often   2 = sometimes   3 = often (a lot)   4 = always

Name:_____ Date:_____

Time Period	Activity	Initiation and completes assign-ments	Accepts assistance	Monitors language style	Copes with stress	Uses graphic organizers	Writes multiple paragraphs
7:45–8:25	Homeroom						
8:30–9:15	Language Arts						
9:20–10:00	Math fun-damentals						
10:10–11:00	Adaptive PE						
11:00–11:45	Social Studies						
1:00–1:45	Science						
1:50–2:00	Music						
2:05–3:15	Resource Room						
	AVERAGE POINTS						

IEP GOALS:

1. I ask for clarification as needed and complete assignments 80 percent of the time.

2 When I'm feeling stuck and people try to help me, I focus on their words and any visual supports and use their help to solve my problem at least 80 percent of the time.

3. During conversation within my social group, I use appropriate words, tone of voice and facial expressions.

4. In my academic classes, I respond to situations using a socially acceptable statement and tone of voice.

5. I can identify my stress level using a five-point scale and ask for a break to calm down if I need it.

6. I can use graphic organizers to help me with my work.

7. I can write a report with at least four paragraphs, including an opening paragraph, two body paragraphs and one closing paragraph.

Acknowledgments

If you are fortunate in life, you will have, in addition to your close relatives, a couple of very special people in your life—individuals who love you unconditionally and who support you no matter what the circumstances. I have been blessed to have in my life more than my fair share of such people. Without them, this book would not have been possible.

From the day we met, more than twenty years ago, my husband, Ernest, has always been my biggest fan and supporter. Whether it was starting my own law firm, creating a nonprofit organization or venturing into the world of publishing, he has always been there with words of encouragement, expert business advice, an attentive ear and a strong shoulder to lean on. Words can hardly express my gratitude to him.

Ernest's supportive spirit set the tone for my two daughters, Michael and Morgan, who through this entire process pitched in and did double duty on the dishes and who didn't protest too badly when we had to cancel our summer vacation in order for me to meet the publisher's deadline.

My incredible son, Marty—whose birth changed my life forever and who never ceases to amaze me. His journey has become a vehicle through which I have the privilege and honor to help so many families. I am grateful to Marty, for his resilient spirit inspires me to do more.

And although they have passed on, thank you to my beloved mother, Doris, who was always so proud of me; and my grandmother Doveanne and godmother, Ethel, who gave unselfishly of themselves to raise me and who believed in me even when I didn't recognize the importance of doing so.

To my aunt Lois, the matriarch of my family, thank you for being there for me and encouraging me every step of the way.

To my father Ronaldo and stepmother, Kathleen; brothers, Eric, Tony, Rodney and Tory; my many cousins in St. Louis, Chicago and Peoria; my surrogate mom Luvenia; and aunts Luveta, Christine, Gwen, Barbara, Alberta and Ida; thank you for supporting me and teaching me important life lessons.

To my Los Angeles family, the Martin, Neely, Crosby, Goins and Taylor clans, who have always supported and encouraged me, thank you for your love and support. I also acknowledge and am eternally grateful to my many sister friends, Robin Miller, Terri Hamilton Brown, Patricia Brown (cousin), Cheryl Gully, Sherna Foucher, Karen Frison, Antonia Routt, Dr. Ruth Creary, Dr. Debra Frenchie and Vivian Mitchell, some of whom I have known since elementary school, and all of whom have supported me, encouraged me and loved me no matter what.

Thank you to the incredible staff at my law firm, Martin & Martin, LLP.—you helped me keep it all together and worked diligently to represent our clients while I was on sabbatical writing this book. I am grateful to you all for pulling together and allowing me the comfort of being away from the office in order to write. You are my dream team!

The amazing volunteers, staff and board of directors of Special Needs Network—Sonjia White, Annette Hollomon, Jan Davis, Kevin McCarthy, Dr. Andrew Yellin, Clarence Harris, Linda Vo, Elizabeth Bedart Ghani, Todd Hawkins and Pat Grayson Dejong—who work side by side with me to give a voice to underserved and underrepresented families, thank you for your support and, most of all, your friendship.

To the many clients of Martin & Martin, families of Special Needs Network, and friends who allowed me to share their very personal stories, this book would not have been possible without you. You are true heroes and I will never forget your generosity and kindness.

Thanks go to the professional team whose leadership has been invaluable to me from the writing of the book's original proposal almost two years ago and whose brilliance made this project possible. To my collaborator, Donna Beech, thank you for helping me find my voice. You are an amazing woman and talented beyond belief! I look forward to many more projects and years of sharing information and knowledge on topics that we both care so much about.

To my research assistant and parent extraordinaire, Prudence Baird: Our journey together began over a cup of tea at a local coffee shop and we haven't stopped collaborating and brainstorming. You are an amazing and compassionate advocate. Your assistance for this and so many of my projects has been invaluable.

To my agent, Laney Katz Becker of the Markson Thoma Agency, thank you for having the vision for this project, for pushing me to make it better and for being relentless in your quest to find this project a home.

To my publicity team, Jacquelyn Carrera, Leslie Garson and Michael Wright, you are the best in the business. I appreciate you and all that you have done to help me make autism and the struggles of families a widely talked about subject in the media.

To my editor, Tracy Bernstein, and the Penguin family, thank you for believing in me and partnering with me to make my dream a reality. Your support and expertise have been invaluable resources.

To my Special Needs Network fellow board member, attorney, law school classmate and good friend Bonnie Berry LaMon, you have been such a source of strength and inspiration to me. I truly appreciate you and your expertise.

To my fitness trainer, Del Millers—you told me to start writing, and every day during your grueling workouts you encouraged me. Thank you for keeping me in shape and for pushing me when I needed it. To Michelle Smith, Claudette Roche, Suzanne Sena, Jennifer Bryan, Eduardo Lucero, Rae Jones, Yvette Chappel and Reggie Ingram—your professional advice, expertise and smarts keep me looking good, feeling good and on top of my game.

To Los Angeles County Supervisor Mark Ridley-Thomas, California Senator Curren Price, Jr., California Assembly Speaker Karen Bass, United States Congresswomen Maxine Waters, Dianne Watson and Laura Richardson, Los Angeles City Councilmember Herb Wesson, Jr., California Senator Darrell Steinberg, Dr. Lou Vismara, Dr. Barbara Firestone and Dr. B. J. Freeman—thank you for your leadership on legislation, policies and issues that impact children and adults living with autism and related disorders. Your pioneering efforts are changing lives and communities.

To Dr. Lynn Koegel, thank you for agreeing to write the foreword to this book. Your work on behalf of children with autism is awe-inspiring. And most of all, thank you for spending a summer with Marty and me and for allowing us to experience your brilliance.

Thank you to Reverend Cecil "Chip" Murray for believing in me and inspiring me to write this book years before I even started the project;

for supporting me in the early days of Marty's diagnosis; and for teaching me some of life's most valuable lessons.

Thank you to Dr. Jim Sears, Professor David Wilkins and Suzanne Wright for your endorsement of the book. You all are doing amazing work and I am humbled by your acknowledgments.

Last and definitely not least, I am grateful to Dr. Phil McGraw, Jay McGraw and the entire team at Stage 29 Productions. Dr. Phil, thank you for endorsing the book, highlighting autism on your show, and for giving me a platform and a medium from which to talk openly about autism. Launching the book on your show is not only a dream come true, but an amazing opportunity to reach millions of Americans. Thank you, Jay, for giving me opportunities I never dreamed of. Dr. Phil and you have assembled an incredible team and I am honored to be a part of it.

Endnotes

INTRODUCTION: ADVOCACY MAKES A DIFFERENCE

1   Obama, Barack, "A More Perfect Union," Speech, Constitution Center, Philadelphia, PA, March 18, 2008. http://www.huffingtonpost.com/2008/03/18/obama-race-speech-read-th_n_92077.html (accessed August 2009).

2   Bush, George H. W., Ceremony for the signing of the Americans with Disabilities Act of 1990, July 26, 1990. http://www.eeoc.gov/ada/bushspeech.html (accessed August 2009).

3   Gray, C. Boyden and A. Stephen Hut, Jr., "Statement of Former President George H. W. Bush as Amicus Curiae in Support of Respondents," *The Board of Trustees of the University of Alabama, et al., vs. Patricia Garrett, et al.* Supreme Court of the United States, Case No. 99–1240. http://www.bazelon.org/issues/disabilityrights/incourt/garrett/presidentbushbrief.html (accessed August 2009).

4   Bush, 1990.

5   Kushner, Eve, "The Life and Spirit of Ed Roberts (1939–1995)," *The Monthly,* http://themonthly.com/feature-03-09-1.html (accessed August 2009).

6   Olkin, Rhoda, *What Psychotherapists Should Know about Disability* (New York: Guilford Press, 2001), p. 139.

7   "A Look Back at Section 504: San Francisco Sit-In a Defining Moment in Disability Rights History," National Public Broadcasting, http://www.npr.org/programs/wesun/features/2002/504/ (accessed August 2009).

8   Cone, Kitty, "Section 504 History: Disability Rights Education and Defense Fund," October 1996. http://www.dredf.org/504site/histover.html (accessed August 2009).

9   Mayerson, Arlene, "The History of the ADA: A Movement Perspective."

http://law.marquette.edu/s3/site/docs/psconference/history-of-ada.pdf
(accessed June 2009).

CHAPTER 1: FACING FACTS: GETTING A DIAGNOSIS

1   "Autism Speaks Responds to New *Pediatrics* Autism Study: New Findings Reinforce the Urgency of Autism as a Major Public Health Crisis, Requiring Intensified Action from the Public and Private Sectors,"Autism Speaks. http://www.autismspeaks.org/press/autism_nchs_prevalence_study_1_in_91.php?tr=y&auid=5412135 (accessed October 5, 2009).

2   England, Christina, "Autism, Cold Parents or Cold Society?"American Chronicle, March 29, 2009. http://www.americanchronicle.com/articles/view/96372 (accessed July 2009).

3   "Autism Spectrum Disorders, Changes in the California Caseload—An Update: June 1987–June 2007." http://www.dds.ca.gov/Autism/docs/AutismReport_2007.pdf (accessed June 2009).

4   Wallis, Claudia, "A Powerful Identity, a Vanishing Diagnosis," *The New York Times*, November 2, 2009. http://www.nytimes.com/2009/11/03/health/03asperger.html?_r=2&ref= (accessed November 2009).

5   Goldberg-Edelson, Meredyth, "Link Between Autism and Mental Retardation Lacks Data," Williamette University, August 7, 2006. http://blog.willamette.edu/news/archives/2006/08/link_between_au.php (accessed June 2009).

6   "Symptoms," Mayo Clinic, http://www.mayoclinic.com/health/autism/DS00348/DSECTION=symptoms.

7   Biel, Lindsay, and Nancy Peske, *Raising a Sensory Smart Kid: The Definitive Handbook for Helping Your Child with Sensory Integration Issues* (New York: Penguin Books, 2005).

8   To speak with an attorney about special-needs rights and/or legal concerns, contact me at www.martin-martin.net.

9   Special Needs Network is a grassroots nonprofit organization that I co-founded in 2005 to meet the needs of families and underserved communities who have been impacted by autism. For further resources on autism and special events, please visit: www.specialneedsnetwork.org.

10 Click the "Community" tab at top, then "Resources link" on the drop-down menu, then "State" tab for a list of facilities and professionals who will give a diagnosis of autism and a list of facilities and professionals who specialize in early intervention.
    For early intervention: http://www.autismspeaks.org/community/fsdb/category.php?sid=6&cid=83.
    For autism diagnosis: http://www.autismspeaks.org/community/fsdb/category.php?sid=6&cid=110.

11   Under the "For Parents" tab on the home page, the "Find a Pediatrician" link, which will take you to the "Referral" page. Accepting the legal release will open the page allowing you to fill in "Medical Specialty" or "Special Interest" for a list of relevant pediatricians. https://www.nfaap.org/net forum/eweb/dynamicpage.aspx?site=nf.aap.org&webcode=aapmbr_ prsSearch.

12   To find an ABPN-certified neurodevelopmental disabilities specialist: Click "Find a Board-certified Physician," then "Search Options." In the drop-down menu, click "Specialty/Location." Then "Child Neurology" and/or "Neurodevelopmental Disabilities."

CHAPTER 2: A NEW PERSPECTIVE: STEPPING UP

1   Sprang, Ginny, PhD, and John McNeil, DSW, *The Many Faces of Bereavement: The Nature and Treatment of Natural, Traumatic and Stigmatized Grief* (Routledge: New York, 1995), pp. 6–9.

2   LeMaistre, Jo Ann, PhD, *After the Diagnosis* (Berkeley: Ulysses Press, 1995), p. 5.

3   *New York Times* http://www.neurodiversity.com/main.html (accessed, June 2009).

4   Sinclair, Jim, "Don't Mourn for Us," International Conference on Autism, Toronto, 1993. http://ani.autistics.org/dont_mourn.html (accessed, October 2008).

5   Murphy, Wendy, Comment, Autism Resources, www.autism-resources.com/advice-to-parents.html (accessed June 2009).

6   "Rainfall Autism Theory," *BBC News*, November 4, 2008. http://news.bbc .co.uk/go/pr/fr/-/2/hi/health/7703072.stm (accessed June 2009).

7   Crawford, Laura Krueger, "Holland Schmolland," http://www.autismsociety .org/site/DocServer/Holland_Schmolland.doc?docID=3183 (accessed June 2009).

8   Sinclair, "Don't Mourn."

CHAPTER 3: ADVOCACY 101: THE PRINCIPLES OF ADVOCACY

1   Champy, J., "The Hidden Qualities of Great Leaders," *Fast Company*, December 19, 2007, 76: 2.

2   "Accepting Personal Responsibility," Livestrong, http://www.livestrong .com/article/14698-accepting-personal-responsibility/ (accessed June 2009).

3   Davis, Renee, "Three Hidden Qualities of Great Leaders," Men Today Online. http://mentodayonline.com/workplace/leader.html (accessed July 2009).

4   Rees, James E., and Stephen Spignesi, *George Washington's Leadership Lessons* (New York: Wiley, 2007).

5   Covey, Stephen R., *Seven Habits of Highly Effective People* (New York: Free Press, 2004), p. 206.

6   "Quotes of the Heart," HeartQuotes, http://www.heartquotes.net/teamwork quotes.html (accessed July 2009).

7   Covey, *Seven Habits*, p. 209.

CHAPTER 4: FAMILY CHALLENGES: ADVOCATING TO YOUR FAMILY

1   "The GFCF Diet for Ausim and PPD," AutismWeb. http://www.autismweb .com/diet.htm (accessed July 2009).

2   Harris, Sandra, PhD, "Sibling Issues,"Autism Society of America, June 21, 2009. http://www.autism-society.org/site/PageServer?pagename=life_fam_ sibling (accessed June 2009).

3   Kelly Anne Dolan Memorial Fund. http://www.kadmf.org/caring_IllChild. htm (accessed June 2008).

4   Harris, Sandra, PhD, *Siblings of Children with Autism: A Guide for Families* (Bethesda, MD: Woodbine House, 2003).

5   Mozes, Alan, "Health Needs of Autistic Children Often Unmet," HealthDay News, December 1, 2008. http://www.healthscout.com/template.asp?page =newsdetail&ap=1&id=621768 (accessed June 2009).

6   Seligman, Milton, and Rosalyn Benjamin Darling, *Ordinary Families, Special Children: Systems Approach to Childhood Disability* (New York: Guilford Press, 1997).

7   McGraw, Phil, PhD, "Life Strategies: Take Responsibility for Your Life," Dr.Phil.com, http://www.drphil.com/articles/article/230 (accessed July 2009).

8   Bickle, Laura, "Parent Time: 10 Habits of Happy Couples—Simple Ways to Keep Relationships Strong," *Today's Parent*, February 2006. http://www .todaysparent.com/lifeasparent/article.jsp?content=20060105_123722_ 4820&page=1 (accessed July 2009).

9   Godin, Seth, *Tribes: We Need You to Lead Us* (New York: Portfolio, 2008).

CHAPTER 5: FAMILY CHALLENGES: ADVOCATING TO YOUR GROWING CHILD

1   Kaufman, Raun K., "Building a Bridge: Breakthrough Strategies for Reaching Our Children," Autism Treatment Center of America, *Good Autism Practice Journal*, October 2002. http://www.autismtreatmentcenter .org/contents/reviews_and_articles/building_a_bridge.php (accessed June 2009).

2   Field, S., and A. Hoffman, "The Importance of Family Involvement for

Promoting Self-Determination in Adolescents with Autism and Other De-velopmental Disabilities," *Focus on Autism and Other Developmental Disabilities*, Spring 1999, 14:1, pp. 36–41.

3   Irwin, Marilyn M., "Sexuality Education for Children and Youth with Disabilities," National Dissemination Center for Children with Disabilities (NICHCY) News Digest, vol. I, no. 3 (National Information Center for Children and Youth with Handicaps, Washington, D.C., 1993). http://www.iidc .indiana.edu/CEDIR/sexuality.html (accessed June 2009).

4   Myles, Brenda Smith, Melissa L. Trautman, Ronda L. Schelvan, *The Hidden Curriculum: Practical Solutions for Understanding Unstated Rules in Social Situations* (Shawnee Mission: KS Autism Asperger Publishing Company, 2004).

5   Harrington, Kathie, MA, "Teaching the Person with Autism How to Drive." http://www.parentpals.com/gossamer/pages/Detailed/585.html   (accessed June 2009).

6   Irwin, "Sexuality Education for Children."

7   Ibid.

8   Although the name of the organization has changed, the acronym has remained the same as it was for the previous name: the National Information Center for Children and Youth with Handicaps.

9   Irwin, "Sexuality Education for Children."

10 "Autism Spectrum Disorders: Pervasive Developmental Disorders." http://www.nimh.nih.gov/health/publications/autism/complete-index.shtml (accessed July 2009).

11 Laugeson, E. A., et al., "Parent-assisted Social Skills Training to Improve Friendships in Teens with Autism Spectrum Disorders," *Journal of Autism and Developmental Disorders*, April 2009, pp. 596–606.

12 Irwin, "Sexuality Education for Children."

13 Wood, Daniel B., "Teens, Sex and Power of Parents," *Christian Science Monitor*, September 5, 2002. http://www.csmonitor.com/2002/0905/p01s03-ussc.html (accessed August 2009).

14 Irwin, "Sexuality Education for Children."

15 Ibid.

16 Harrington, "Teaching the Person with Autism."

CHAPTER 6: EMPOWERMENT CIRCLES: AVOIDING ISOLATION

1   Gratton, Lynda, and Tamara J. Erickson, "Eight Ways to Build Collaborative Teams," *Harvard Business Review*, November 1, 2007. http://harvardbusiness.org/product/eight-ways-to-build-collaborative-teams/an/R0711F-PDF-ENG (accessed July 2009).

2   Ferazzi, Keith, *Who's Got Your Back* (New York: Broadway Business, 2009).

3   Kerr, S. M., and J. B. McIntosh, "Coping When a Child Has a Disability: Exploring the Impact of Parent-to-Parent Support," *Child Care, Health and Development* 26:4, pp. 309–21.

CHAPTER 7: BALANCING A CAREER AND AUTISM: MAKING YOUR LIFE WORK

1   Schneider, Barbara L., and Linda Waite, *Being Together, Working Apart: Dual-Career Families and the Work-Life Balance* (Cambridge: Cambridge University Press, 2005).
2   Mozes, Alan, "Health Needs of Autistic Children Often Unmet," Medicine Net. http://www.medicinenet.com/script/main/art.asp?articlekey=94608 (accessed August 2009)
3   Katsarelis, Katrina, "Setting Boundaries at the Office to Balance Work, Family," *USA Today*, November 2002. http://www.usatoday.com/money/jobcenter/workplace/lifeworkfamily/2002-11-26-set-boundaries_x.htm (accessed May 2009)
4   Shiffrin, R. M., and W. Schneider, *Psychological Review* 84, (March 1977), pp. 127–90.
5   Briley, John, "When a Loved One Has a Serious Illness: Balancing Caregiving and a Career," RevolutionHealth.com. http://www.revolutionhealth.com/healthy-living/caring/caregiver/work/career-balance (accessed July 2009).
6   Katsarelis, "Setting Boundaries."
7   "Five Key Laws for Parents in Califiornia," Paid Family Leave California. www.paidfamilyleave.org (accessed August 2009).
8   "Strengthening Families and Communities," Organizing for America: BarackObama.com. http://www.barackobama.com/issues/family/index_campaign.php (accessed August 2009).

CHAPTER 8: NAVIGATING THE THERAPY MAZE: EDUCATING YOURSELF

1   Carlson, Doug, "First Words Can Speak Volumes," FSU Med, (Talahassee, Florida State Unitversity Press), Fall 2009, p. 24. http://issuu.com/fsumed/docs/fall2008 (accessed August 2009).
2   Geddes, Linda, "Earlier the Better for Autism Therapy," *NewScientist* 2657:6–7, May 21, 2008.
3   NICHCY was originally entitled the National Information Center for Children and Youth with Disabilities. When the name of the organization changed to the National Dissemination Center for Children with Disabilities, it was decided that the well-known abbreviation NICHCY would not be changed to match the new name.

4   "Overview of Early Intervention," NICHCY. http://www.nichcy.org/babies/ overview/Pages/default.aspx (accessed June 2009).

5   Taylor, Beth, "Microsoft Employees Collaborate to Craft Autism Benefit," *Puget Sound Business Journal,* May 10, 2002. http://seattle.bizjournals.com/ seattle/stories/2002/05/13/focus6.html (accessed July 2009).

6   Seo, Seonjin, Anne G. Bishop and Lisa K. Langley, "Special Educator Supply and Teacher Quality: The Critical Role of Teacher Induction," 2004 CEC Annual Meeting, New Orleans, LA. http://www.coe.ufl.edu/copsse (accessed September 2009).

7   "California Regional Centers See Big Jump in Clients with Autism," California Healthline, May 7, 2009. http://www.californiahealthline.org/ Articles/2009/5/7/Californias-Regional-Centers-See-Big-Jump-in-Clients-With-Autism.aspx (accessed August 2009).

8   "What is the Lovaas Method?" National Autistic Society, http://www.nas .org.uk/nas/jsp/polopoly.jsp?d=528&a=3345 (accessed July 2009).

9   "ABA. The Lovaas Method," *The Approach,* Lovaas Institute. http://www .lovaas.com/services.php (accessed August 2009).

10 Ibid.

11 Lindblad, Tracie, M.Sc., M.Ed., "ABA in Schools—Essential or Optional?" ABACUS: Help for Parents, September 2006. http://www.abacuslist.ca/ Client/ASO/ABA.nsf/object/ABA+in+School+full+article+edited/$file/ABA+ in+School+full+article+edited.pdf (accessed August 2009).

12 Lovaas, O. Ivar, "Behavioral Treatment and Normal Educational and Intellectual Functioning in Young Autistic Children," *Journal of Consulting and Clinical Psychology,* vol. 55(1), February 1987, pp. 3–9.

13 Reinke, Tom, "States Increasingly Mandate Special Autism Services," *Managed Care Magazine,* (August 2008.) http://www.managedcaremag.com/ archives/0808/0808.autism.html (accessed July 2009).

14 Landau, Elizabeth, "Choice Autism Treatment Offers Benefits, Has Limits," CNN, March 31, 2009. http://edition.cnn.com/2009/HEALTH/03/31/autism .applied.behavior.analysis/index.html (accessed September 2009).

15 Lovaas, "Behavioral Treatment."

16 "Practitioner Review: Psychological and Education Treatments for Autism," *Journal of Child Psychology and Psychiatry* 39:307-22, (March 1998).

17 "New AAP Reports Help Pediatricians Identify and Manage Autism Earlier," AAP News Release, October 29, 2007. http://www.aap.org/advocacy/releases/ Oct07autism.htm (accessed June 2009).

18 http://autism-therapy.suite101.com/article.cfm/biomedical_therapies_for_ autism

19 http://www.autism.com/DAN/index.htm

20 "The Price of Autism," Bio-Medicine.org. http://www.bio-medicine.org/ medicine-news/The-Price-Of-Autism-9735-1/ (accessed July 2009).

21 "Mich. part of growing push for autism coverage," MSNBC April 2009. http://www.msnbc.msn.com/id/30181325/ (accessed July 2009).

22   Matlock, Michelle, "How to Convince Health Insurance Plans to Pay for Autism Treatment." http://www.insure.com/articles/healthinsurance/autism.html (accessed May 2009).

23   PRNewswire (June 19, 2009). Blue Shield of Michigan. http://www.reuters.com/article/pressRelease/idUS189408+19-Jun-2009+PRN20090619 (accessed July 2009).

CHAPTER 9: LEGAL CONSULTATION: MAKING DECISIONS ABOUT YOUR CHILD'S EDUCATION

1   IDEA, 20 U.S.C. Section 1414.

2   Ibid.

3   Ibid.

4   "Number of Charter Schools by State," U.S. Charter Schools. http://www.uscharterschools.org/cs/r/view/uscs_rs/2030 (accessed August 2009).

5   http://www.uscharterschools.org/pub/uscs_docs/sp/index.htm.

6   "School Boards: Charter Schools Low on Special Ed Innovation," Special Ed News, November 15, 2000. http://www.specialednews.com/educators/ednews/charterreport111500.html (accessed August 2009).

7   Pardini, Priscilla, "The History of Special Education," Rethinking Schools Online, Spring 2002, 16:3. http://www.rethinkingschools.org/archive/16_03/Hist163.shtml (accessed August 2009).

CHAPTER 10: LEGAL CONSULTATION: OUR FAMILY'S CHOICE FOR INCLUSION

1   Koegel, Lynn Kern, and Claire LaZebnik, *Overcoming Autism: Finding the Answers, Strategies, and Hope That Can Transform a Child's Life* (New York: Penguin, 2005).

CHAPTER 11: LEGAL CONSULTATION: PLANNING YOUR CHILD'S EDUCATION

1   Andrea, "The Art of IEP Meetings," My Autism Insights blog, November 14, 2008. http://autisminsights.today.com/2008/11/14/the-art-of-the-iep-meeting/ (accessed August 2009).

2   Laviano, Jennifer, "STOP the IEP Meeting, I Want to Get Off!" Connecticut Special Education Lawyer blog, June 26, 2009. http://www.connecticutspecialeducationlawyer.com/occasional-rants/stop-the-iep-meeting-i-want-to-get-off/ (accessed August 2009).

3   34 C.F.R. 300.320(a)(4).

4   34 C.F.R. 300.34.

5   458 U.S. 176 (1982).

6   20 USC, Section 1414(d)(1)(A)(i)(lll).

7   34 C.F.R. 300.1(a), 20 U.S.C. § 1400(d)(1)(A).

8   34 C.F.R. 300.320(b).

9   Rudy, Lisa Jo, "Tips to Help You Plan for Your Autistic Child's Future,"About
     .com: Autism. http://autism.about.com/od/financialresources/a/tipsmoney
     .htm (accessed August 2009).

10   34 C.F.R. 300.530(e).

CHAPTER 12: IN THE COMMUNITY: INTEGRATING YOUR CHILD

1   Ogintz, Eileen, "Traveling with an Autistic Child," CNN. http://www.cnn
     .com/2008/TRAVEL/traveltips/08/04/autism.traveling/index.html (accessed
     June 2009).

2   Scott, Elizabeth, "Traveling by Plane with an Autistic Child," Suite 101.com.
     http://autistic-child-parenting.suite101.com/article.cfm/traveling_by_
     plane_with_an_autistic_child (accessed July 2009).

3   Maurice, Catherine, "ABA and Us: One Parent's Reflections on Partnership
     and Persuasion," Address to the Cambridge Center for Behavioral Studies
     (CCBS) Annual Board Meeting. http://www.behavior.org/autism/catherine_
     maurice.pdf (accessed August 2009).

4   "A Prom Night to Remember for Teens with Autism and Other Special
     Needs: Dance Lessons at the Help Group Teach Students All the Right
     Moves," The Help Group. http://www.thehelpgroup.org/whatsnew.php (ac-
     cessed August 2009).

5   "Autistic Kids' Outbursts Stir Furor and Guilt: Recent Cases of Public
     Disruption Reveal Complexities to Being Considerate," MSNBC, August 13,
     2008. http://www.msnbc.msn.com/id/26182016/ (accessed August 2009).

6   Maurice, "ABA and Us."

7   Section 504 covers only those public accommodations that receive some
     federal funding. This can include, for example, a private day-care center or
     club that accepts federal subsidies to run a program, such as a basketball
     league or meal program.

8   Davis, Kim, "Making Camps Accessible for All," Indiana University. http://
     www.iidc.indiana.edu/irca/socialleisure/accessiblecamps.html (accessed Au-
     gust 2009).

9   "Autistic Kids' Outbursts Stir Furor."

10   Ibid.

EPILOGUE: IT BEGINS WITH HOPE

1   Obama, Barack, "A More Perfect Union," Speech, Constitution Center,
     Philadelphia, PA, March 18, 2008. http://www.huffingtonpost.com/2008/03/18/
     obama-race-speech-read-th_n_92077.html (accessed August 2009).

2   Bowe, Frank, "The Time to Rise Will Come Again," Ragged Edge Online,
      November 21, 2005. http://www.raggededgemagazine.com/departments/
      closerlook/000631.html (accessed August 2009).

ACRONYMS AND APPENDICES

1   Baird, Prudence, *Treasure Chest of Tools* (Los Angeles: Special Needs Network,
      Inc., 2009).
2   Ibid.
3   Ibid.

Index